SPARK

In the Shadow of the Refinery Fires

DEBORAH S JUCKES

DEDICATION

To my sons, Josh and Jake who deserved better.

To my friend, Christi, the proverbial Energizer bunny. I never understood your eternal optimism and positive outlook. How I wish I'd learned more from you so much sooner in life. I apologize for not remembering more of our Artesia buddies, but I'll never forget you.

To the powers that be at Ponca City Refinery for staying in business long enough that I could retire. To those who gifted me with so many, many opportunities to learn and grow.

To the supervisors that failed to see the passion beneath the belligerence,
or the reality beyond the perception.

To all of us "square pegs" that don't fit the "round hole" norms.

We may have missed opportunities to be better, but that can change.

CONTENTS

ACKNOWLEDGMENTS

Thanks again to Theresa and Jim Blazek for their time and thoughts.
Thanks to Wesley Young for encouraging me to tell the things I didn't want to tell.

Thanks to all the supervisors that taught me so many, many things.
Thanks to the one who told me I was different, that I didn't fit in, and unwittingly made me realize my worth.
Thanks to the one who opened doors to my potential, then slammed them in my face.
Thanks to the one who believed in me, but failed to champion me.
Thanks to the one that taught me what leadership was, and showed me what it wasn't.
Thanks to the one who listened to my ranting and raving, and showed me the value of calm, stable leadership, and shared those magic words.
"It's fine. Everything is going to be just fine."

Thanks to all the animals in my life who have helped my sanity and well-being.
Thanks to the F'ing Fritos that helped me overcome my fears.
Thanks to the cupcakes that tipped the balance, and set me free.
Thanks to all of you who read my story, if for no other reason than to figure out how Fritos and cupcakes fit into the great scheme of life.

INTRODUCTION

This is the story I thought I would never tell. I am a female who worked in a major oil refinery for forty years. It was amazing but difficult, fulfilling, yet frustrating, and also downright dangerous.

People have asked me what the most difficult thing was being a woman working in a predominantly male role. Was it the time I could have died in the flare drum explosion? Was it the time when the fan exploded, coming within inches of crippling me? Was it the day of the massive fire that caused so much damage it twisted and warped the huge steel beams in our unit?

No. It was trying to fit in, trying to belong. Trying to be recognized and appreciated for all my hard work. Wanting to be valued and not thought less of because I was a woman.

Let's lay some background. At nineteen years old, I was hired on as a laborer at the Conoco Refinery here in Ponca City, Oklahoma, in 1978, which later became ConocoPhillips, or CoP. Eventually, our refinery split from CoP and became Phillips 66 Refinery. I retired after forty years, at just fifty-nine years old in 2018.

Since I'll be writing about a very powerful company and very powerful people, I'll either not give a name because I have little or no respect for them or more likely because I'm afraid I'll get sued, or maybe I just don't remember. I'm definitely going to make up names just to make the writing go smoother and/or to really confuse those who think they know who the hell I'm talking about.

Figure 1 *This was from a card given to me by my friend, Peggy. I've always thought of it as a perfect example of what it is like for a female working in the refinery.*

I want to tell you about those forty years, but I must warn you, I am going to straight-talk about my life as a female in a traditionally man's field. I am going to talk about relationships and will most assuredly digress to traumatic past events in my personal life, events that shaped who I became. In essence, I am going to try to stack the straws on the camel's back in such a way that you will understand why they became the burden they did.

I am going to talk like I talk and not sugar-coat anything. If you are offended by foul language, I apologize in advance. As I said, this is me. I am also going to give a few very basic, very generic descriptions of different types of equipment or operating processes in the refinery just to build a better understanding of what was physically happening. Those of you knowledgeable in refining, please don't roll your eyes at my overly simplistic idioms. This book isn't to teach anyone how to operate a refinery unit. This book isn't going to give away any trade secrets. This book is to help people navigate their personal hardships, thoughts, or demons that plague so many of us just trying to fit into a place others say we don't belong.

"Spark." You might wonder what is so different or special about my life, my career. What would possibly make a plain, ordinary old woman like me believe she has a unique story to share? It's that, ever so tiny, spark of fire—life—soul, or let's say, *passion*, that we all have deep down inside of us. I have felt that spark flicker and dim so many, many times. I have felt that spark burst into a roaring inferno that I feared would consume the essence of who I was. I have seen that spark shadowed by the brighter, louder, more dangerous fires around me. And yet my spark survived. My spark was never extinguished, no matter how feeble and insignificant it seemed at times. We all have that bright, powerful source within us. I want to help you nurture and appreciate yours.

I've heard so many people look back on their lives and say, "If I could do it all over again, I wouldn't do anything differently because it made me who I am." To that I say, bullshit. If I could do it all over again, I would do everything different. As for my life, to put it simply, at sixty-five plus years old, this has been one fucked up ride and I'm sad to say, so much of that is on me. Most of it, but not all. So maybe you'll see a little of yourself in me. Maybe you'll learn something that will help you emotionally handle what you're going through right now and hopefully you'll laugh a little.

Which brings me to the subtitle of my book, *In the Shadow of the Refinery Fires*. What would you think is the worst, scariest, and most dangerous thing in an oil refinery? Fire? Seems logical. Did you know it is also one of the most crucial components? Nothing would be accomplished without the wicked, difficult-to-control, impossible-to-handle, scar-you-for-life, bright, hot, dangerous, beneficial, multicolored fire. (Did you know that hydrogen burns a lovely pale blue color that at times can be practically impossible to see in the daylight?) In a refinery, when all other efforts just aren't enough, fire is even the last line of *defense*, the flare. These are the tall stacks you commonly see burning every night and day in any refinery. In an emergency, anything that can't be controlled and contained is safely burned at the tip of the tall stacks of the flares. So yes, fire is the villain or the hero. Fire can change your life for the better or horrifically end it in one fateful flash. There is also something else that is often overlooked, something hidden in the shadows cast by the bright light of the fires—what about the spark? No fire, good or bad, happens without that one tiny spark. The most essential core of your entire being is your spark. You must learn to control it, but even more importantly, you cannot let it be extinguished by anyone, not even—especially not even—by yourself.

If you're still with me, what you're about to read is my memories of actual events, thoughts or rambles. I have no idea if they are wholly accurate or not, if they are 100% factual, or if my memory has twisted them to fit my active imagination. I'm not going to intentionally lie to you as I try to explain my interpretation, my *perception*, my memories of events. Memory, what a fickle bitch she is. I am, however, wise enough to know that not all things are as they seem, and I have, on more than one occasion, been my own worst enemy. Go ahead, nod your head if you ever felt that way.

CHAPTER 1
(1957/58) THE FIRST FATEFULL FIRE

I'm going to try and explain what led me to make the choices that sent me down my life's path. The life that led me to be who I am, what I'm made of, and why I made some of my choices. My early years were difficult because we moved so often. My father, Charles Juckes, worked for Conoco pipeline and he was transferred often in the early years, so my siblings and I were scattered from state to state. Steve was born in California, Charley and then I, in New Mexico. Diana came along a handful of years later in Montana. The youngest, Dotti, would have been born in Illinois, but when Mom found out she was pregnant (once she quit crying as Dotti was a … big, happy surprise) Mom didn't want her born in a place where she had no family. That brought us back to New Mexico for Dotti's birth before eventually coming back to Oklahoma.

Talking about the early, formative years, I have to discuss the accident. It was to be the first time that fire would touch our lives and mold it for all the years to come. It may have happened before me, in 1957 or early '58, when the boys were very, very young and living in New Mexico. As a matter of fact, now that I try to put it all together, Mom might have been pregnant with me at the time, but hey, I don't remember. There are mixed stories of how it happened, but the one thing that remained the same was that it was a horrible accident. My mother was a smoker and always had this silver Zippo lighter. Most of us kids cut our teeth on that lighter. Yeah, probably not the best idea to feed your kid lighter fluid, but I imagine the cool metal felt good on achy, teething gums. There are no safety devices on a Zippo lighter. Once lit, it would just keep burning. Like most accidents, it just takes a second for your whole life to change. That day, the lighter somehow ignited; it fell on Charley's baby blanket, a blanket with no fire retardant, and like dry tinder it immediately burst into flames. Charley's feet and lower legs suffered severe burns. Most of his toes were burned off, leaving only nubs on the top of his foot.

The doctors at the local hospital didn't give Charley much hope, telling my folks he would lose both feet. Mom refused to believe them and hauled Charley out of the hospital and went to either Roswell or Albuquerque. I'm not sure. She had barely walked in the hospital door when a doctor took Charley from her arms and began peeling the burned, black crust off of his feet and legs. I'm not trying to gross you out here, but imagine a hotdog roasted over a fire. You see the skin start to bubble up, then start to brown and then blacken. If it stays in the fire, the skin starts to split, exposing the moist flesh beneath. The skin continues to char and thicken as the moisture from within begins to boil. The same thing happens with human flesh. The pain associated with burns is horrific, as anyone who has been burned to any degree knows. I can only assume that this was the beginning of Charley's road to drug addiction in the honest attempt to alleviate his pain.

The new doctors were much more hopeful about Charley's prognosis and waited to see if he would possibly lose one foot, as it had minimal circulation. Mom told me that she sat by Charley's bed, her hand always wrapped gently around the bandages on his bad foot. Finally, she felt warmth from the foot and in no time at all she said it felt like a hot potato. Charley would keep both feet. It would take him a long time to learn to walk, but since it happened when he was so young, he was able to adapt.

Charley had only part of one big toe left and it was tapered to a point like the small end of a carrot. Many years later, that toe would try to grow a nail. It never came in like a real toenail. Instead, it was a razor-sharp, cat-like claw. We've had a lot of cats growing up and being clawed by them was nothing compared to

14

Charley stabbing you in the side with that damn toe, raking a gouge in your flesh every time.

Charley's feet caused problems his whole life. He would develop skin ulcers frequently, especially on his heel. He received numerous skin grafts over the years, but there was one that was especially memorable. By this time, we were old enough that I was driving Charley back and forth to the hospital. He had developed a deep ulcer on his right heel. Skin grafts normally are very thin layers of skin, but this would require a much deeper repair. The surgeons believed the only way to do that was for the grafted skin to still be alive with blood pumping through it until it had time to adhere, to heal. To do this, they cut a three-sided flap on the top of Charley's left leg, just above the knee, where the skin was unharmed and healthy, even hairy. His right heel was then placed under the flap and sewn into place. To keep the foot at the proper angle, they drove a metal rod through the bottom of his heel and up into his leg. Both legs were then put in casts to further prevent movement. He was sent home for a couple of weeks with lots of painkillers and muscle relaxers. I don't believe anyone really thought about drug addiction back then.

The rod was eventually removed, and the flap cut loose from his left leg. It worked beautifully. The patch on the right heel healed nicely. So well, in fact, that the hair that had been growing on his left leg now grew on the patched right heel.

I have no idea when Charley started taking non-prescription drugs, but I understand it was at a very young age. He was definitely on drugs when he tried to burn the church down in Montana. He was definitely on drugs the day he beat the hell out of me. I assume he was on drugs when he abused other family members as well. He struggled with his addictions and eventually, the drugs and booze took his life.

My own childhood was much less physically traumatic anyway. Oh, I'm sure I may have had a small dose of "middle child syndrome" even though I need to google that and see what it really means. I know a lot of my childhood was spent sitting alone in doctor and hospital waiting rooms while Charley was being cared for. I vividly remember one visit where Charley's screams seemed to go on and on. Some days I still hear them. I wonder now if this was the beginning of my feelings of hiding in the shadows?

I do remember the fantastic times we had as a family. I remember hugs from family and friends and always being told, "I love you." I didn't realize how many kids grew up never hearing that. Every child deserves to be loved and hugged. Every child deserves to hear those words, "I love you!"

CHAPTER 2
(1960s) TOMBOY FROM MY SKINNED NOSE TO MY DIRTY TOES

My mother may have stuffed my chubby baby butt into dresses, but once I was big enough to argue, I changed all that, much to her dismay. I was a grubby, dirty, outdoorsy, bare-footed, skinned-knee, split-lip, wrestling, fighting, animal-loving, dyed-in-the-wool tomboy. Mom would occasionally drag me indoors, kicking and screaming, to get cleaned up. I hated having my hair brushed, which only made it worse when Mom tried to make me presentable with a ponytail or puppy dog ears. I do believe she may have intentionally pulled waaay too tight just as payback for me being a little hellion. I've got to admit, my favorite school picture, I had my hair in puppy dog ears, short bangs, a skinned nose and chipped tooth from falling on my face just a few days earlier. If forced to wear shoes, I insisted on cowboy boots, which made Mom roll her eyes. Even though Mom was a tomboy herself growing up, she really hated that I wasn't feminine.

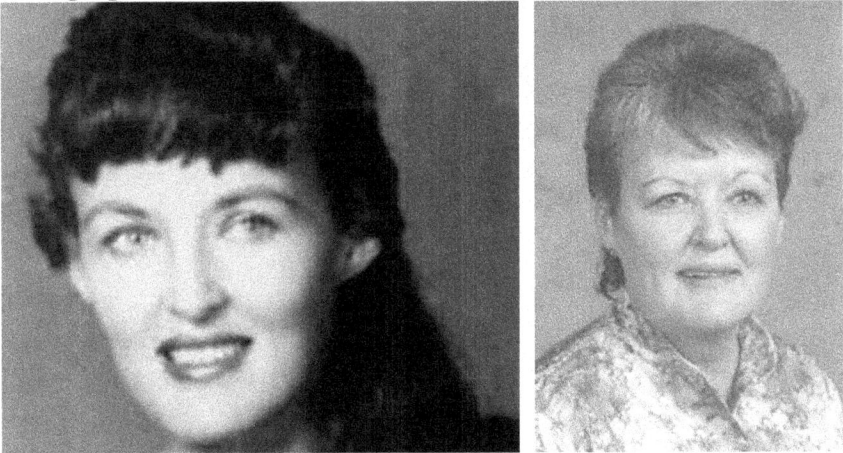

Figure 2 *My mom, Sue Juckes.*

I don't know if I became a tomboy being raised with two older brothers, or if I was just born that way. I think I was born that way, just as my youngest son, Jake, was born gay and my cousin, transgender. I don't believe it's something we choose; it's something we are. Although I'm a tomboy, I could never imagine being physically attracted to women. I like men a lot. I couldn't make myself want to be with a woman sexually. I assume my son is the same way. He is attracted to men and was lucky enough to have found a wonderful man, John, to marry and share his life with. I am so happy for them. My point is, we didn't make these choices. It's what we feel deep down in our hearts and soul and, I believe, in our chemical composition. I don't claim to understand why we are like we are. There are so many things I don't understand because I've never felt it. I have empathy, but I'm not naïve enough to think I could ever walk in someone else's shoes with absolute understanding. I can only try my best to respect other's feelings. Something I wish we all would do.

Being a tomboy, I did rough and tumble with my brothers. The oldest, Steve, hated to wrestle with me because I could grab on and never let go. Where the boys led, I would follow. So much so that my mother would ask me, "If they jump off the roof, does that mean you have to?" Instead of being chastened, I would jump up eagerly, wanting to know how they got on the roof. I didn't want to be left behind. Besides, the only time I remember jumping off the roof was in Montana, but we landed safely in the snow.

Figure 3 Billings, Montana, 1961, Steve, Charley, & Me. This
would be the house where we jumped off the roof.

There was also the time in Montana when the boys tried to
throw me through the wall in the basement, but just demolished
the sheetrock on one side. We took one of the mattresses off the
bed and stood it up to cover the hole, thinking Mom would never
see it, but she wasn't fooled.

That Montana basement is where Charley and I played darts.
That is until he lipped off to me and I came after him with the
darts. I still clearly remember him racing up the stairs screaming
bloody murder with a dart stuck in the back of his head, bouncing
like crazy as he ran away. Oops.

There was another accident in Montana and I'm even more
fuzzy on those details than on Charley's accident. I remember
Charley and I riding our bicycles. We were supposed to be home

already, so we were racing to get back as fast as possible. Charley was in the lead and took a shortcut through the cemetery—the cemetery beside the dog pound. We were really young, maybe five and six years old. It was just starting to get dark. I remember flying down the narrow road, headstones on either side. The dogs were barking and howling in the increasing darkness. Charley looked back, yelling at me to hurry. I remember the handlebars starting to shake, and the front tire beginning to wobble. Then I don't remember anything.

Charley was still looking back when I lost control, flying over the handlebars and landing head first on the blacktop road. I suffered a concussion and had memory problems for quite some time. I don't know if it was the cause for my continued memory issues or if that's just my weakness, my faulty short-term memory. Come to think of it, my long-term memory too? I don't know, I can't remember. (Sorry, I couldn't help myself.)

It was the mid to late 1960s when we left the snow of Montana for the tornadoes of Oklahoma. After a couple of houses in town, we moved out to "The Osage," where we lived in a little trailer house.

Osage County is home of the Osage Indian Nation, the Tall Grass Prairie Preserve, and underneath it all, crude oil. Many atrocities befell the Osage Nation in the early 1900s as their people were murdered and lands stolen, all for greed of black gold.

I loved that our trailer sat on a couple of acres of woods. We never jumped off the roof of the trailer house, but we did make our own zip line in the oak trees. Of course, it wasn't very professional. You'd have to climb up one tree, throw an old set of handlebars over the cable, and hang on for dear life as you rocketed down the line to the base of a neighboring oak tree. The real trick was letting go before you smacked face first into the second tree. Charley wasn't very good at the letting go part. He always crashed into the bottom tree. He was also the one that was zipping when the handlebars wore through, and he tumbled out of the tree. Good thing kids bounce.

I think that's probably the same tree where we hung one of our little sisters, Diana. Well, we didn't hang-hang her. We were a little smarter than that. Mom had saddled us with babysitting, and we didn't want the little twerp getting in our way. We put a heavy jacket on Diana. One of the boys picked her up, then we wrapped the rope around her waist and tied it off, making sure she couldn't touch the ground. It seemed like a good idea at the time. Not such a good idea when Mom found her and then lined us three older kids up and swatted our asses good with a switch off that damn oak tree—and I was third in line. I had to watch and listen to the boys scream and bawl before I got my whipping. Each time that damn switch would break, we would be sent to get another one for her. I don't know how old I was before I found out that when Mom found Diana, she thought it was so funny that she left her hanging there and went back to the trailer to get a camera and take pictures before finally untying her. Later, she even brought us all back to the scene to reenact the crime for more photos. I guess the whippings were for our own good.

I went to several grade schools, but my favorite by far was McCord. Our principal, Mr. Able, was also our sixth grade teacher, our track and basketball coach, and the meter outer of punishment (Charley in the coat closet getting his ass paddled). He was also a baseball fan, and I remember watching ball games on TV during class.

(1970-1971) I hated leaving our trailer house in Oklahoma to go to Illinois. There were more kids in my first period class than in the whole school back in Oklahoma. We lived in a trailer park that was close to the city dump. Oh, don't get me wrong—that was the fun part. The boys and I found an antique wheelchair in a nearby dump and built an obstacle course so we could race.

21

Charley always won, but then he had lots of experience with wheelchairs and crutches. We also found an old claw-foot bathtub down by the creek. We would work our butts off dragging it up the embankment, jump in and whoosh over the side to crash into the creek. You might wonder that any of us lived through our pre-adolescent years, let alone all three of us. Sure, there were many accidents. I learned all about tetanus shots running around in that dump and getting a nail from an old board driven clear through my foot. I couldn't get loose from the board until I raised my foot up and Steve stomped on the board. That would be my first tetanus shot of many to come. Good thing the shot lasts for many years, or I'd be a pin cushion.

While I was young and supposedly malleable, Mom kept trying to entice me over to the girly side, but it just wasn't for me. She was encouraged when I liked the movie *Mary Poppins* and bought me a…doll for Christmas. I had to explain to her it was the magic I loved and certainly not any girly doll.

She finally came around and the next year, when the boys got their GI Joes, I got a Jane West doll. I was shocked at first, but soon came around because Jane had a horse with a saddle and bridle…and a rifle. Oh, yeah. We rode down into the GI Joe camps and trampled everything, whinnying and riding off into the sunset.

If my love of horses came from my mother, my love of motorcycles came from my father. My folks liked to tell the story that after us kids were born, Dad would bring us home from the hospital on the motorcycle. I think that might have been a slight exaggeration, but we weren't much older. One of my earliest memories was sitting in front of my father on his motorcycle and being so tiny that the gas tank in front of me looked enormous. The chrome gas cap and handlebars glinted in the sunlight, and I yearned to reach out and touch them. I had that flashback so many times when looking down at my own motorcycle gas tank from a much higher altitude.

School was tough as we continued to transfer from one state to another. I became more and more shy, not making many friends before we'd move again. I did get lucky and attended the same high school for my final three years.

My sophomore year, I enrolled in Naval Junior ROTC and absolutely loved it. I advanced during my three years of high school until achieving the rank of Cadet Lieutenant JG. I was a part of the color guard that performed at sporting events and parades. I still, to this day, get choked up every time I hear the *Star-Spangled Banner* or see a military color guard in their crisp, starched uniforms, rifles carried at the ready to protect our flag.

Figure 4 Senior Picture, Cadet Lieutenant Jr Grade Juckes.

I was also a top competitor in advanced individual drills. If you've never seen military drill teams, you need to check them out. I loved the precision synchronization of the drill team, the sound of boots hitting the ground, hands snapping smartly against rifles. I can't dance to save my life but give me a synchronized march and I'm all in. As much as I loved the drill team, I also excelled at individual drill. To my knowledge, I was the only female in individual competition at the time. Surely, there were others back then.

Figure 5 Men's ROTC drill team.

The opposing Army ROTC performed drills with balsa wood rifles. Balsa wood is extremely lightweight. I performed my drill routine with a 1903A3 Springfield 30-06, weighing nine pounds, six ounces when outfitted with the shoulder strap, minus, of course, the bayonet.

Figure 6 *Me competing in individual drill.*

Our teacher, Chief Paltridge, did not let me use a bayonet since I'd already hurt myself during a previous drill practice. During that practice, I had dropped the rifle and unknowingly lost the sight guard. This guard was for the sight at the very end of the rifle barrel. The sight is a pointy, triangular piece of metal meant to help you aim. The guard, of course, was to protect me during the drill. I didn't realize I'd lost the sight guard and on the next toss of the rifle, the sight jabbed through the skin, embedding itself into my forearm. I stared at the weapon now standing upright from my arm, the sight buried under my skin. I continued to watch as the rifle finally toppled over, tearing through my flesh as it did. Let me tell you, that one took several stitches.

Although not allowed to use a bayonet, I did perform an exhibition drill with a flaming rifle. My most memorable performance was at a hockey game. They rolled a carpet out onto the ice, and I stood at the end. Once the muzzle end of the rifle ignited, they dimmed the lights. The fire reflected beautifully on the mirrored surface of the recently Zamboni'd ice. I was nearing the end of the drill when I heard booing start. I was shocked but continued my drill until the final move, where I had to keep the rifle spinning in a circle with only one hand, the other hand in a salute, and continue until the very last of the fuel was expended. As the flame went out, the lights came up, and the audience went wild. It was absolutely thrilling for me. Chief Paltridge later explained that the booing was directed at the opposing hockey team when they prematurely came out on the ice, and thankfully not at me. He also said the team quickly retreated when they spotted me, or maybe it was because of the flaming rifle.

There was another moment in ROTC that was monumental for me. I never attended any high school proms, as I was never asked. However, Chief Paltridge ordered me to attend the Navy Ball as I was an officer and therefore must attend. No way in hell was I going to wear a dress. It was all I could do to put on my women's navy uniform (skirt) but that's how badly I wanted to be in ROTC. Then something odd happened. Another ROTC officer asked me to the ball. He was one year ahead of me, tall, quiet, and shy, good looking too. Others told me that Chief Paltridge had ordered him to ask me to the ball. I don't know if that's true or not. I was just thrilled to be asked. I think it was the very first "date" I'd been asked out on.

I even managed to find "The Dress." It was everything I was not. It was floor-length formal, all delicate lace and satin in a soft ivory hue. For the first time in my life, I remembered feeling like a beautiful young woman.

We arrived at the ball, me in my gorgeous dress, on the arm of a very handsome man in uniform. We went through the reception line shaking hands with Captain Raley, Commander Martin, and then Chief Paltridge—who fucked it all up. He reached down and jerked my dress up above my knees. I about fainted. I jerked my dress down as he explained to the hysterically laughing onlookers that he was checking to make sure I wasn't wearing my jeans underneath.

I don't remember the rest of the evening. I don't remember if I danced. I don't remember if my date kissed me goodnight. I hate that I lost that memory to trauma. I don't know what happened between my date and me that night, or afterwards, but I know I've always thought of that gentleman as the one that got away. If things had worked out differently, it's possible both my kids would have been tall. By the way, I still have that dress.

During my junior year, our ROTC company was able to attend one week of basic training at Orlando, Florida. It was a blast. We trained in survival techniques in the water, including how to make flotation devices out of your clothes. We trained in firefighting and first aid. We even went to the firing range and were allowed to shoot. We shot from the prone position. I laid down with my rifle and took a little extra time fitting the sling around my arm. Our Navy instructor told me I was doing it all wrong and suggested I remove the sling. Chief Paltridge patted the instructor on the shoulder and told him to let me do it my way.

We fired ten rounds, then waited as our targets were retrieved. I had hit the bullseye every time but one (as long as they touched, and the bullseye was hit, they count as a bullseye). That one "wild" bullet hole to the top left, very nearly touched the edge of the others. You'll notice, however, that it did actually touch the bullseye.

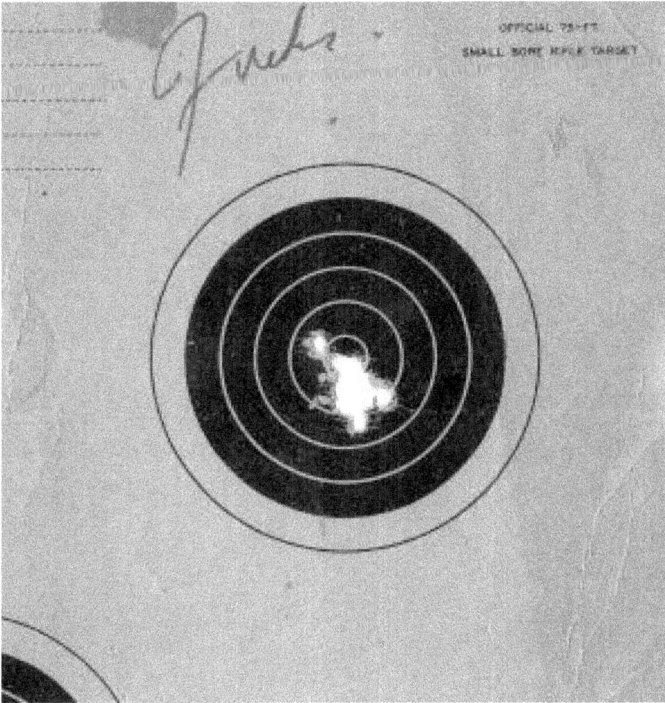

Figure 7 Target from Orlando.

Word got around before we left Orlando and they ended up doing an article on me, which, of course, my mother kept.

JANUARY 1975

Cadet Juckes Enjoys Her Military Life Discipline

CADET LT. (j.g.) DEBBIE JUCKES is an outstanding marksman, hitting the bull's eye every time but one on a visit to the shooting range while at the Naval Training Center, Orlando, Fla. The miss was less than a quarter-inch. She is commander of the Po-Hi NJROTC color guard and drill team. On her crisp light blues, she wears award ribbons for aptitude, exemplary appearance, color guard and drill team participation and rifle marksmanship.

Poised, Confident, dynamic... These are just a few words that could be used to describe Cadet Lieutenant Junior Grade Debbie Juckes, a member of Ponca City, Oklahoma's Navy Junior Reserve Officer Training Corps unit, which trained last week.

Commander of the unit's drill team and color guard, Cadet Juckes is also the Battalion Administrative Officer.

With her crisp, pressed light blues, she wears award ribbons for aptitude, exemplary appearance, color guard and drill team participation, and rifle marksmanship.

Her earliest ambition was police work. She then joined NJROTC, hoping to combine police work and the military.

"I know it sounds strange, but I like the military discipline," she explained.

She thinks she'd like to be in the Military Police, although her company commander, talked with her of joining the Navy in the Master-at-Arms rate.

She has advanced in rank faster than any other woman in her area and is the only woman individual drill exhibitionist that she knows of.

Debbie's school day begins at 7 a.m. She enjoys English and creative writing next to her NJROTC activities. She leaves school at 5 p.m. and goes home to practice her drill routines. "I taught my 11-year-old sister all of my routines," and she added, "and my baby sister says 'other', 'yes sir', 'no ma'am'."

Before becoming so involved in her NJROTC ACTIVITIES, Debbie accumulated "a small collection" of two swimming trophies, one bowling trophy and 21 swimming medals, two

of which she earned at the Explorer Olympics. She also earned a rifle medal there and has attended the Junior Olympics in swimming competition.

In her small amount of spare time, she enjoys taking her dog for motorcycle rides and studying the martial arts of aikido and judo.

To earn a little extra money, she exercises horses for people who haven't the time, or who cannot handle a particular horse.

After one and a half years in NJROTC, Debbie says, "I have one more year to go; maybe I won't like the military by then. But right now, I really enjoy it."

Cadet Juckes attended school in Artesia and was member of the Waterdog swimming team.

She is the granddaughter of Mr. and Mrs. Jim Juckes.

Figure 8 Article from trip to Orlando, FL.

I didn't realize it at the time, but I had begun to develop a reputation at school, a reputation of being tough, of not backing down from fights, and I'd been in a few fights. There was even a time at school when I squared off with a guy nicknamed "Oklahoma Tank." Whew, what a day, but I did get my stolen belt buckle back. It wasn't just the fighting, either. I think because I

30

was so introverted that people maybe thought I was mentally off. Is introversion, shyness, a sign of a mental disease? Technically? When I look back on high school, I realize now that I was so weird, I am sure if you had a checklist of potential "crazy" attributes, I would check most of the boxes. That's when I really perfected my "don't fuck with me" face. There was one thing that set me apart from the real bad guys, although nobody ever knew it—because I didn't let them know it. I never, ever, wanted to hurt anyone. I would. I could. But I ached with the idea that I might have to cause injury to anyone. I worried about being put in a situation where I would have to fight and how badly I could hurt someone. I always thought I'd never fight unless forced into it, but I've been in a couple of really, seriously bad places and each time, once I realized I had to fight, I had every intention of making it count, of doing whatever I had to do to survive. I also started to learn that I would quickly risk taking a beating to protect someone else.

There were times, however, when I refused to fight, or tried to refuse. That unfortunately led me to one of the worse beatings I've ever had in my life, at the hand of my own brother, Charley. At the time of the beating, I had an injured wing. My right arm was bandaged from wrist to elbow due to a burn suffered from hot bacon grease that Charley had thrown on me a few days before. He had been cooking bacon and was startled when it popped, and I chuckled at his reaction. I guess in his mind that was reason enough for him to throw the hot grease on me. The day of the fight, Charley came home that afternoon, and I don't know if he was drunk or stoned, but he thought I'd stolen a pack of his cigarettes. I told him I hadn't stolen anything from him. He got really pissed, really loud, really angry, and repeatedly threatened to kick my ass if I didn't admit guilt. I just got quieter. Finally, for some stupid reason, these words just slipped right out of my mouth, "I guess if you don't believe me, you'll just have to kick my ass because I didn't do it." I seem to have an uncanny knack for saying really stupid shit when I'm trying to be cool, or be accepted, or just trying to fit in. Sometimes we have good intentions but maybe a little electrical spark in our brain gets redirected to the "stupid shit you should never say" file and BAM, you're a dumbass.

Charley's drug of choice was speed, but there's no telling what drugs he was doing that day. I believe the dust-up started in the kitchen. He hit me upside the head so hard I dropped like a rock. He waited for me to stand, and he hit me again. Several blows later and we were in the living room. I hope, for your sake, that a muscled-up dude has never punched you in the face. It sends shock waves through your body. Blood fills your mouth and drains down your throat. It fills your nose and sinus cavities. Your face quits working correctly and you can't understand what's wrong with your vision, your balance, your brain. Every punch knocked me to the ground and Charley would wait for me to stand. Each time I did, I reminded him that I wasn't guilty, that I didn't do it and that I didn't have to defend myself because I had done nothing wrong. BAM, another punch knocked me out the front door. Another solid blow to the face knocked me off the porch and into the yard. I noticed a crowd was gathering on the sidewalk near the street. I felt ashamed. I didn't want anyone to see Charley acting like this. I stood up again and tried to tell Charley we needed to stop; we needed to go back inside. That's when he punched me in the throat.

I don't know how long I laid on the grass trying to catch my breath. As my head cleared a little, I could see that a cop was now in the crowd near the street. It was so quiet outside, Charley waiting, me panting. Then I heard someone tell the cop to do something, to help. The cop's response shocked me. "It's private property. If she wants help, she'll have to ask." I think I actually laughed in my head. I sure as hell couldn't out loud because I could barely swallow, barely breathe. I rolled to my side and curled up into a ball, clutching my burned arm. I concentrated on breathing, all the time watching the cop. I didn't get angry, I just realized I had to do something. Being innocent was not going to protect me. I had to take care of myself because no one else was going to. I stayed close to the ground, rolling more so that I could start getting my feet under me. When I came off the ground, I launched myself with every ounce of strength I could muster. I hit Charley square in the face and followed through with all my 140 pounds behind it. Charley was flipped head over heels, but he didn't stay down. He jumped up and raced off down the street. The cop took off after Charley, but I don't know if he ever caught him.

By the time my parents got home that evening, I was black and blue from my scalp to my collarbone. Dad sat me down at our round kitchen table and asked what happened. I didn't want to get Charley in trouble. After all, I had been his defender all those years when kids made fun of his legs. I couldn't stop that now. I told Dad that one of the girls from school did it. He said he didn't believe one girl could do that to me. I told him it was one girl and her friends. I still don't know how he did it. Dad wasn't very tall, and he had really short legs, but he managed to reach across the table and backhand me to the floor. This would be the last time my father would ever strike me. I had just sat back down in the chair when Charley walked in and told Dad he'd done it. Dad sent us to bed, and that's the last either of my parents ever mentioned it.

I did have one teacher, though, Chief Paltridge, that didn't take it so lightly when he saw me the next day at school. He took one look at me and even though I wouldn't tell the chief who had done it, they came and hauled Charley and me both off. We had to talk to a counselor of some sort with the city. I think her husband was the District Attorney or something like that. She spent several hours asking me questions, then spent twenty minutes with Charley. Afterwards, she brought us together and explained that it was all my fault, that I just wanted attention. She was trying to explain my shortcomings, my failures, when Charley called her a stupid bitch. He said he'd done it because he was stoned and angry and just how fucking stupid could she be? He got up and left and I sat there wondering what the hell to do, so I got up and followed him out. I wish I had escaped before the seed was planted—before a person of influence and power told me that being abused was my fault, my plea for attention. After all, I wanted attention, didn't I? Was this really my fault?

Now, in my old age, I can tell you without a single shred of doubt in my mind—it wasn't my fucking fault! I don't care how much I chuckled, or what I said, or even how much I wanted attention. I am not responsible for my brother's actions, his abuse. Anyone suffering from abuse should report it. Find someone who will listen. Talk to your parents, your school counselor, your teacher, or preacher. Report it to the police. Don't be ashamed to ask for help. I don't know if my parents took any steps that I was unaware of, but if so, I never saw the outcome. I know that in the past I have harbored resentment towards my parents for the incredible abuse that Charley inflicted on family members, and my parents seemed oblivious to it all. I do believe that if Charley's abusive behavior to me had been dealt with, then maybe it could have prevented him from abusing others.

It was true that my heart still begged for attention and warred with my desire to never, ever draw attention to myself. It was high school, and the most horrific battle was to come—speech class. How many of us have been there? This could be one reason why Charley dropped out of school. Forcing me to do something that makes me physically ill, that terrified me beyond reason— speaking in front of other people—sent me on a personal, silent tirade. Just thinking about it made me want to puke in the teacher's trashcan. So, what did I do? I made one of the stupidest mistakes of my high school years. I gave a speech on *Murderers and Motives*. I found the book, the psychology actually, fascinating to read. (Another check on the list?) What made people do such awful things to other human beings? Well, hell, I thought, if they are going to force me to do this, I really want to shock them, to punish them. It wasn't until I started trying to speak that I realized what the hell I had done. Kids looked at me like, "Yeah, I knew it; she's a total whack job!" And then, of course, I mispronounced a word.

I was a very avid reader. I read all the time. I remember so many times I'd ask Mom what a word meant, and she'd tell me to go look it up. Back in those days, that meant picking up an actual, physical dictionary and thumbing through the pages to find the word. Too many times, I didn't take the time to learn to pronounce the word, especially if I was really wrapped up in a story and didn't want to go look it up. Most of my books were about animals, dogs, horses, and happy endings, not murderers and motives. During my speech, when I was reporting on a "severed" head or hand, I pronounced it severe, as in a severe case of dumbass. When they started laughing at me, albeit nervous laughter from some, I felt the outside door in my mind shut a little tighter, separating me even further from my peers. Yeah, school was rough for me.

Sadly, my senior year, Chief Paltridge left and was replaced by Chief Spalding. We struggled with the new chief. I never knew what made him so resentful and hateful. Cadets picked up on his attitude and soon started coming to me for direction. That did not go over well, to say the least. I was a Cadet Lieutenant JG when Chief Spalding arrived. He soon busted me down to Cadet, taking my officer stripes from me. His reason was, "I was too over-dominant and powerful of a leader." I still remember those exact words. Um, I thought that's what we were trained for. I was confused, but never considered fighting it. I don't remember if my folks said anything. I can't imagine my dad didn't do something. But then, he pretty much left Mom in charge of parenting unless a whopping with the belt was needed.

Things didn't change until Chief Spalding tried to schedule another trip to Orlando. He called to arrange the visit and just happened to talk to one of the officers, an admiral actually, that met me the previous year. The admiral was very enthusiastic about our company coming to his base again and said he couldn't wait to see me personally. Chief Spalding explained that I wasn't good enough to come and would not be attending. The admiral's response was quick and concise. If I wasn't good enough, none of our company was. The trip was denied.

Now that stirred the pot a little. It wasn't much later that the admiral showed up in Ponca for an inspection. I stood at attention as he walked down the line, and I tried not to smile when I recognized him. I tried harder not to smile when the admiral leaned toward me and whispered, "I'll have your (officer) bars back before the end of the day."

I was not able to attend the meeting at the school that day. I do know that some of the parents attended. In fact, I heard that the meeting ended when the mother of one of the female cadets punched Chief Spalding in the face.

I did get my bars/stripes back that day, but ROTC was never the same after that.

Figure 9 *Me in my Army helmet.*

My love for ROTC, and no doubt my dad's service in the Marine Corp, sparked the thoughts of a career in the military.

Figure 10 *My daddy, Charles Juckes.*

My Dad, Charles Juckes, was a member of Reconnaissance Company, Third Marine Division FMF. They were the first company to initiate "Scout Swimmers," or frogmen as my dad called them, and the first recon company to send members to Fort Benning, Georgia, to attend parachute courses. One of Dad's marine buddies told me that they were, in fact, the forerunner to the Seals. Now that is badass.

Dad's frogman days may have also inspired me to be a competitive swimmer. I swam on the Water Dogs team in New Mexico and continued to compete when I came to Oklahoma. Our team was so small in Oklahoma that I often had to compete against the guys.

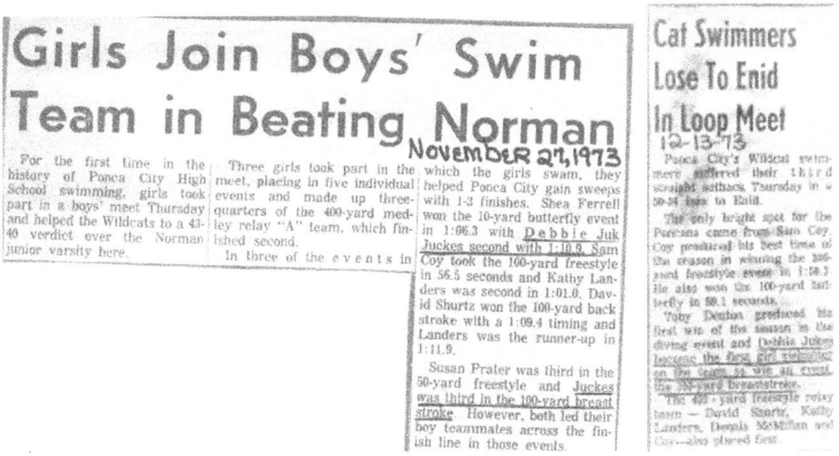

Girls Join Boys' Swim Team in Beating Norman
NOVEMBER 27, 1973

For the first time in the history of Ponca City High School swimming, girls took part in a boys' meet Thursday and helped the Wildcats to a 43-40 verdict over the Norman junior varsity here.

Three girls took part in the meet, placing in five individual events and made up three-quarters of the 400-yard medley relay "A" team, which finished second.

In three of the events in which the girls swam, they helped Ponca City gain sweeps with 1-2 finishes. Shea Ferrell won the 10-yard butterfly event in 1:06.3 with Debbie Juckes second with 1:10.5. Sam Coy took the 100-yard freestyle in 56.5 seconds and Kathy Landers was second in 1:01.0. David Shurtz won the 100-yard backstroke with a 1:09.4 timing and Landers was the runner-up in 1:11.9.

Susan Prater was third in the 50-yard freestyle and Juckes was third in the 100-yard breast stroke. However, both led their boy teammates across the finish line in those events.

Cat Swimmers Lose To Enid In Loop Meet
12-13-73

Ponca City's Wildcat swimmers suffered their third straight setback Thursday in a 50-34 loss to Enid.

The only bright spot for the Felicats came from Sam Coy. Coy produced his best time in the freestyle event in 1:58.3. He also won the 100-yard butterfly in 59.1 seconds.

Toby Deaton produced his first win of the season in the diving event and Debbie Juckes became the first girl swimmer on the team to win an event, the 100-yard breaststroke. The 400-yard freestyle relay team — David Shurtz, Kathy Landers, Dennis McMillan and Coy—also placed first.

Figure 11 Mom kept all the newspaper articles.

All that led to me thinking about a military career. But life took a turn. It was 1976, my senior year in high school. I was seventeen years old and engaged to be married to the one guy I thought wasn't afraid of me. Just weeks before graduation I turned up pregnant, and he ended up skipping town.

As a kid myself, I had a choice to make. This is not an easy decision for any girl or woman to make. So many things go into deciding what the right thing to do is, and each and every instance is different. So many things are factored into these decisions—health, love, family, support, money, selfishness just to name a few. How can one insignificant human being decide what is best? It is an agonizing decision and one I believe belongs to the mother.

My son, Josh, was born just two days before my eighteenth birthday. After that, my main goal was to take care of my son, to give him all that he deserved. I needed a job.

CHAPTER 3
(1977) JOINING UNCLE SAM'S ARMY

I didn't want to jump from job to job as I tried to support my son. I wanted a career that would pay well. I was also willing to pay my dues, so to speak, and knew I had to start somewhere. I also hated the idea of being separated from Josh. Then, of course, there was the question whether I would even be accepted into the military being a single mother.

I talked to the Army recruiters in town, and they made things sound so great (don't believe this bullshit). The biggest problem was just as I had feared; I couldn't join as a single mother. I would have to let my parents legally adopt Josh. I knew it was temporary, and that Josh would be well cared for, but it still frightened me. I elected to try the Army Reserve instead of the regular Army just so I knew I could come home to Josh. If things worked out, I could always switch over to the regular Army. I signed up as a 63b, light wheeled vehicle mechanic. After basic training and towards the end of my AIT, Advanced Individual Training, I was told I was going to be shunted to supply instead of the mechanical pool, so for that reason, and so many more, I got out of the Army. No way was I going to be shut up in an office worrying about inventory. So, yeah, I had to eat crow years later as I took my yields (inventory) job at the refinery. I've gotten ahead of myself. As much as I hate to, I need to tell this story. I have no idea what the military is like for women now. But back in 1977, at least where I was, there was extreme abuse happening. Physical abuse was one thing. Add to that the mental abuse and the perfect setting to groom young women for sexual abuse. It was atrocious.

I started my Army career as a PFC, Private First Class, due to having been in NJROTC in high school. Being a PFC got me out of a lot of work like having to serve in the mess hall or scrubbing toilets. It did, however, put me up front and visible, a target you might say.

On the first day of basic, we were loaded into cattle cars (not the actual cars used to haul cattle but similar in design, semi-trailers with holes cut into the sides to allow for ventilation) and driven to our barracks. They unloaded us and immediately dropped everyone on the ground to do pushups. A large group of drill sergeants (male and a few female) then proceeded to inform us of what despicable, useless, pieces of shit we were and how we would never amount to anything. Drill sergeants remarked on our lineage and what types of animals fucked our mothers to spawn worthless shit like us. Crazy stuff. It didn't take five minutes until I heard crying coming from all around me. There was one drill sergeant in particular that was bouncing around like the Energizer bunny, yelling and screaming. I couldn't help it. I started laughing. He hunted me down as if I was a rabbit for dinner and he was fixing to skin me alive and fry me up in hot oil. Drill Sergeant dropped on the ground in front of me and started doing pushups in cadence so that he could yell at me face-to-face. I couldn't help it, I laughed harder. All the other girls were settled into the barracks before I was allowed to stop doing pushups.

I was so tired I could barely pick up my duffle bag and climb the stairs to the barracks. I walked down the hall looking for a bunk. As I passed the drill sergeant's office and heard that unmistakable voice, I chuckled again. What an ass. I just sat down on a bunk when I heard the drill sergeant screaming my name. He didn't pronounce it correctly, of course, but that could have been on purpose. Juckes is pronounced "jooks," like Jukebox, or I've seen it misspelled as Jewks. Drill Sergeant always called me Jucks, as in rhymes with sucks or fucks. I ran down the hall and stood at attention, giving the proper pronunciation of my last name, for all the good that did. He looked at me in disgust, rolled his eyes and said, "It had to be you." The paper he was holding

42

said I was to be assigned as squad leader. I didn't laugh that time, but I definitely heard several other drill sergeants laughing. I might have smirked. Yeah, I smirked.

Once bit of advice I had been given was to never volunteer for anything while at basic. Our second day of training they asked for volunteers without any mention of what the hell it was for. My hand shot up in the air like it had a mind of its own. I'm used to my mouth engaging before my brain—or the look on my expressive face that just can't be controlled, but even I was surprised to see my hand in the air. I had just volunteered to be a driver. It wasn't a bad gig. On our off time, I drove recruits back and forth to the hospital as needed. I had a cot at the end of the staff sergeant's desk and could even catch a few Zs on quiet nights though there weren't very many of those. It also got me out of most of the long, forced marches wearing full gear. Instead, I drove a truck and picked up recruits that dropped out. I might not have marched, but I sure didn't get much sleep.

I also drove supplies out when we went on bivouac—a weeklong camping excursion into the swamps of South Carolina. We slept in small, two-person tents along with any spiders, snakes, or other critters that needed a little extra warmth during the night. They'd just come right on in and nestle down beside you like your favorite dog or cat back home. The reactions they evoked weren't nearly the same though. You always knew when one of the girls had an unexpected guest. I saw a couple of tents get torn down from the inside as the ladies tried to fight their way out.

Once I arrived at bivouac, I met up with my squad and went through all the training with them. As the squad leader, I was the first to go into the tear gas chamber. We went in masked, got our bearings, and then a drill sergeant ordered us, one by one, to remove our mask. Drill sergeants also barred us from exiting the gas chamber until we had recited our name, rank, and serial number. It was actually my second experience with tear gas. The first time was during our training at the Naval base in Orlando. Let me tell you, it doesn't get any easier, but at least I knew not to panic when it felt like my skin was burning off and my eyeballs had been seared out with red-hot pokers.

I led the way on the daylight marches and brought up the rear on the nighttime marches. Drill sergeants bombarded us with tear gas, flash grenades, or firing their M16s. We went on marches through all kinds of terrain. I'll always remember those huge trees with Spanish moss hanging down from them. The gray tendrils started looking like snakes hanging from the branches the deeper into the woods we marched.

One night we were following a shallow creek, the water just above our boots. That's when the firefight really started. Gunfire came from all around us. Explosions sounded from both sides of the creek; flashes lit up the night sky. Smoke rolled down the hill and Drill Sergeant gave the order to drop. I was at the end of the line, making sure we didn't lose anyone. I still remember looking up and seeing all these helmets bobbing in the water like a bunch of turtles as the smoke rolled over us. I hope my laughter didn't carry across the water where Drill Sergeant could hear. We belly crawled for what seemed like forever down that creek. I was just hoping all the smoke and noise kept the water snakes away.

Now that everyone knew exactly what tear gas felt like, we had gotten really fast at donning our gas masks. Nothing like the proper incentive. Each time we stopped for a break, Drill Sergeant would have errands for me so that I never got a chance to rest. Then he would lay back against a tree and pull that wide-brimmed hat down low on his face so he could sleep. Not a smart thing for him to do. It doesn't matter how fast you are, when a tear gas canister lands at your feet and your gas mask has mysteriously gone missing while you were napping, you're gonna cry like a baby. The memory still makes me smile.

Figure 12 *Washing dishes while out on bivouac. Yep, those are trashcans.*

Drill Sergeant did everything he could think of to knock me down. Even during our crucial, final physical training (PT) test. This was the PT test where we had to make a high enough score to move on. Fail the test, and you had to go through basic training all over again. That day, we marched to the PT field before the sun came up. As soon as we arrived, Drill Sergeant said he'd forgotten his paperwork and sent me to run to the barracks to fetch them and to be sure and run all the way back while the platoon waited and rested. I did as I was ordered, ran the whole way, picked up the papers he'd mentioned, right where he said they would be, and ran back. I handed him the BLANK sheets of paper and we immediately started our final PT test without any time for me to rest. At the end of the day, the scores were tallied. Being my drill sergeant, he was the one that had to give me my award for achieving the highest score of the whole company on the test. He was also the one that had to give me the Expert Marksman medal after M16 rifle qualifications. He was not pleased.

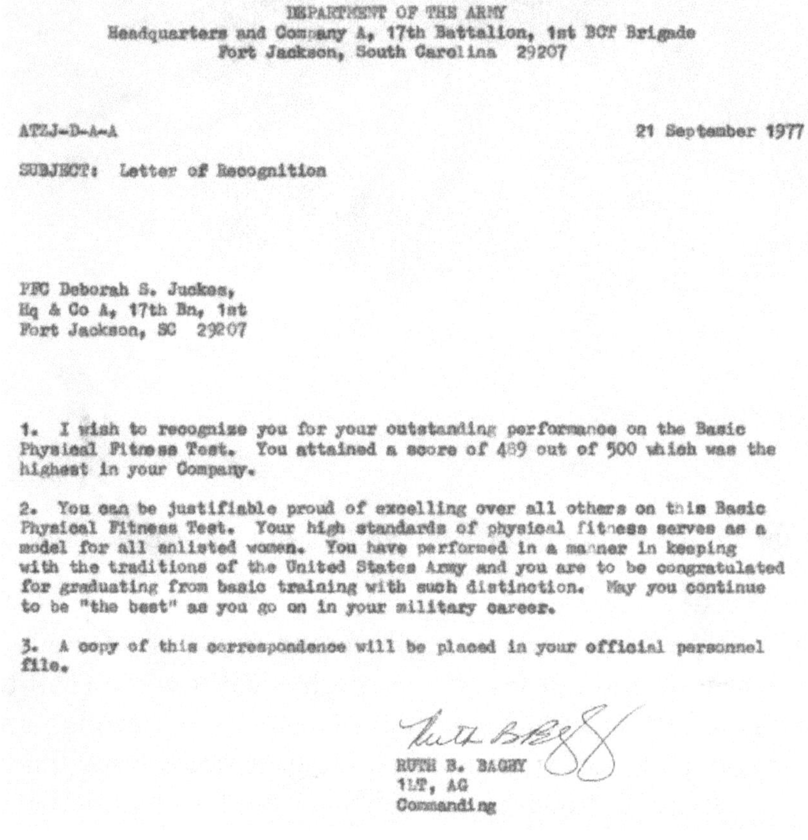

DEPARTMENT OF THE ARMY
Headquarters and Company A, 17th Battalion, 1st BCT Brigade
Fort Jackson, South Carolina 29207

ATZJ-D-A-A   21 September 1977

SUBJECT: Letter of Recognition

PFC Deborah S. Juckes,
Hq & Co A, 17th Bn, 1st
Fort Jackson, SC 29207

1. I wish to recognize you for your outstanding performance on the Basic
Physical Fitness Test. You attained a score of 489 out of 500 which was the
highest in your Company.

2. You can be justifiable proud of excelling over all others on this Basic
Physical Fitness Test. Your high standards of physical fitness serves as a
model for all enlisted women. You have performed in a manner in keeping
with the traditions of the United States Army and you are to be congratulated
for graduating from basic training with such distinction. May you continue
to be "the best" as you go on in your military career.

3. A copy of this correspondence will be placed in your official personnel
file.

                                    RUTH B. BAGHY
                                    1LT, AG
                                    Commanding

Figure 13 High score on PT test.

Things didn't always go well for me though. Really bad things can happen when you put some men in charge of a group of women on a twenty-four/seven basis. Training, living, sleeping, eating, even showering. We had a couple of female drill sergeants, and I often wondered if they had any idea what was going on. I didn't find out myself until the last week or so, how many women

46

were being abused. I felt like I had let my people down. I hadn't protected them. I had failed.

So, here it is, the story I have never told...anyone...ever.

We were close to graduating basic training and everyone was in high spirits. We had the day off and I spent it ironing my uniforms and polishing my boots. It was after dark when I received a message to report to Drill Sergeant in a place we normally never went to in our building. This was enough to make me suspicious. I found the door, knocked, and heard a male voice giving me permission to enter. The room was large and dark with only dim light glowing in several places. One sweep of the room and I froze. I couldn't make out faces but I knew what was going on. It was literally an orgy. Drill Sergeant stood just inside the door and had to yell at me several times to get me to focus on him. I had totally blanked out. My mind shut down yet at the same time it was like a constant screaming in my head. You've heard of fight or flight? There is also—freeze. My brain refused to work; my feet were rooted in place. I finally realized Drill Sergeant was talking to me, giving me orders, but it's like the noise in my head didn't allow me to make sense of any of it. I was so frozen I could barely turn my head, but I did notice there was a second drill sergeant standing close by, watching, just watching. Drill Sergeant yelled at me again and since I was rooted in place, he moved closer. Then I understood what was happening. Drill Sergeant was going to get his final revenge. I would pay for all those times I laughed at him. He was going to assert his dominance and prove to the other drill sergeants that he was in control; that he had absolute power. Nothing would prove it more than to force me to his will in a submissive sex act. He was trying to force me to participate. He didn't want it to be rape. He wanted me to do as he ordered—as I had been programed to do, as I had been trained to do—follow his orders. After all, he couldn't get in trouble if I was a "willing" participant.

He ordered me to my knees, and I have no idea why my body betrayed me. I couldn't think with the screaming going on in my head. I was following orders, after all. This had to be what I was supposed to do, wasn't it? Yet the screaming silently continued. Drill Sergeant moved closer still and unzipped his pants—his United States Army issued uniform pants. He pulled his dick out and stuck it in my face, ordering me to suck on it. I wanted to faint. I wanted to run. I wanted to fight. I wanted to fucking disappear off the face of the Earth.

It is nearly beyond my comprehension why I, and doubtless many other women, felt we had to submit to authority figures no matter what the situation was or what it would cost us. Everything told me how wrong this was, how much I should fight. But, some programming deep in my brain (From birth? From generations ago?) told me it was my "job," my "duty" to obey, as a soldier, as a woman.

To my horror, I opened my mouth, and he shoved his dick in deep. I can't be sure what he said next because the buzzing in my ears was so loud, but my brain had finally engaged. I don't know exactly which came first—the order not to bite—or the bite itself. Then, there was the screaming. I really can't say how much of it was mine and how much was his. His reaction was immediate and brutal. He doubled up his fists and began hitting me in the face. The howling and cussing coming from Drill Sergeant finally drowned out the screaming in my head. I had fallen to the floor and was gagging and spitting up blood. I was vaguely aware that the other drill sergeant was trying to help, was trying to drag me away. I don't dwell on what might have happened if it hadn't been for the other drill sergeant. He pulled me out of the room and helped me back to my barracks. Not to the hospital, but at least I was safe. Due to the swelling and bruising, I was unable to attend the big graduation day for basic training.

I still carry the shame of that day, but only for not having contacted the authorities. I have no idea if the other women were willing participants or not. What I had gone through was something that should not have gone unpunished. But I didn't tell anyone. I just packed my duffle bag and prepared to leave Fort Jackson behind.

No one deserves this type of treatment at anyone's hands. If you or anyone you love has been treated in such a way, speak up, speak out, and get help. Believe me when I say that keeping this buried down in your soul will eat you alive from the inside. It will make you question everything around you, everything you do, and everything you say. It will make you question your worth as a human being. That's what abuse is—losing control of your own mind, your innocence, your spirit, your internal beauty as a human being. Stand up for yourself in whatever manner you are able. Stand up for the victims who will most assuredly follow. The trauma I endured wasn't from the sexual assault, or even the physical beating. That abuse happened to me, was not my fault, and was nothing I had control over. I believed I failed as a decent human being by not reporting the abuse and saving other women from the same fate. I branded myself a coward, and it has taken me so many, many years to heal. You have the power to heal yourself from such a tragedy, but most of us need help to figure out how. Also, I'm not naïve enough to think all the bad guys will be caught and punished. But I do believe you heal just from taking action. Don't be afraid to act. Don't be afraid to ask for help.

I had a couple of buddies at basic, Jo and BJ. Our original orders stated that after basic, all three of us would be assigned to the same fort for our Advanced Individual Training (AIT). Things changed at the last minute. I received orders to report to a different fort. It was the most difficult loss of friends I've ever been through. I really could have used some friends right then. Someone I could/would talk to about how to handle my issues.

Figure 14 Jo & BJ.

Figure 15 Jo & BJ saluting.

AIT was definitely an experience. My company was one of the first experimental training cycles where the women trained side by side with the men. In the first few days, we were even bunked with the men, but they sorted that out after a few sleepless nights; but then all my nights were mostly sleepless. At AIT, all of our drill sergeants were male.

I trained as a light wheeled vehicle mechanic but tended to hang out with the group in EOD, Explosive Ordinance Division. Those guys take partying seriously and I ended up getting my first…and only, tattoo one night after a really bad drunk. I did not pick the tattoo. My drunk Army "friends" did. It was a simple little butterfly on my shoulder blade so it could have been much worse. I don't know how many times over the years my pain-in-the-ass brother, Steve, would smack that tattoo in an attempt to "get the bug off me."

Compared to basic, AIT was relatively painless. Being a mechanic meant they taught us how to read equipment manuals, gave us a vehicle, and told us what to go do each day. Our shop manuals were the only guidance we had for the maintenance we performed. I really enjoyed working with my hands. I loved dismantling and putting machines back together. I even enjoyed changing tires.

Although AIT was a breeze, I did get into one bad fight. I was walking back to the barracks one night, across a big, empty field, when a couple of guys jumped me. I don't know what they wanted. I don't know what their intent was. I do know I lost my fucking mind that night. One guy hit me a couple of times with a pipe before throwing it down. What kind of dip shit, hillbilly, motherfucker starts a fight and then drops his weapon? I picked it up and had every intention of crippling them both, but after a few solid blows to ole dip shit, they high-tailed it out of sight. After returning to the barracks, the on-duty watch called an ambulance, and I was taken to the hospital. Once again, however, I didn't report the two individuals. I just wanted it to be over.

I still remember the day I came home from the Army. One of my drill sergeants gave me a ride home.

Another lesson—not all drill sergeants are evil bastards—not all men (or women) are pieces of shit. Don't lump people together and judge them. You are not like anyone else. Don't ever think that another person carries the same taint of someone that has hurt you in the past. Judge people by their own actions, not the actions of others.

I remember exactly what coming home felt like. I dropped my duffle bag on the floor and finally let my shoulders drop, my arms relax. I quit looking over my shoulder. Then I went to see Josh who was sleeping peacefully in his crib. He was wearing a blue shirt and blue denim pants and smelled like baby powder. I woke him up and snuggled him, but he didn't seem to mind. The second-best thing was a long hot shower, by myself, with nobody watching. I still take long, hot showers as if I think I can wash away memories.

The very little experience I had in the Army Reserve was enough to make me appreciate the friendship and bonds that formed. I wish, I wish, so much, that things had gone differently. I have so much value for the military and really believed that would be my career. Many years later, Josh would go on to serve in the Army, trained as a combat medic. His tour ended right before the war but, his wife, Christina, went on to serve a tour in Afghanistan. I felt like I held my breath every single day she was gone.

Figure 16 *My son, Josh.*

Figure 17 My daughter-in-law, Christina.

CHAPTER 4
WORK, FAMILY, AND FINDING
WAYS TO HEAL

After the Army, my fear of public places and people in general, which was bad enough to begin with, had ratcheted up about 100 percent. I didn't realize it at the time, but I believe now that I was suffering from PTSD. When I came home, all I wanted was to be with my son and take care of him. My parents, however, had decided that they shouldn't legally change Josh's guardianship yet. They would allow him to live with me and I could take care of him, but they would not sign over custody. They may have sensed that something had changed In me, that something wasn't quite right. Unfortunately, I kept my problems locked up tight and shoved way down into a dark hole so I couldn't see them. I wouldn't talk about it. Understandably, they refused to legally give my son back. I had to prove to them that I was good enough. At the time, it felt like the worst betrayal of my life but now, I appreciate everything they did for Josh.

I had hoped to work for my dad in his shop building gas meter test equipment, something Dad and his brother, Jimmy, had invented. It was a side job for him, but he still spent a lot of hours there. Mostly I wanted to learn to weld. Dad wasn't really big on the idea. He wanted the boys to work for him and I don't remember if Steve ever did or not, but Charley sure as hell never did. Dad gave me piss ant jobs that didn't amount to anything and never really taught me much. One day I was grinding some metal with my back turned to the door, hunched over, wearing a face shield, heavy coat, and gloves, when one of Dad's friends came into the shop. I stopped grinding just in time to hear him say, "I see you got one of your sons to come to work for you." Well, damn, that was the end of that short career. Only time I've ever been fired. Dad just couldn't handle it.

Dad decided I should go to work for a friend of his as a waitress in a tiny café right across the street from the refinery. I hated it. I hated dealing with the assholes. I hated the men that thought they had every right to touch me as if I was there for their entertainment. I hated that my father would put me in this position. I didn't want to be flirted with and patted or rubbed on and I wouldn't hesitate to tell them to keep their fucking hands to themselves, no matter how many times the boss ripped me for it. I hated the total lack of respect for me as a woman, as a human being. I just wanted to do my job. I hated the job, but I wanted to work, I had to work.

As much as I hated the dirty old men, I was also susceptible to some flirting. I didn't just hate all men, and I really wanted to be loved. I wanted to be wanted. I was dumb enough, gullible enough, naïve enough to believe some of the bullshit that was thrown at me. I fell for one guy, an out-of-town contractor (red flag). Long story short, we got into a friendly, though somewhat rough, football game, I tackled him and a few hours later his appendix ruptured. He did make it back to his hometown before it actually ruptured, and I felt guilty, so I went to visit him. That's where I met his wife. Surprise! How could I have been so stupid? Truthfully, that's an easy answer. I wanted so badly to be loved that I was willing to believe just about anything.

Josh and I left shortly after that to go back to Artesia, New Mexico, for a short vacation, a recharge really. The dumbass contractor followed me out there and tried to make amends. He offered me a beautiful ring. That ring may still be out there somewhere in the New Mexico sand; I have a really good throwing arm. I had finally come to a realization—"I deserve better." Say it with me folks, anyone who has ever been there. "I deserve better."

Josh and I spent some time with Grandma and Grandpa Juckes, the two dogs, Sir Snuffy Smith and Don Pedro Rojas. I just wanted, needed, to bake in the hot New Mexico sun of home. Once I felt my backbone stiffen, I came back to Oklahoma, back to that crappy café job. I had to work.

Many times in my life when I've been knocked back like this, it took the breath right out of my body. I felt defeated, lost, alone, and even unlovable. Sometimes I just had to find a safe place and let the sun burn the bad feelings away. Once I let go of those self-defeating thoughts, I would feel my old self return, my strength, my compassion, my power. During times like this when I had horses, I would mount up and head away from the barn. It didn't matter where I went, I just wanted the feel of the horse under me and the sun above me, then I would start analyzing my problem. Often, I needed to make a decision. I made a pact with myself not to turn back until a decision had been reached. Yes, total exhaustion often played a part in forcing me to focus and reach a conclusion. It's amazing how the sound of horse's hooves, the jangle of the bit, the squeak of the leather, and the earthy aroma of the sweet, salty sweat coming off of a horse could ease my troubled mind. You might laugh at that but then I'd bet you'd never buried your nose in a horse's neck, in that little hollow just above the shoulder. Buried your nose and breathed in that heady aroma. If only men's sweat smelled like that.

***Figure 18** Me and my quarter horse mare, Lady.*

Figure 19 *Ready for Western Pleasure competition.*

Figure 20 *Horse show with Walking On Clouds as a yearling.*

Figure 21 *Horse show with Mom's miniature stallion, Sonny.*

Soon after my return from New Mexico, back at the crappy café job, I started talking to a guy, Butch, that had a roofing business. Butch came in for lunch one day and mentioned he was hiring and agreed to give me a shot at roofing. I hung up my apron, picked up a menu, and ordered lunch. I was going to need a hearty meal, after all, before starting my new job.

I really liked roofing. It was hard, hot, and rewarding. I could immediately see the results of my work. I could measure how much I had done, how much I had left to do. The day the old man slipped and fell, knocking us both off the roof wasn't enough to get me to quit. I just used the opportunity to pick up a bundle of shingles and carry it up to the roof so I could get more work done.

The worst thing about roofing is that work depended on job availability and weather, no consistency. I had to work. I started looking for something more reliable. I don't know who it was that told me the Conoco Refinery in town was hiring. I was really torn. My dad had worked for the Conoco pipeline company my whole life and worked shift work. His job often took us to multiple locations in several states. I went to so many different schools and left so many friends behind. Each time we moved I made fewer friends. Don't get me wrong, I always had a couple of good friends at each place, and it was very hard to leave them. It seemed like Dad wasn't around a lot. But we did take a vacation together every year. I loved those vacations.

It wasn't until I finished writing this book that the puzzle pieces fell into place, and I realized exactly how important those family vacations were to me. I've had a shrink tell me that it is critical to get away from the house, to take real vacations. Time and time again, I put off taking vacations because of work and so many other stupid reasons. But then finally, very late in my career, I took a real vacation, and my life changed. I'll explain how later.

We had two very memorable vacations. When I was younger, we took a trip from Billings, Montana, back down to Artesia. My brothers and I rode in the back seat of an old station wagon, the backend full of luggage and Christmas presents. To keep us occupied, my parents suggested we play a game of hide and seek—in the back seat of the station wagon. We did, until Charley hid so well, we couldn't find him...or so we believed.

Figure 22 *This may be the vacation where we "lost" Charley in the back seat of the station wagon playing hide and seek.*

On another vacation when I was a bit older, my dad and I rode his BMW motorcycle from Bethalto, Illinois, to Artesia, New Mexico, over 1,000 miles one-way. That was a great trip. We bundled up in snowmobile suits to stay warm. I sat there, still as could be, only my mind in constant movement. Dad would often reach back and touch my leg just to make sure I was still there. I was so happy on the back of my father's bike. The changing scenery captivated me. Often, as we drove the highway, my imagination rode a horse beside us, thundering over the surrounding terrain, leaping over fences or roads as if carried on wings. I could hear the sound of the hoofbeats in sync with the beat of my heart. I really, truly, loved those vacations.

Reflecting more on Dad's career, things changed in 1972 after we moved back to Oklahoma and Dad quit working for Conoco and went to work for Williams Brothers Pipeline. He went overseas, and the family stayed in Oklahoma. This was the beginning of the end for Mom and Dad but then, those things happen. So now I had to decide whether to, at least partly, follow in my father's footsteps. I thought about how many times growing up I had told myself over and over, that I would never go to work at the refinery or the pipeline.

Years later, I worked one semester as an adjunct teacher for "Intro to Refining" at a nearby community college. My boss at the refinery asked me to be very forthcoming with the students on what it would be like to work in the refinery. One of my first assignments for the class was to write a letter to their children telling them why they wouldn't be home for Christmas. More than one student complained about how difficult the assignment was when they had to address the letters to their actual children. It made it too real. There was one student that I'm aware of that chose family over the refinery after taking my class. By this time, I had come to realize what a shitty mom I had been to my kids. I had become more obsessed with the job instead of my family. I had become my father.

CHAPTER 5
(1978) THE START OF MY CAREER IN A "MAN'S" JOB

I was nineteen years old when I applied at the Ponca City, Conoco Refinery and was hired soon after. I remember asking if I was hired because I was qualified or because I was a woman. I did not get an answer. Back then, folks were hired for mechanical (daylights) or operations (shift work). I was told when I got hired that I was going to be assigned to operations. Well, that just figures. My background was mechanical, and I had no idea what operations would involve, other than the dreaded shift work. How would I take care of Josh? Who would watch him while I was working all night and sleeping part of the day? Part of my parents' requirements was that I had to take care of Josh. Mom would not babysit for me. I had to figure out how to take care of things myself. Stress and anxiety started mounting, and I hadn't even started work yet.

I developed my first ulcer at nineteen years old. Doc Palmer was flummoxed. He asked me what in the world could stress me so much. I asked him what time it was. He stared at me for a minute, shook his head, and pulled out his prescription pad.

Doc Palmer and I went through several ulcers over the years before he treated me for the bacteria that causes some ulcers. He also spent some time coaching me about not stressing, relaxing, and having fun. I just shook my head and told him my mother would never approve. He pulled out his prescription pad again.

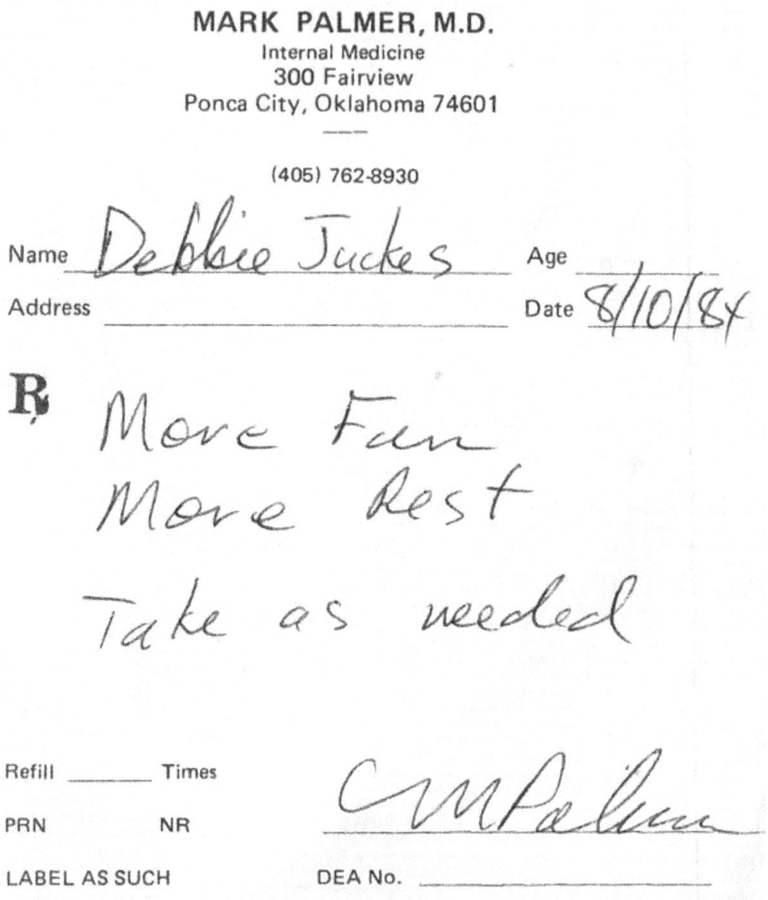

MARK PALMER, M.D.
Internal Medicine
300 Fairview
Ponca City, Oklahoma 74601

(405) 762-8930

Name _Debbie Juckes_   Age _____

Address _____   Date _8/10/84_

R̸

More Fun
More Rest

Take as needed

Refill _____ Times

PRN   NR   _C M Palmer_

LABEL AS SUCH   DEA No. _____

Figure 23 *I wish I'd taken a lot more of this remedy.*

My stomach problems continued and since I didn't know how to destress, I took more prescription drugs for ulcers. Eventually, I had horrible side effects from the drugs. How crazy is it that ulcer medicine would have a side effect of extreme anxiety? So how did they treat it? More drugs. I had to take drugs to combat the drugs that were supposed to heal me.

Fortunately, the second type of drug worked, and I strove to get weaned off of all the medicine. My mother was raised

Christian Science (no doctors, no drugs) and a part of me wondered if maybe she was on the right track. But after she nearly died from pneumonia, I seriously doubted it.

I've worked really hard over the years to control my emotional state, not very well at times, but it's better than taking drugs and turning into a zombie. However, let me clarify that statement—I believe there are times when the chemicals in your brain get so far out of whack that they need a boost to get things back on track. This is when you should unashamedly take the prescribed meds. Always couple the meds with the mental work that goes into getting better, whether on your own or preferably with the help of a great counselor.

My first day at the refinery was weird. They gave me a push broom and told me to sweep up around this one area, the area I had been assigned to as an operator. They explained I wouldn't begin my operations training until after an upcoming turnaround at the Alkylation unit. (Turnarounds were scheduled shutdowns of equipment or units in order to do maintenance work.) Back then, they pulled as many folks out of operations as they could to help with the turnarounds. So, I swept. It was easy to keep busy but being in the refinery was something I'd never experienced. I was shown where the lunchroom was, the control room, the bathroom, and where to sweep. That was it. I have to tell you about the lunchroom. It had these long metal steam boxes along the wall. That was how we heated our lunches up. If you had a sandwich wrapped in foil, it didn't take too long to warm up, about thirty minutes (I guess time is relative). If you had more substantial leftovers, you might have to put it in the steam box for a few hours to get nice and piping hot. Ah, the good old days.

The refinery is loud. With noise from all the pumps, fans, furnaces, steam, it is crazy loud. At least they did offer earplugs, and I was glad to wear them. Back then, we didn't have fireproof clothing, but we did have hard hats. Hard hats take some getting used to. My hair was relatively short in the beginning and easy to put up in a ponytail and tuck up inside the hard hat, so that was no big deal. Long hair was forbidden (to hang down loose) so you had to keep it tucked up so it wouldn't get caught in moving equipment. Hard hats have a webbing inside of them that provides a few inches of space between the outer protective shell and the much more fragile human noggin. Therefore, after spending nineteen years knowing exactly how tall I was and exactly how far I needed to duck when walking under things—big, solid, non-moveable things—I had to relearn my new combined height after jamming my neck several times when I failed to duck low enough for my stupid hard hat to clear.

I spent day one sweeping the concrete around huge, loud, and sometimes even burn-your-skin-off-it's-so-damn-hot equipment, so of course I tried not to touch anything.

In a simplified explanation of an operating area: product moves from one piece of equipment to another through various sized pipes that are generally located in overhead racks. When you get into a compacted operating area, there are many places where the sun doesn't come through the racks but it's generally not dark, just shady. Some areas even had multiple decks with heat exchangers (horizontal cylinders) near the tall towers (vertical cylinders). So, there I was, sweeping away, when I noticed something odd. There were guys hiding behind the concrete stanchions that hold up the pipe racks. What the hell? I'd later recognize some of the men as operators I would be working with. They were all old dudes. Remember, I was nineteen, so they all looked old. But how weird was that? I thought I was socially awkward but here were grown ass men trying to hide to get a peek at the new girl.

The next week I started on the turnaround. Work started a little differently for me, I suppose, than it did for the guys. First, they had a great time making fun of my boots. We were required to wear leather boots, and I had a perfectly good pair of Army combat boots (literally) so that's what I wore. Unfortunately, they were spit-shined as usual. It took me a while to break the habit of shining my boots. Though most of the guys laughed at me from a safe distance, one fellow took a more personal approach to try and get to know me. He sidled up to me, close, really close, leaning over to whisper into my ear, "What would you do if I kissed you on the neck?"

Remember, this is my second day at work. I sidled a fraction closer and whispered in his ear, "What would you do if I kicked you so hard your balls got lodged in your throat?" He gulped and left.

Once the pleasantries were out of the way, I was assigned to the tower crew. The first thing they did was send me to the tool trailer to pick up some supplies. Actually, they told me to go to the tool trailer and get a "donkey dick." I kept my mouth shut, went to the tool trailer, and the guy asked me what I needed. I scanned the items hung on the walls and stored in bins until I finally spotted what looked most like a donkey dick and asked him for a grease stick, about 2" in diameter and 12" long. Okay, from what I've seen on the farm, it might have been a little donkey. I took it back to the crew who all waited expectantly and told them I'd found a dick in case any of them were missing theirs.

The tower crew's job was to clean out and repair the internal parts of the towers. Cool, I was excited to get to work. I quickly learned what job not to have—standby. The standby's job was to stay on the landing outside of the tower and be the safety link to the workers inside. You have to keep track of who goes in and out of the tower and watch for safety hazards outside of the tower such as fires or tornadoes. Did I mention this was Oklahoma? The standby job is extremely important, actually the most important and the absolute worst job. You just sit on a bucket and don't do a damn thing other than freeze your tits off in February. I learned to immediately grab tools and jump into the tower first, so I didn't have to be a standby.

Work inside the towers was fun as long as you were not claustrophobic. You entered the tower through a round manway that in normal operation was covered by a flat, heavy, metal head that bolted into place on the drum flange.

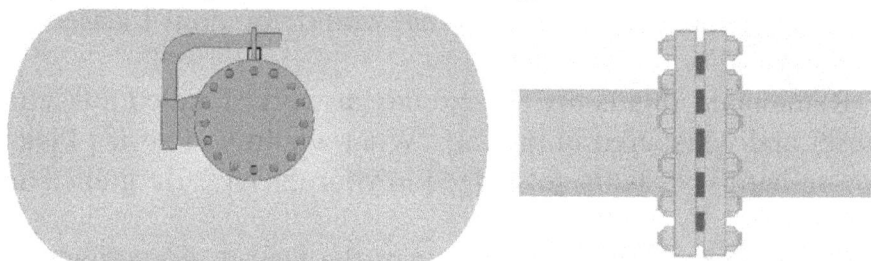

Figure 24 Left—typical closed manway on a horizontal drum; right—pipe flange.

This manway flange is basically the same as a pipe flange. It allows two sections to be bolted together, such as the flat head to the drum manway, or a flange that connects two pieces of pipe. The flange is the outer ring that the bolts run through.

I learned to always be the first person to go in and always to go in feet first so you don't leave your ass hanging out for someone to grab because they would definitely make you wish you hadn't. Going in/out feet first gives you the opportunity to kick the shit out of anyone who thinks they're going to fuck with you. And no, that is not an exaggeration. Back then, not a lot was said if there were "shenanigans" going on. In self-defense, I've kicked, punched, and on one occasion, bashed a guy in the head with my pipe wrench (he started it). I did actually try for the hard hat but those knock off too easy when you're swinging a 24" pipe wrench. Over the years, things got less physical between workers as company tolerance decreased. That is, if the company found out. But there were years of abuse, what they liked to call "horseplay," before that. On one occasion, HR even told me they wished I had whipped another gal's ass, and they would have looked the other way. I was getting wiser by then and knew this was a not-so-subtle ploy by the company to get me to make a big mistake and get rid of two proverbial birds for the price of one.

Back to the towers. The towers have quite a few metal trays in them designed to hold a certain amount of the heavier liquid while also allowing the lighter vapors to bubble up through vents in the trays and rise up the tower. This liquid and gas exchange helps clean the product(s). During turnarounds, workers (like me) enter the towers to clean, inspect, and repair the trays to keep the towers operating efficiently. Each tray has a removable inspection plate that allows access to the next tray. Once we had removed all the inspection plates, we could begin cleaning and replacing worn or nonfunctioning parts or in the worst instances, we would replace the entire tray. Depending on the tower, these horizontal trays could be several feet apart or a whole lot closer together. I've worked in towers where you lay flat on your stomach and have just enough room to work your wrench to remove the nuts and bolts from the inspection plates while bumping your head on the tray above you. That's where the claustrophobia can kick in. It wasn't just from working in a confined space. It was that, combined with the way the guys liked to joke (aka screw with you). Being inside the tower, you have to rely on mechanical light sources. It seemed my flashlight never had working batteries, and my drop light kept getting "accidentally" unplugged. If I was working with a real douche bag, they might even swing the manway cover closed and in worse cases, put a bolt and nut in to prevent you from kicking it open. They also liked to tell stories of other new hires that were accidentally stuck in towers and died when steam, gas, and then hot oil was pumped into the towers. They got graphic about what that would do to a body and how there wouldn't be any traces left by the time the tower was opened again for another turnaround. The important thing here was to never show the guys fear of their stupid stories, especially since my logical mind didn't believe any of the bullshit. But I have to admit, I had some wicked nightmares.

I enjoyed working inside the tower alone and at my own pace but then they moved me to the big tower. This tower had a double set of inspection plates so two of us were sent in to work side by side, though several feet apart (it was a big tower). We had the same tools, the same number of trays, but not the same work ethic. By lunchtime, I was quite a bit further ahead of my coworker. Several of the guys cornered me in the lunchroom and explained that I needed to learn to pace myself, that I was making them look bad. I told them maybe they needed to try and keep up. I didn't give a damn what they thought. At least that's what I told them. Of course I gave a damn. I wanted to be appreciated and noticed for my hard work. I wanted to be respected. Instead, I retreated into the shadows, into silence. That may have been when I realized my horrible habit of not standing up for myself, not defending myself. I had this weird idea that if I argued or tried to defend myself, it would just make me look that much worse with the guys. I feared it would alienate me even further. I really, truly believed it. I wanted so badly to fit in, to be a part of the crew, to be accepted. I didn't want to be "that girl." You know, what the guys referred to as a prude who complains about every little thing, always whining, bitching, and causing trouble. This is probably one of the biggest regrets I've had in my life, not standing up for myself, not fighting harder but instead just taking the shit thrown at me (figuratively speaking) full in the face and letting it drip slowly off as people stood and laughed. Or worse yet, let it dry on my face where I could smell the stink forever and never again be able to look myself in the mirror without seeing the stain of shame. It is so strange to me too, that I turned into the kind of person who would do that. I think my family thought of me as tough. My mother definitely hated the fact that I wasn't feminine, that I liked to play rough and dirty—you know, like actual dirt or even better—mud. I loved good hard work and play that left you sweaty, stinky, wrung out, and exhausted. I loved it.

Let me expand a little on the "that girl" moniker because I felt it or thought it many times in my career. On one hand, I say stand up for yourself; don't take shit off of people. Yet on the other hand, I refer to what I call the whiny little bitches. Here's where I differentiate—don't take a job where you're going to get hot, tired, and dirty, if you don't like to get hot, tired, and dirty. Don't take a job working with mostly men, or mostly women, if you don't like working with men/women. Don't take a job working with a group of folks if every look, joke, or comment is considered a horrendous insult or too inappropriate for your delicate ears. Yes, you'll find this in every group or situation, whether it's vulgarity, racism, sexism, hate, or even haughty disdain. Before you revolt, please read on. I know there are times when looks, jokes, and comments are way out of bounds. It is all in how you handle these issues. People will test your limits, your boundaries. There is a tough balancing act between not letting everyday bullshit remarks piss you off (which just encourages the scoundrels) and stopping blatant assholishness. The best way to handle these situations is to keep it between you and the asshole if possible. For instance, there was a guy who asked me in a group setting at work, what I thought of oral sex. I told him I thought it was something private between two people and not something to be discussed at work. That was it. It wasn't ever mentioned again. Just a test to see how I would react. Had it been a recurring topic of conversation, that's when you tell them it is inappropriate and to stop. You don't have to explain, just tell them to stop. You can also be crystal clear by telling them that if it doesn't stop, you will report them. It is important to set boundaries and communicate them. If you are offended by some type of behavior and don't say anything, you are in fact communicating that the behavior is acceptable. You <u>don't</u> want to try and ignore the inappropriate behavior until it gets so bad you lose your cool and fly off the handle. I've found that when I did this, the final straw was something small and insignificant when looked at as a single incident. I looked like I was totally overreacting to what happened. Nobody knew that, for me, it was an accumulation of events. Events that tipped the scales and sent me down Crazy Street going the wrong way on a one-way avenue.

Worst-case scenario, if they choose to be a dumbass and continue the inappropriate behaviors, report them. You have to make a judgement if those folks are just trying to test your boundaries, or if you're dealing with someone who needs to be dealt with. I will tell my story of when the boundaries were crossed, and action had to be taken in Chapter 11. Do not go jumping ahead. Read the story, follow the flow.

My many years at the refinery were not all doom and gloom. I really liked the work and most of the people. Too many times, I was in over my head without any idea of what I should be doing. Trial by fire some people would call it. In a refinery, that could be literal. Like the day of the tower fire where the heat was so intense that the surrounding iron structures were warped and twisted. Or, the tank fire that horribly injured a couple of employees. Worst of all, the awful fire that took the life of our coworker. But I'm getting ahead of myself again.

CHAPTER 6
OPERATIONS, SHIFT WORK, AND COOL OLD DUDES

After my first turnaround, I started training at my new operating area. There were a few young guys there but mostly, there was the oddest assortment of some of the coolest old dudes on planet Earth. I remember thinking that we (young people) would never have the exaggerated personalities this group of old guys did. I really didn't have many big problems with the older guys. Oddly enough, they were the ones that accepted me. Like Bobby, dear sweet, adorable Bobby. He always made me think of an elf. If ever there was a Santa's elf in disguise, it would have been Bobby. He was kind, quiet, and always there if you needed help. I remember working hoot owl shift and we made paper airplanes. Bobby worked very intently, peeking through his little round spectacles, folding the paper so precisely. He had just sent one airplane flying when the production supt (pronounced "soup," short for superintendent—they were actually called night supts back then) came in the door and the damn airplane lodged in the guy's ear. I also remember being at the hospital for Bobby's heart surgery. Before they took him in, I held his hand and tried to think of only encouraging words. His family hadn't arrived yet and although I didn't know them, I just couldn't imagine why they weren't there. I gave him a kiss on his grizzled, chipmunk cheek and told him I would see him at work when he was recovered. I waited at the hospital through the surgery. Afterwards the doctor came out and asked for his family and thankfully, they were there. Then I knew it was okay for me to leave. You would think it would be normal, or expected to introduce myself to his family, but I was afraid. So many people jumped to the wrong conclusions about my relationships with my male coworkers. I couldn't stand it if they thought that about me and Bobby, not for my sake but I couldn't stand the possibility that anyone would dare think anything salacious about Bobby. Many guys I worked with were great to me at work, but outside…outside they would pretend they didn't know me. It is amazing just how invisible you can become. That was something that plagued me my whole life, the feeling of being invisible.

There was also Adler. He was the physical opposite of Bobby, large and looming. He had a wicked sense of humor and had the rare ability to say sexual innuendos, then waggle his big, bushy gray eyebrows and make me crack up each time. Not one time did I ever think Adler meant anything by his words other than goofing around. I understood his INTENT. Had I taken his comments personally, as an insult, I would have missed out on so many hard belly laughs. Adler was such a unique gentleman. He smoked a pipe, and I had a horribly bad (got to four packs a day) smoking habit myself. We had a tiny little shed with bench seats that served as our designated smoker. Several of us would be sitting around smoking, maybe talking about work or just idle gossip. Adler would take a puff on his pipe, lean over towards me, and quote a line from a song: "If I said you had a beautiful body would you hold it against me?" Then, of course, the inevitable bushy eyebrow waggle. Still cracks me up.

There were other guys though that weren't gentlemen like Bobby and Adler. One old dude never spoke to me again after a woman, who I later found out was his wife, called one evening asking for him. He wasn't on shift, so I checked the schedule and told her he was on vacation for the week. She seemed surprised and asked me to double check. I did, same outcome. He came back on shift a week later and although he'd stopped speaking to me, he told anyone who would listen what a bitch I was for ratting him out to his wife. I told him I wasn't about to lie to her and the problem wasn't my actions but his, but it didn't matter, I was invisible. Some of the other guys looked at me differently too, like I had betrayed the pack.

The time came when the company decided to make me permanent. All hourly, union represented workers came in as temporary and then the company had fewer problems getting rid of us if we didn't measure up. Made sense. However, the union had a limit on the time so the company couldn't drag it out and keep us from making the higher pay/benefits. I went to HR to do my paperwork. I remember they slid a paper across the table and told me to sign a bid sheet for the operations job. I raised an eyebrow and reminded them that I was still temporary, and only permanent employees can bid on jobs. Bidding on an operations job would force me to stay with the twenty-four/seven shift work job and not give me an opportunity to bid on a mechanical job working daylights with weekends and holidays off. They told me to sign the bid sheet and then they would sign the papers making me permanent. Being me, I reminded them again that this wasn't following proper protocol. They pushed the bid sheet closer and waited. It's amazing how many thoughts, images, and feelings can pass through your brain in any given moment. They say that happens when you die but it happens to me all the time. Yep, I'm an over thinker. There was the part of me that wanted to be the hero, the person that didn't let anyone cram anything down their throat, the tough bitch. There was the mother who wanted to take care of her son, make sure he had clothes, food, and a place to live. The mother who would have the opportunity to give him better things. There was the bitter, choking anger and once again, being forced to do something, something that was not right, that went against the publicly documented rules and regulations for proper, ethical (in my opinion) behavior. There was the logical side of me that remembered something that I had heard already, "The company is going to do what the company wants to do." I remember thinking I couldn't fight this; I shouldn't fight this...I wouldn't fight this. I signed the paper to bid on the operations job and then HR made me permanent.

You may have caught my comment about the situation being unethical "in my opinion." Our company had very strict, very explicit, very well-documented rules on ethics. Any actionable violation had to fall under one of the categories. In other words, if it didn't fit neatly into one of the specific categories, it wasn't a violation. We had to hope that the company was so brilliant, so insightful, so perfect in its compilation of offenses, that nothing, let me repeat, nothing unethical would fall outside of their documented rules. I wonder if they thought the same thing when they documented safety protocol for Chernobyl?

There was indeed some comfort to having a permanent position. The union would protect me, and the company could no longer fire me without just cause. Nevertheless, I continued the habit of watching my ass in those early years. For instance, our control room had paper strips and pens that recorded different operating parameters, like the paper strips from an EKG. These recorders covered the upper half of the walls from one end to the other along with a few dial or column type indicators. We would change out the paper and refill the ink cartridges as needed. I was doing this one night, standing on a small step stool to reach the instrument, not thinking about my back, or my ass to be more exact, being turned to the guys. When I backed down off the stool, one of the old dude's hands clapped up solidly between my legs. I spun around, so furious I'm sure my hackles were literally standing up. I briefly noted the surprised expression on the old guy's face. It's possible he had just been clowning around and showing off for the boys, pretending to grab my butt, when I unfortunately stepped down right into his hand. His expression turned to fear as I felt my face burning with rage and humiliation. I wanted to tell the son-of-a-bitch to never lay a hand on me again. I wanted to make an example of him and scream at the top of my lungs. I went after him, and he backed away so fast I thought he was going to fall and hurt himself. I wondered what would happen if I'd put this guy in his place, like I should, like I needed to. What would happen to my reputation with the other guys? Would more of them shun me? I was still struggling so hard to try to figure out how to fit in and be a part of the group instead of an individual, an unwanted stray, a female they were forced to endure. What if they complained about me to HR, said I didn't fit in? They do that you know. My brain ratcheted through all of this in the time it took me to back him up against the opposite wall. My throat muscles clenched so tightly I choked on the words, but I needed this job. I needed to work. Unspoken, my words died with my pride, and shame of myself replaced it as I walked silently away.

Instead of things getting better as time went on, they got worse. The work was fine. I really enjoyed my job. I loved working with tools and being outdoors even in harsh weather. I loved the paycheck. I could buy things for Josh; not just things he needed but stuff I wanted him to have like his first tricycle. I have absolutely no fashion sense and my personal taste went to the darker, fade-into-invisibility colors. But I didn't want that for Josh. I remember buying so many clothes for him, OshKosh B'Gosh and Garanimals because they coordinated the outfits for you. I wanted Josh to fit in with other kids—to be as well dressed, not looking like a reject, not looking like me. Back then, I thought I was really being crazy, wild and fun when I dressed him in blues and greens and matching outfits. Years later when I found out he liked the color orange it shocked me. I looked back on the kids' time with me and wondered how much I might have hampered their outlook on life, their choices, if they had stayed with me. Back then, it never occurred to me that they (Josh and later Jake) might like something different than I did, that I should expose them to different things and let them make those choices.

Clothes were the least of our worries. I was still in shift work, three rotating shifts, days (6 a.m. to 2 p.m.), nights (2 p.m. to 10 pm) and hoots (10 p.m. to 6 a.m.). Mom was working then too since Dad was gone overseas. They weren't divorced yet, but that was coming. She helped a little when I worked hoots. I tried hiring individuals to babysit, but it was hard finding someone to trust and someone willing to work those hours. I did eventually get him into a great daycare. I still can't believe how wonderful those ladies were. The only problem was the hours. They didn't open before I had to be to work on days and I got into some serious trouble for being late to work. One of them, and I hate myself a little for not remembering her name, let me bring Josh to her house so that I could get to work on time. She was a lifesaver, but that only helped for the early shift. Childcare was a constant problem, and I never understood why the company didn't help. I guess most of the workers were male and didn't bear the responsibility for taking care of the kids—yes, I understand what a horrible generalization that is, but you really didn't hear much about single men raising kids back then. My sincere apologies to any men out there who agonized the same way Josh and I did. There is one guy that comes to mind that I know raised his kids on his own. It still upsets me that to this day that a company who has shift workers doesn't provide a safe, nurturing environment for the employees' kids. A job in the refinery is a big enough risk but just imagine how much your mind would ease if you knew your child was somewhere safe and well cared for. I just don't get it.

I personally feel that providing quality childcare is how more big companies could make a difference in attracting dedicated, long-term employees. Especially today with so many women now entering once male-dominated fields. Many companies offer incentives to young engineers. These folks have made commitments to getting their education and are just starting or hoping to start families now that they have their degrees. The company has a great "New Hire Network" that offers lots of socializing and exposure. Why not offer something more practical like childcare? Nobody would benefit more than the operators working twenty-four/seven shift work or the mechanical personnel working hours and hours of overtime, often unscheduled.

I know the company looks at the cold hard cost of such a thing as on-site twenty-four/seven daycare. But, how do you quantify a parent's ease of mind knowing their child is cared for and protected? How much better and safer is the work performed when an employee isn't distracted with worry? Whew, that was a great soapbox moment.

CHAPTER 7
A LIFELONG COMMITMENT TO SAFETY

Safety was/is a big thing for me. It's really pretty simple. I wanted to go home at the end of each shift. I wanted to be able to walk in the door with all my fingers and toes. Safety was something I never took lightly. I had two goals for my career: safety and retirement. They actually fit together. My main goal from the first day of work was to retire. In order to retire, I had to live long enough; I had to be healthy; I had to do my work safely. I had to work efficiently to make the company profitable enough that they would, after my long and illustrious career, pay me a fortune to leave.

I kept safety in mind every day at work and I wasn't the only one; it was drilled into us. Safety was something the company truly believed in, supported, taught, and demanded of us. I can never appreciate that enough. Still, I sure had some narrow escapes I think you might like to hear about. This will jump around in time a bit but once I get on a roll telling these stories, it's hard to stop. So here goes.

As with most jobs, the new employee gets the hind tit, the dirty job, the least desired job, and the senior employee usually stands at a safe distance and watches. On just such a day, my trainer, John, and I went out to check a newly repaired fan on the cooling tower. The controls for the fan were located on the ground so we didn't have to climb the tower each time we made changes to the fan speed or direction. To test the fan would require one person on the ground switching the controls and one to stand at the same level of the fast-moving blades of death to make sure everything was working properly. Guess where I was!

Let me explain the cooling tower a bit. Water is used as a cooling agent for many of the refinery processes. As the water heats up from the exchange, it then needs to be cooled back down so that it can be circulated back through the system. This is done by trickling the water down through a cooling tower. The tower is a large rectangular wooden structure with vented sides and huge fans on top located behind tall fiberglass shrouds. You've probably seen these with vapor clouds rising out of them in colder weather.

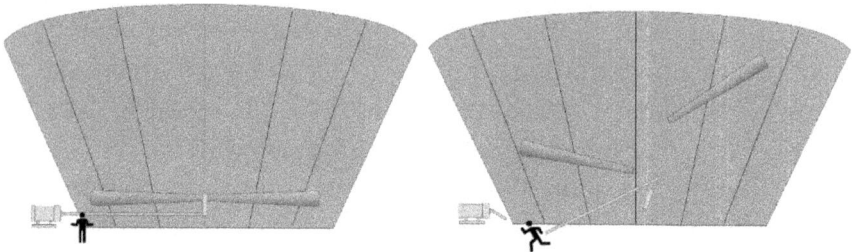

Figure 25 *Cooling towers shroud with motor and fan blades inside the shroud (left) and after catastrophic failure (right).*

The fans are engineered to run forward or backward, much like a normal ceiling fan, either forcing air down into the cooling tower or in normal operation, pulling the hot air out of the tower. The fans lay parallel to the top of the tower and a drive shaft runs from the fan to a motor sitting outside of the shroud. My job that day was to check that the fan ran smoothly in both directions and that there was no excessive vibration. An electrician was also on hand to check the repair. I stood close to the motor and watched the fan through a small hole bored through the shroud. I radioed John and told him to try the fan in reverse. Everything seemed normal, so I told John to shut the fan down. After it had quit turning, I radioed John to switch it into low, forward mode. Again, things looked great, and the electrician seemed satisfied. I radioed John again and told him to kick the fan on high. I immediately heard racket inside the shroud and noticed the drive shaft begin to buck up and down. I heard the electrician yell, "RUN!" I meant to run, I really did, but the sight of the motor caught my attention.

The large motor, securely bolted to the sturdy wooden deck, dipped downward, forcing the wood flooring down, and then suddenly sprang back up. I watched as the drive shaft broke loose from the motor and was sucked into the shroud. The banging inside was deafening. I saw enormous chunks of shrapnel (fan blades) flying out of the top of the shroud. My mind and my feet finally synched, and I turned and ran. Although I couldn't fully appreciate my timing, there were several witnesses to the incident. From their vantage point, it looked as if I'd just been killed. I simultaneously ran away from the shroud just as the massive shaft harpooned itself through the fiberglass, right where I had just been standing. They found fan pieces scattered across the refinery, but I lived another day closer to retirement.

I was low enough in unit seniority that I still spent time in the yards doing labor work. I didn't mind because at least I'd be working day shift. It was less pay but worth it. One of the most traumatic stints in the yards was cleaning the old lead tanks. When a tank is emptied, they do what they can to clean them by mechanically flushing them out. Part of the cleaning success depends on where the outlet pipe is located. Since some products may have contaminants entrained in them, the outlet piping could be above the tank floor. This allowed any solids to fall out and not get pumped to the next location. Even tanks that have a lower outlet pipe can still get crap laying on the floor, though not nearly as much. Since these tanks were going to be demolished, they needed to be clean, especially in a case like this where you had the health hazard of the lead additive. Those of us working inside the tank were required to don supplied air masks (full-face mask with a long air hose running back to fresh air cylinders). We manually shoveled the sludge off the floor and into five-gallon buckets, which we then carried back to the manway two at a time. Workers outside the tank dumped the buckets into tubs that were later hauled off for disposal. I don't remember how long it took us, but it was several days.

Since we were working with a known contaminant, lead, we had to follow extra safety precautions. Every morning the crew supervisor would give me a fresh pair of white coveralls with the explanation that the lead would show up red on the white coveralls. It seemed odd because they were so stained with red blotches that I wasn't sure how I would know if I got a fresh stain. I was also told that to mitigate contamination I couldn't wear any—ANY—of my own clothes. I was given a pair of white socks, and the males were given socks and underwear. My supervisor didn't think it was fitting for a woman to wear men's underwear, so I had to go without. Of course, they didn't have any type of bra either. Before every break, lunchtime and quitting time, we had to take a shower and don regular coveralls before going to the lunchroom. After break, we'd get back into the white coveralls to go back to work. At least they did have a women's locker room and shower. I am immensely grateful for that. Each day the supervisor would give me coveralls with buttons missing or broken zippers. Some had tears in strategic areas. Maybe the guy's coveralls had the same problem. I don't know as I never looked that closely. After the first day, I carried a good supply of paper clips and duct tape. Each morning, I would spend a few minutes repairing my coveralls and closing all the gaps. As the days went by, I got goosier as I used more and more paper clips and duct tape to hold my coveralls together. Everyone knew what the white coveralls meant and several commented on my fancy repair jobs. The looks and comments chaffed as badly as being naked underneath the rough coveralls.

I really appreciated that the crew I worked with treated me respectfully. Maybe it was because I filled and toted just as many buckets as they did. I still had the habit of being the first one to jump into the work. The contractors, however, were a lot more vocal. Vocal I could handle, but as I have already said, I'd learned to watch my ass. What happened that day, happened so fast, I really didn't plan it. I was in my white coveralls, walking down the middle of the road just outside of the lunchroom on my way to the tanks. I suppose it happened there so that plenty of people could watch. Remember, refineries are noisy, and I never heard the guy come up behind me. I did feel him goose me in the ass and I was wired so tight I just reacted. I whirled around and hit the guy full in the face with every ounce of force I could muster. He went over backwards like a felled tree and just laid there not moving a muscle. I don't know what happened after that. I just turned around and went to the tank, grabbed my tools and went to work. I never saw the guy again and fortunately never got called to HR about it. I did hear a lot of whispers in the lunchroom, but nobody goosed me again. Once we finished with the tanks, we went to medical to get a blood test done to measure our amount of lead exposure. Mine tested, "within acceptable limits."

There was another gal, Pam, who worked at the refinery for a long time that was even goosier than I was. I heard one guy got her really good, and that she was going to get her revenge. Pam, who had a sweet, happy personality, was all kinds of tough, physically tough, like tear-your-head-off-with-her-bare-hands tough. I was sitting in the smoker one day with the alleged gooser and a couple of other guys when the tiny little screen over the tiny little window was bashed in. I saw the look on the dude's face as he was grabbed around his jacket collar and then, woosh, he disappeared head first out the window, the soles of his boots the last I saw of him. The whole building rocked because I believe that guy was actually slightly bigger than the window. We heard quite a ruckus outside but none of us dared to even take a peek. We just sat plastered against the walls, flinching away from the window. The poor guy did survive the incident, but I think he did a much better job of not goosing people after that.

Since we're talking about Pam, I need to tell the story of how she almost accidentally killed a coworker, Raymond. Fortunately for him, I was there to save his life. I mentioned that Pam was strong. She had a habit of sneaking up on Raymond and getting him in a chokehold. It was damn near impossible to break Pam's hold once she had you in a headlock. On this day, I was reading up the board, writing down the flows, temperatures, and pressures from the paper charts. I heard a commotion going on behind the board. Raymond had a work desk behind the board, so I went around the corner to check on him. What I saw shocked me. It looked like Raymond had been sitting at his desk, on his normal high-chair-type stool. Pam had obviously snuck up on him from behind and now had him in a chokehold. Normally, Raymond was good about tucking his chin so that Pam couldn't actually choke him. He must not have been fast enough that day because Pam's arm was firmly under Raymond's chin, and he was already turning different shades of red and blue. Pam had pulled him backwards and due to the tall stool, Raymond couldn't get his feet on the floor. The poor guy was in a terrible situation and Pam had no idea. It looked like he could pass out at any minute.

I looked at Pam and in a slow, unhurried drawl, told her, "You'd better turn him loose. I'm not going to give the son of a bitch mouth-to-mouth."

Pam immediately jerked her arm away and poor ole Raymond toppled over backwards, chair and all. He hit the ground with a loud, "woof" and began sucking air. He tried to talk, but it took him a minute to catch his breath. Pam and I moved closer to try to make out the words. Finally, hand over his heart, Raymond said, "She loves me! She saved my life." I rolled my eyes in mock disgust and left him lying on the floor to return to my work. I made sure and waited until I got back around the board before I grinned from ear to ear. I'm sure glad ole Raymond didn't die that day. He was one heck of a character.

CHAPTER 8
(1980) UNION VS COMPANY, THE STRIKE

Contract time was always nerve-wracking, no matter if you were union (represented) or company (non-represented). If you were represented the contracts being negotiated would reflect your pay and benefits. If you were non-represented, you had to train to fill in should the union call a strike.

I hadn't worked at the refinery very long when we went out on strike. It was a relatively quiet event in the big picture, non-violent by most accounts, but there were some issues. The first day of strike, we had picketers packing all the gate entrances. We kept cars stalled for as long as we could before allowing them to drive into the complex. Company people were required to work during the strike and some "scabs" (union represented workers who didn't honor the picket line), were also allowed to work. Not all of the people crossing the picket line handled it amicably.

For those company folks who had to work, I didn't blame them. After all, my dad had worked through a few strikes himself as a non-represented employee and it was a lot more violent, back in his time. For the scabs that worked, I really hoped it was because their financial situation demanded they must. Many scabs, however, just worked because they made a tremendous amount of money. For these people, life was hell when the union folks came back to work.

The first day of the strike was very tense for everyone. As we union employees blocked traffic and crowded around the cars, I can see where it might have intimidated some folks. One driver decided he was going through the picket line regardless and pushed his car into the crowd at low speed but still striking several picketers. The reaction was as expected, and several picketers began pounding on the car. I saw the antenna get broke off the car, but it was a weird accident. The driver lurched forward a second time and caught a picketer from behind. The picketer threw his arm out to catch his balance and hit the antenna with the back of his arm, breaking it off. I don't think the guy who did it even realized; he was just lucky he didn't fall and get run over. Another picketer spotted the antenna on the ground and picked it up. Suddenly, in the midst of all this panic with so many of us worried that we would get run over by a car, the cops swarmed in and hauled off the guy with the antenna. For some reason, it was okay for the douche bag driving a—how much does a car weigh?—approximately two-ton car into a group of picketers, but the union guy with a wimpy antenna gets hauled off to jail for having a "deadly weapon." I heard there were several other union folks hauled off by the police but that's the only one I witnessed.

The strike calmed down after the first day when the union received an injunction that covered the acceptable conditions of our picketing. The rules covered the duration of time company employees could be detained before entering the refinery complex. Only one person would be permitted to walk in front of the vehicle before allowing it to pass through the gates. So obviously, there were a lot less people walking picket after that first day. Many union folks went out and got temporary jobs to be able to pay their bills while the strike continued. For one brief moment of insanity, I thought about finding a waitress job and then wanted to beat my head against a wall—literally. I had to take care of Josh. I had to work. I stressed even more as the union dug in and warned us, they were ready to fight as long as it took. The union did have a fund to help those who were in desperate need, but I just hated to do that unless absolutely necessary. Then I got lucky. A friend of mine asked me to walk picket for her. The union put out a schedule telling us when and where we were supposed to walk picket, and it included all the union folks if they had taken up part-time jobs or not. To meet those requirements, they would hire someone to walk for them. Janie had a good job, so she paid me a decent wage to walk for her, and then someone else did, and someone else. I made enough money walking picket to pay my bills and take care of my son.

I spent enough time walking picket that I got pretty bored. I started thinking of different ways to entertain myself. One day I took Josh's small, maybe sixteen-inch tall toy robot out on the picket line with me. When a car approached, I would hold my hand up from the side to stop them. Nearly everyone did, but some would just drive through. I'd wind up the robot, set it on the ground and it walked in front of the car. Many drivers got a kick out of it. I also made the mistake of taking a volleyball, and if I remember right, dragging my little sister, Diana, with me one day and we volleyed the ball back and forth. That ended tragically when the ball bounced out into the street and met its end under the wheels of a city dump truck.

I walked picket and watched while truckloads of supplies went inside. One day a pickup truck drove through with the backend full of booze. Many of the employees working through the strike stayed inside the complex so they didn't have to cross the picket line each day. In a way, it honored the picket line by not brazenly, in your face, driving across it every day. The folks worked, ate, and slept inside the complex so a lot of supplies were needed. Several of the delivery drivers were sympathetic with the strike and would give us part of their provisions, cigarettes, food, or snacks. Not sure if anyone scored booze or not.

The union also delivered food and drinks to us. It was cold, so we had a lot of hot chocolate and chili. One really cold, late night, (did I mention we picketed twenty-four/seven?) my brother Steve, who also worked for the refinery, another gal, Dora, and I were scheduled at the south gate. Damn, it was cold, but we had our chili and hot chocolate. All three of us crawled into Steve's truck to stay warm until we saw a vehicle coming. Then one of us would jump out, walk in front of the vehicle then jump back into the warm truck. Sadly, it doesn't take much in the wee hours of the night to get sleepy. Dora was the first to drift off. That's when I guess the chili kicked in. She started farting truly competition worthy farts. Believe me, I know what it takes because I had two brothers, and we did a lot of fart competitions. As much as we should have been immune, due to exposure therapy, Steve and I had to bail out of the truck. Man, that was a long cold shift.

The most dramatic event for me during the strike was the day I took Josh's tricycle to the picket line. At first, I would just jump on the tiny trike, knees poking high in the air as I tried my best to pedal my way across the gate in front of the vehicles. I'm not really tall, just 5' 9" but that was a really small trike, and I imagine I looked like quite an idiot. That day, I was working by the gate closest to the railroad tracks and the loading docks. I saw a truck coming down the road beside the docks on its way out of the complex. I jumped on my trike and took off full speed ahead, which was actually slower than I normally walk. I raced to reach the truck to make sure I could delay him from going home to be with his family, to do my union duty, to serve a purpose in life. He reached the gate first and slowed, maybe to allow me to do my part? He hadn't come to a full stop though, so I ducked my chin and really tried to crank those pedals. That is when the accident happened.

Head ducked, chin tucked, knees about ear level, elbows jutting out behind me like the wildly flapping wings of a drunk seagull, I plowed into the tire of the truck. I bounced off and in dramatic fashion, slow motion, fell over sideways in a tangled ball of dedicated striker and tricycle. The rear wheel spun slowly as I lay unmoving on the ground, feet still on the pedals.

As I mentioned earlier, it was very cold during that strike. I had so damn many clothes on that I probably could have jumped in front of that volleyball-killing dump truck and still survived. I lay there frozen in fear wondering how much trouble I had just gotten myself into. I could be fired for this. Had I just screwed up my career over some stupid little stunt? I heard the muffled voice of the truck driver through my stocking cap and ear warmers. I finally released my death grip and rolled off the trike worried that I might have damaged Josh's toy. Security showed up, and they didn't look happy. They asked the driver if he wanted to file charges and without hesitation, he said no. Thank you, sir! Security said they would let me off the hook this one time, on one condition. I have to admit, I was terrified. They explained that they had me on tape and there was no denying what had happened. I just about fainted. They repeated they had it all on tape, all of it except the fall, and would I please do it again. I finally made eye contact with them, and they burst out laughing saying that was absolutely the funniest thing they had seen in a long time. After more guffawing and discussion, we concluded it would be reckless to attempt my foolhardy adventure a second time and maybe we'd best leave well enough alone.

Years later, when I was working non-union represented jobs, I had to train to work potential strikes. One year I was put on standby to go to Lake Charles in the event their refinery went out on strike. The training isn't easy, especially if you're required to train on units in which you are unfamiliar. Normally, I was lucky enough to be assigned locally to the area I had worked previously. There is a lengthy test also and you might think that if we really didn't want to work the strike, we could just play stupid and fail the test. But, once you're on the company side, your pay/benefits aren't set in stone. Raises, bonuses, etc., are meted out by the work you do, the money you make the company, how much they like you, and possibly where you go to church, or your kids go to school (…in my opinion). Oh, but I've jumped way down a rabbit hole there, haven't I? I'm sure I'll touch on this again.

Fortunately, in my forty-year career, we only had the one strike. My opinion of strikes? It may seem like a feasible option when passions are running high. "We'll bring the company to their knees!" "They'll never be able to operate without us!" Yada, yada, yada. I know that did work in the old days. But today, even if it works and you get a portion of your demands met, you will never recoup the losses it took to get there. Fortunately, union workers will make this sacrifice to ensure the needs of future employees. How I wish that both sides could sit across the table from each other and work respectfully to reach mutual agreements. There has to be give and take. The only way to be truly successful is if both sides want the other to succeed long term.

CHAPTER 9
(1980/82) BOBBY JACK, BEGINNINGS, AND ENDINGS

Post-strike, I continued my training in operations and took it very seriously. So seriously in fact, that when I met my first husband, I cussed him for getting in my way at work. I was in the control room when we got an alarm that a compressor had failed. I grabbed my hard hat, wrenches, and gloves and ran out the back door. Our control room, located just yards from operating units, was designed to be blast proof, so even the doors were substantial. I threw my shoulder into the door as I hurried out to handle the emergency. I took about two steps and ran straight into this dumbass that was just standing there on the porch. I hit him so hard that it knocked me on my ass but didn't seem to faze him. I was pissed! The compressor was down, and I had to get it running again. That took some time and this asshole had just slowed me down. If I had any doubts whatsoever that this guy was an asshole it was actually written right there on his hardhat—ASSHOLE. I called him a few other choice names and then ran off to the compressor building.

Later that day, emergency handled, one of my fellow operators, Rick, told me that he had a friend that wanted to meet me. The guy was a contractor that was currently working in the refinery. Like I mentioned before, I didn't hate men, and I really wouldn't mind dating. I was just too shy to really get into it, but I said yes. I'll be damned if Rick's friend didn't turn out to be the ASSHOLE. He was tall, dark, and his beard made him look like a pirate. It turned out the asshole had a real name, Bobby Jack Stieber, and Bob loved kids. He had a daughter, Sasha, who was close to Josh's age.

Bob and I were dating when the flare drum fire happened. Bob was working somewhere out in the plant, and I had been pulled into the yards for another turnaround.

I was working as a pipefitter helper assigned to install blinds. Blinds are solid metal, pancake-like discs with a long handle (picture a flat skillet) that are inserted between the flanges. Our job that day was to put blinds into the pipes coming off the huge flare drum to prevent any hydrocarbon, steam, or contamination intrusion into the drum through connected piping. Once isolated that way, the drum could be safely entered, cleaned, inspected, and repaired. Scaffolds were erected around the horizontal drum to allow us to climb onto the top and install a huge blind. I think there were at least six of us because the blind was so big and heavy. We were all geared up in fresh air hoods with attached air lines that ran back to a wagon on the ground with fresh air cylinders. This was required because the flare drum is a dangerous character in itself. All sorts of gasses are vented to the flare drum where any liquid is caught and drawn off. The gases that aren't recovered are then vented to the flare. The flares are just what you might imagine, tall torch-like stacks with a flame on top to burn up the vented gas which destroys the contaminants, thereby protecting the environment. A flare is a last line of defense. Every effort is made to never put any type of hydrocarbon to the atmosphere, but in an emergency when a unit over-pressures, the flare drum and then the flare, is a controlled way to safely handle any releases. The flare itself is normally situated well away from the flare drum. It sits in an open area in case the flare is overwhelmed with liquid that could potentially be released to the atmosphere. There were a few times long ago, when flaming liquid was spewed to the ground, burning the grass at the base of the flare; but that was long ago.

I do want to take a minute to say how proud I am of our company for all they have strived to do for the environment. I believe they have always been proactive in their efforts to minimize the refinery's impact on the environment. They have made great strides over the years and meet extremely strenuous air quality targets today. They also worry about being a good neighbor to the community.

Back when I was a kid living in Ponca, we'd come back to town after being on vacation. I always looked for the refinery towers and flares looming high in the air to know we were almost home. I thought of the brightly burning flares as a welcome home light. But you really realized you were almost home when the odors from the refinery assailed you. You could smell all the oily stuff but also the waste gas that made your nose burn and caused headaches. That was a long time ago and like I mentioned, the company has made great strides in environmental quality. Today, I love looking out my back door and seeing the refinery lights and all I smell is the fresh air. I know that my relatives and my neighbors are being looked after as the refinery has done their best to be a good neighbor. They strive to always maintain rigorous environmental standards and monitoring and about the only smells you get today are the smell of the bugs. Yep, the refinery has bugs, but they have them intentionally and they serve another great purpose in keeping the environment clean by eating contaminants. Occasionally there might be a "bug kill" and then those little dudes stink. But, let's get back to the flare drum.

I want to paint a clear picture of that day. The flare drum is a large, horizontal drum with rounded ends, capsule shaped. Piping comes out of the top of the flare drum, drops down, and runs straight to the flare off in the distance. The point being that when you're on top of the drum, you can clearly see the pipe that goes to the flare along with a clear view of the flare itself. As mentioned earlier, there were several landings of scaffolding erected on the ends of the flare drum to allow us access to each pipe.

One of the workers that day was Don, an old, laid back, never-in-a-hurry pipefitter. I had trouble working with Don just because he could drag his feet with the best of them. I would get so frustrated waiting on him to get his tools, waiting on him to tell a story, waiting on him to think. So, yep, I was working with him that day.

We got all our tools and the fresh air hoods on top of the drum and suited up. The hoods fit down over the head with a clear plastic face shield and the same type of headband as in our hard hats. The hood material comes down over the torso and then belts on tightly at the waist to hold it in place. An air hose runs up your back and fastens to the hood to supply a constant flow of fresh air. It is not a sealed respirator, just a hood with air pumped in. We made sure we had enough air hose to move around and do our work then we got started on opening up the flange.

As soon as we loosened all the bolts and oxygen was able to enter the drum, I heard a deep rumbling. The drum started vibrating beneath my feet. I stopped my work and turned to look as I heard the rumble move out of the drum and through the pipe headed for the flare. It was so loud and caused enough vibration that you could see it moving through the pipe, like a snake swallowing a mouse. I just stood there and watched, unaware of what was going on around me due to the reduced visibility from the air hood. The rumble started up the flare and burst out of the top of the stack in a huge ball of fire, and then, crazy as hell, it sucked in on itself and started back down the flare. I heard the rumbling again, but it was much louder and much faster. I turned back to the flange we had been opening up and was backing toward the scaffolding at the same time. That is something you should always keep in mind while in a refinery—where is the escape route. I felt and heard the explosion hit the drum and watched as fire shot out of the very narrow opening we had made when we unbolted the flange. I finally got my shit together, turned, and ran to the scaffold, dragging my air hose behind me. The drum began to BOOM, BOOM, BOOM, shaking and hammering under me. I reached the scaffold, grabbed the handrail with one hand and leaped over the side, swinging myself toward the ladder. I'll be damned if the old pipefitter, Don, hadn't beat me to the ladder. He served as the perfect backboard as I bounced off him and began to fall. On the way down I remembered wondering how in the hell that old man had outrun me to the ladder. A second later, I slammed into a horizontal scaffold pole. My legs must have scissored, and I hit hard on the inside of my upper thigh. Okay, that could have been much worse. I still had falling momentum, thanks gravity, and flipped head over heels falling to the next level. You guessed it, I hit the next pole, flipped again and fell some more. Finally, my air hose pulled taut, inexorably tangled above me on the scaffolding and jerked me to a halt. I still heard the BOOM, BOOM, BOOM, behind me, or maybe it was my heart. I really wanted to run then, run as far and fast as I could. Instead, I thrashed around like a puppet on an air hose string, dancing with my toes just inches off the ground. I had no idea where my air hose was hung up, but I couldn't get loose. The belt on my hood was so tight I couldn't budge it to free myself from the hood and tangled air hose. This must be what seatbelts do when you're in a car wreck. They save you one minute and the next they hold you prisoner.

I mentioned before that the job of standby is the most important on in the refinery. That day we had two standbys, one male, and one female. I remember looking at the guy straight in the eye as I struggled to free myself from the tangled air hose and hood. That is until he sprinted off. You just can't imagine the horrible sense of being left alone, of being abandoned in a time of such great need. Or sadly, maybe you can. Suddenly, I was hefted up so that my belt loosened. I quickly freed myself and fell to the ground a bit wobbly. The female standby grabbed my arm, and we hotfooted it out of the area.

I was transported to the company's on-site medical office to check out my injuries. The only thing that hurt was my leg. It hurt so damn bad I thought it was broke but knew it wasn't as I could still walk. We had an actual doctor on site too. At least I think he was. Okay, I know he was. It's just that I am always suspicious when a male doctor gets embarrassed with a female patient. Like I said, it was on my inner thigh, way up high. I peeled my coveralls off and saw I was already turning black and blue from my crotch halfway to my knee. Doc had me lay down on the table and he looked like he was going to faint. Finally, his hand hovered over my leg. He turned his head, gently touched my thigh, squeezed it slightly a couple of times, then jerked his hand back and told me I was just fine. What an asshole. I've grown up with male doctors my whole life. I don't necessarily like it but hadn't thought much about it until the doc acted like we were doing something wrong. What must it have been like for all those women who came before me? I've read horror stories of women long ago being committed (usually by their husbands) to asylums because of PMS or even just being strong willed. Before that, they were accused of witchcraft and typically hung, but there were some burned at the stake.

NOTE: This was the same company doctor who later decided I had "beaver disease." Yes, you read that correctly—beaver disease. Okay, quit laughing, it's not what you think. He explained that you catch the dreaded beaver disease from drinking out of streams or rivers where beavers live. That is in fact, a real thing. I did ride horses, up, down, around, and across streams and rivers. Although I allowed the horses to drink the creek water, I always stuck with my canteen or better yet, the wine coolers tucked in the ice chest back at the truck. I got a second opinion, and we discovered I had a kidney infection. Humph.

The whole refinery soon knew about the flare drum incident. There were several explosions inside the drum but no external damage. Still, it caused quite a stir. Bob came rushing to the site as he knew I'd been working there that day. He was told several different stories up to and including one story saying I'd died. He was also told I had been taken to medical, and that's where he found me, alive and pissed off. Pissed at the doctor who made me feel embarrassed and ashamed. Pissed at the damned old pipefitter who was obviously a whole lot smarter than I was and was getting the hell out of Dodge while I was standing there like a dumbass watching. Pissed at my supervisors for putting me in such a dangerous position. I had no idea how much more I would be pissed off in the next few minutes.

Shortly after convincing Bob I would live, I was told to report back to the flare drum. The fire had burned itself out and the drum still needed to be blinded. "They" thought it would be good for me to "get back on the horse." I straightened my big-girl panties, thankful I hadn't shit myself actually, gathered up my tools and went back on top of the drum. Part of the PPE (personal protective equipment) required at the unit was rubber boots over our normal leather work boots, so of course I had mine on. The drum was still so hot from the internal fire that it melted my rubber boots in a matter of minutes. We worked as fast as we could because you couldn't touch anything without getting burned, the metal was still so hot. We installed the blind without further incident, but by the time I was back on the ground the soles of my work boots were also melting. I rode that proverbial horse to hell and back that day.

Bob and I didn't date very long before deciding to get married. Although this was a first for me, Bob had already been married twice. His mother said she really did not want to put his family through another wedding/reception/etc. I said I understood. I wanted to say I had never pictured myself in a wedding dress but maybe I had. I said I didn't really want a wedding, but maybe I did. I just couldn't rock the boat. I was afraid that if I did anything to screw this up that I would lose my chance at having a husband and father for my son. I really wanted a family. A real wedding just wasn't my style anyway, and I was actually happy with simple. My mother got married to my father in blue jeans and a checkered shirt—both times she married my father come to find out—another surprise. I went a little crazy and bought an ivory colored, regular ole dress (as you know by now, any kind of dress was crazy for me). Bob and I went to the courthouse and were married by the Justice of the Peace. Remarkably, my parents let Bob and I adopt Josh and I finally had my family. Strange that I had to adopt my own son, but it was necessary after my folks adopted him when I went into the Army.

Now that I was married, I had to make some more decisions. I wanted a normal life. I wanted the Monday through Friday, family together at the dinner table, weekends spent playing together, kind of life. A strange twist of fate happened, the stars aligned, and I was qualified to bid on another job, a normal daylight job at the Compounding and Packaging, or C&P, unit. It was still a part of the refinery so I would retain all my seniority, which was great. It would be for a lot less money, but Bob was working three jobs, albeit sporadically, when we met. I had no doubt that together we could make it; together we would be fine.

And then that bitch, Fate, slapped me awake again. The ink hadn't dried on my bid sheet when the loading dock job went to two shifts. Still, it was daylights and evenings but no hoots and a skeleton crew on weekends. Just to rub salt on the wound they didn't pay a bigger shift work bonus like they had in operations. Still, I told myself the sacrifice would be worth it.

My marriage to Bob was not everything I dreamed it would be. Maybe it was Fate or maybe my mother cursed us when she "accidentally" threw our marriage license away the day we got married.

Figure 26 *Bob and Mom digging our marriage license out of the trash as Steve watched.*

For a short time though, I got to be a stepmother to Bob's daughter, Sasha, from his first marriage. I remember taking her out to the mud runs and later getting in trouble because her mother didn't approve of her getting dirty and boy did we get dirty! I also remember teaching her how to hang a spoon off the end of her nose. Maybe we wouldn't have gotten in trouble for that one if Sasha hadn't waited to show her mother one day—whilst they dined at the country club. Oops. I'm sorry we upset her mother but I'm not sorry for those fun times. Sadly, our time together was too short.

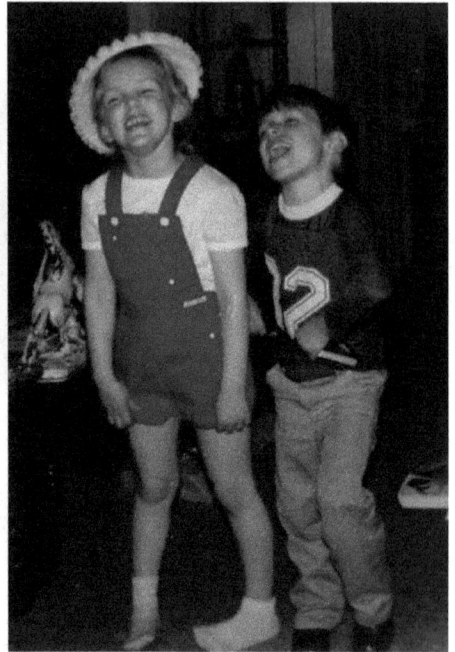

Figure 27 Sasha's birthday – Sasha & Josh.

Although Bob was working his butt off before we got married, he was a contractor, a carpenter, and work was come and go, like when I worked roofing. He tried finding jobs where he could. He even did some roofing jobs and took me along to help. It was shortly after one of these jobs that I had a miscarriage and lost our first baby together. After that, I don't really know what happened between us, but one day I began to realize that no matter how I felt, Bob didn't love me.

Enter, stage left, that old bitch, Fate. Our relationship was pretty much on the rocks when I found out I was pregnant with Jake. I thought maybe this would change things between Bob and I, make them better. That's not why I got pregnant. I still had this fantasy of having a real family. But it just wasn't to be.

I do remember the day I realized I had to get divorced. I was eight months pregnant with Jake and still working at C&P,

loading forty- to fifty-foot-long semi-trailers. We loaded everything from five-gallon buckets to fifty-five-gallon drums.

Fork lifts were used to bring a pallet of four fifty-five-gallon drums, or barrels, into the trailer and then the loaders placed them in the truck. A barrel weighs between 400 to 600 pounds depending on the product. Loaders don't just use brute strength; it's a whole lot to do with balance. You pull the drum off the edge of the pallet, tilting it as it slides off until the rim hits the floor. Then you brace the drum with your foot and leg and pull it back towards you until you feel the center of balance. If you maintain the balance of the drum, you can roll it along on the rim fairly easily. If you pull too far, well you can guess how bad that could be. Sure, it does take some muscle, but balance was the key. Now try doing that when you're eight months pregnant with a big baby boy belly. I was extremely healthy back then, and the doc told me just to keep doing what I normally do. (That is how I ended up getting bucked off a horse the day before Josh was born.) I have a funny suspicion that the doc really didn't understand what I did, or he simply didn't believe me. Anyway, I did have a few truck drivers about faint when they saw me loading their trucks. Some tried to stop me. One driver came in as I was just finishing up his truck, spotted my huge belly and said, "You can't do that!"

"Damn," I said, "wish you had told me that sooner."

I woke up that fateful morning and snuck out of the house. Bob was asleep on the living room floor. He hadn't been employed for quite some time and tended to stay up late. I tiptoed past, careful not to wake him. I drove a few blocks down the road to my friend Nancy's house. It was common for me to stop at Nancy's for coffee. She poured me a cup that day and listened to me bawl as I told her what I had to do. Nancy was—is—one of those people that just makes you feel good about yourself. She is a wonderful, caring person who helped me through so many dark times. Thank you so much, Nancy. I love you. Nancy called in sick, and I called in and started my maternity leave. My second call was to my lawyer.

My mother was very upset about my divorce from Bob. Although she never asked why we were divorcing, Mom warned me that, "Nobody would ever love you like Bob had." I admit I cried for a long time over that. After all, Bob didn't love me. Was it possible that nobody ever would? I do wonder if maybe Mom had some Gypsy blood in her. Maybe I needed to reconsider the possibility of curses.

I went to the courthouse to sign the final divorce papers in front of the judge. The judge was rightly concerned about someone in my obvious condition getting divorced. Finally, my lawyer interrupted and asked the good judge if he knew how to deliver a baby. The judge, frowning, said he did not. The lawyer pointed out that this very day was my due date. The judge whipped his signature out and had me ushered to the door. Thank you, Jake, for waiting another week to come.

I had come to realize that Bob was still searching for that one true love, his soul mate, and I'm happy for Bob that he did eventually find her. Gala would take in both my sons and she treated them like her own. She didn't just feed and clothe them and put a roof over their heads. She cared for them and loved them and gave them a family. No doubt, she made Bob a better man.

I've made it clear I'm an introvert. Bob unintentionally (?) enabled my problem by doing the difficult things for me, those really tough things, you know, like talking to people. I hated needing to go to the doctor because I couldn't make myself call much less actually go to the doctor. After the divorce, I realized I had to change. I had to conquer or at least control my fears. I did this in very slow, very painful steps. First, I got into the habit of going to my dad's favorite coffee shop. I would sit by myself, grab a newspaper, and work the crossword puzzle. It was a great way to keep people from talking to me, but I could surreptitiously watch and listen to them. It took a long time before I felt like I could breathe easily and a longer time to walk in casually and not feel panicked. It worked out better than I would have imagined. There were a couple of game rangers (would soon change to game wardens), John and Joe, that came into the coffee shop and I'll be damned if John didn't work the same crossword puzzle. He had the audacity one day to speak to me and ask what I had for twenty-three down. His easygoing manner soon won me over. It was a huge leap in easing my social anxiety. My sister, Diana, joined me on many occasions and she was great at crosswords. She was also much better than I was at talking to people and making friends. We both became friends with John and Joe. Next, Diana initiated friendships with Bud, the concrete guy, then Fritz the truck driver. I learned a lot from my little sister in that coffee shop.

I also frequented another local restaurant with my sons. Josh and Jake quickly became a big hit with the owner's wife, and she made a special effort to make us all comfortable and happy. I think she was especially charmed by Jake and would bring him a bowl of peaches (his favorite) when we came in. We also became friends with several of the staff and even went to one lady's wedding where I actually wore a dress and made Jake dance the two step with me.

Tragedy struck that small group of friends when they went on a boating trip out on the lake. The boat capsized, and the friends were unable to reach their life jackets. The water was very cold, and they swam for shore. All but one of them miraculously survived. I joined the teams of volunteers that searched the lake for a full week before the drowning victim was recovered. Officer Staz and I were the ones that found the body. After a week in the water, we didn't want to risk pulling the body into the boat as decomposition was really bad. Instead, I leaned over the side and held onto his shirt while we pulled him to the shore, and it was a long way to the shore. Once there, the officials took over. I was asked to wait and talk to the authorities. I waited while the body was removed from the water. I waited while the body was loaded. I waited while law enforcement, lake patrol, and the coroner talked and laughed. I waited in the cold as my wet clothes clung to me. I waited, not able to grieve in front of all these strangers. The strangers that stood laughing next to the van that contained the body. I waited and tried not to think too much, but I heard them. Volunteers had been informed that the search was over and now congregated on the shore in small groups. I heard the laughter and tried to make sense of it. I supposed they didn't know the victim or his family. I have no idea what they laughed about or what they thought. It seems odd that life so callously goes on when death is so apparently present. It is difficult, when your heart is crushed with pain, to understand why unwitting bystanders aren't scorched with the pain burning so hot in your chest. I assume either it didn't affect them personally or maybe they were trying to cope themselves. I admit I did feel a sense of satisfaction for having helped my friend find her husband's body. It did not, however, bring a smile to my face. The smell of death clung to me. It stayed with me for days. I went home, burned my clothes and showered till I ran out of hot water. The scent of death was in my nose, and nothing seemed to help. It did eventually go away but the memory of that smell is still with me. And yet, I'd do it again to help my friends.

I came to realize my social anxieties were based on anything new, even at work. I was comfortable at work as long as I worked the same job, the same area, with the same people. I was comfortable at the coffee shop with a small handful of regulars. New things knocked me back almost to the start line. I considered quitting my job more than once because of it.

I remember another time I had been pulled out to go to the yards again in an area I'd never worked, for a supervisor I didn't know. My anxiety ratcheted up. I showed up early, like always, and stopped beside the brick building just outside of the refinery entrance gate. It was cold outside. I needed to have a hard talk with myself, reminding myself what I needed to do, what I had to do, what I could do. I squatted down against the brick wall and lit a cigarette, watching the blossoming colors as the sun rose. It was so cold. Suddenly I was back in the Army, outside of the barracks smoking…hiding. The sound of the nearby train whistle brought me back. This was work; this was the refinery. I was fine, I could handle it, and I would handle it. I have no idea how our military vets and frontline workers handle their exposure to so many traumatic events during their careers. Fortunately for me, the intensity of the flashbacks has faded.

I should mention that by this time, my two sons had gone to live with Bob and Gala. It was definitely one of the hardest things I've ever done, and I really struggled to make that decision, until the day Josh showed me he was growing up to be just like me.

We were living in a nice house just across from Josh's elementary school. I looked for opportunities to get Josh more involved with other kids and had asked him about Scouts. He was excited about it. I was thrilled to think he might have a chance at a normal life, to not have all my social hang ups. Until the day of the first meeting came. I can still see little Josh standing on the couch, watching out the window to see people arriving for the meeting. He kept his head low, just above the back of the couch and watched, sinking lower and lower as more people arrived. We talked and although he wanted to go, he couldn't. Do you know how unconceivably heartrending it is to realize your child is growing up to be just like you and that it's not a good thing? What it's like to know you're possibly screwing up your child's mental well-being because you yourself are so fucked up?

I wish I'd found help then. I wish I'd reached out and asked someone to help me get over my fears, to be stronger, to be…. Normal. I wish I'd fought for my kids but instead, I thought the best thing I could do was try to save them. They had the opportunity to have a family, a real, loving family with a father, a mother, and even brothers and sisters. They wouldn't bounce from sitter to sitter. They would have some stability, a safe place to call home. Bob might have fallen out of love with me, but he loved all his kids to the moon and back.

I still think I did the best thing I could for my kids at that time, but it damaged me even more. My despair was absolute and drowning. I believed my mother was right. Nobody would ever love me.

I did make one attempt and turned to my mother for help, the first time that I can really remember doing so. Her only help was to tell me she "wished she had killed me before I turned thirteen." Needless to say, it was the last time I ever intentionally went to her for help. There were occasions after that when I would try to talk to her, when she seemed like she really cared and wanted to help. Every damn time I would confess a weakness or fear to her, she would take it and show me how stupid I was, how worthless I was in her eyes. She'd been this way for a while.

My mother did teach me some valuable things. Love your kids. Tell them you love them. Show them you love them. Talk to them, encourage them, hug them. Be honest with your kids while trying to never hurt them. Be respectful to your kids and teach them to respect others. Never forget that you are the adult. Protect your kids as much as you can—when it's appropriate. Admittedly, some lessons may be best learned the hard way.

CHAPTER 10
PROTECT YOUR BRAIN! EVEN IF YOU DON'T THINK YOU NEED IT

Work had become exceedingly boring. I was accustomed to using my brain as an operator. Now, I was just a trained monkey at C&P doing repetitive tasks without any significant amount of intelligence needed.

Let me explain a little about the C&P area. This was where we filled oil cans with different products such as quart cans of your favorite 10w30 motor oil or transmission fluid, etc. We also blended and filled larger containers, including five-gallon buckets, twenty-gallon quarter drums and the big green fifty-five-gallon drums. C&P had three different sections: the barrel barn, canning section, and the loading docks/warehouse. The barrel barn is where we received all the empty containers and packaging. Empty fifty-five-gallon drums were unloaded from semi-trailers and sent up a lift and then down an overhead shaft to the canning/filling section. The barrel barn also stored unfolded, empty bundles of the cardboard motor oil cases. The canning/filling section does just as the name implies. They filled the old, waxed cardboard quart cans (we would transition to plastic quart bottles shortly before I left C&P), buckets, or barrels with product. They would then be stacked on pallets where the forklift drivers would take them to the combined warehouse and loading dock section to be stored until loaded into trucks for sale.

Work at the barrel barn was mind numbingly boring, but we had a fantastic crew, including Nancy, Mary and Ben—dear sweet, laid-back Ben. He knew we had a seemingly insignificant job, and he told people he was just a garbage can roller. Then he would do that wink and slow, sexy smile and in his low, gravelly voice say yes, but he was the best damn garbage can roller there ever was. I really miss him.

Ben was injured off the job in a motorcycle accident. He was alone and not wearing a helmet, so it's not known exactly what happened. Dear sweet Ben was not the same afterwards. I never saw Ben again but thought of him often and what a loss the world suffered when his gentle soul left it.

PLEASE, PLEASE, PLEASE—ALWAYS WEAR A HELMET WHEN RIDING MOTORCYCLES OR BIKES

We also had a very different kind of supervisor, Henry. You know, the kind that creeps you out but doesn't do anything bad enough you can turn him in (especially back then). It was just odd things, like talking about us girls going to the bathroom. Henry would ask why we always had to go together. Was it a harem kind of thing? What did we do in there? Here's the thing; when unloading a truck, let's say of cardboard cases, one person takes the bundles out of the truck and tosses them onto a conveyer belt. The conveyer trundles the bundles to the upper level of the building where the second person takes them off the conveyer belt and stacks them neatly on the floor, separating the bundles according to the product description on the box (30W, 10w30, Transmission Fluid, etc.). Since there are only two of us on this particular job, it just doesn't work for one person to stop work and go pee; it just doesn't. We simple-minded girls (and guys) thought it might be more efficient to grab the intercom phones and coordinate a single quick pee break. I think maybe Henry was the one with harem fantasies.

Then he got creepier. A bundle of cases was maybe one foot tall when laid out on the conveyor belt. Henry would put his hands in his back pocket and lean against the conveyor belt so that each time a bundle passed by it would rub against his crotch. I couldn't make myself pull the bundles off the belt while he was standing there, I'd have to go downstairs and find Ben, asking him to switch places with me. He always would.

One day we were scheduled to unload a railroad car full of empty five-gallon buckets. The tracks ran right next to a large window opening in the brick building. We would offload the buckets from the railcar, sliding them on metal rails through the window to be stacked inside the building. When the railcars were originally loaded, they would stack the buckets in the car and then hold them in place by inserting empty air bags followed by a wooden frame that was strapped in place. Inflating the air bags put enough pressure against the buckets to keep the load from shifting. Unfortunately, they didn't control how the car came down the tracks and if it was parked on the opposite side from how it was loaded, you ended up with a catapult on the far side just waiting to crash a multitude of five-gallon buckets on your head. Usually, if we opened a railcar door and weren't lucky enough to be on the framed, airbag side, the buckets would immediately start falling and you just stayed out of the way. One day, I wasn't so lucky. We did have a few buckets fall after we opened the door, but it seemed like the buckets had wedged together enough that most were still standing. Railcars are tall and the buckets were stacked well above my head. I did of course have on my safety glasses, hard hat, leather gloves, and steel-toed boots. I was the only one working in the car and the rest of the crew was inside, pulling the buckets off the unloading rails, stacking them four high and rolling them across the floor to a nearby storage area.

I'd had buckets fall on me before and although they are lightweight when empty, the thin metal rims can really hurt if they catch you on the shoulder, back, or arm. I was admittedly nervous. I knew that at some point, as I worked my way further into the rail car, that the pressure from the air bags would knock the buckets over. We couldn't intentionally try to pull the buckets down and let them fall willy-nilly because that could damage the buckets and cost the company money and, as mentioned, I wanted to retire. I tried to be careful but at the same time work fast enough to keep the crew inside busy. When the buckets finally gave way and started falling, I could see it wasn't going to be three or four stacks. There were dozens of stacks falling forward. I knew the only safe place was inside the building. Staying in the railcar was not an option. I jumped out of the railcar and through the window into the building. At least I would have jumped through the window if it wasn't for that damn hard hat. I would have cleared it and been just fine, but I had forgotten to allow that couple of extra inches the hard hat added to my head. I hit the edge of the window at about fifty miles an hour, or so it seemed. The hard hat took the blow, but my forward motion pushed the hat down onto my face putting a great deal of pressure on my safety glasses. The metal frames were jammed against my cheek and split my face open just below the eye. I ended up on the floor inside of the building and landed on top of one of those damn buckets. I had no idea my face was hurt. One of my coworkers, Janie, ran to me and for some damn reason, jumped onto me and was holding me down telling me not to move, that I might have broken my back. I told Janie that she was the one breaking my back and to let me up off the damn bucket. As soon as I sat forward, my cheek gaped open. Now that was weird, I thought. I could look down into the gash and see right under my skin.

I was told that a company ambulance had been called, so we wandered up towards the front of the building to meet them. They weren't there yet, so I figured I could grab a quick smoke. I went back to the lunchroom and sat on the picnic table and was smoking when the ambulance driver showed up. He was directed into the lunchroom and when he saw me smoking (from the good side) he figured he'd take a minute and smoke one too. "Sure," I said, "Smoke if you got 'em," like they used to say in the Army.

When we finished our cigarettes, I fully turned towards the guy, and he about gagged looking at the open wound. After that, he quickly got me into the ambulance and trundled me off to our on-site medical. I really liked the doc that was working that day. He said we should get a plastic surgeon to take care of sewing it up and that the company would, of course, pay for it. I remember telling him, "Come on, Doc, look at this face. A few stitches and a scar will be an improvement."

He actually did a good job sewing me up. With the first several stitches, even though I was lying down, each time he would pull the needle and thread through the skin on the lower side of the cut it would pull my cheek out an inch or so from my face where I could see down into the open wound again. Cool. I went back to work and finished unloading the railcar. The company had decided it would be okay for me not to wear my safety glasses for a week, at least until I got the stitches out. I was good with that.

CHAPTER 11
SEXUAL HARASSMENT BY A SUPERVISOR

The bad times came when I left the barrel barn and moved up to the docks. We had multiple supervisors that covered the different areas. That's when the sexual harassment started.

When I first started at the loading docks, the women didn't have a restroom. Even the one at the barrel barn was co-ed. Instead, we had to leave the docks and go to another building. More than once, I was chastised for taking too long and I'd remind them that there was some travel time involved. I wasn't reading a magazine or anything. I remember being barely pregnant with Jake and maybe it was hormones, but I got a bit testy and told them if I slipped and fell on the icy sidewalks going back and forth to the bathroom that there would be hell to pay.

We eventually got a women's bathroom that was just off the lunchroom—literally, you went through the lunchroom to get to the bathroom. One night as I came out of the restroom, one of the supervisors, we'll call him, Moe, was there in the tiny alcove just outside the door. He grabbed me and kissed me. I pushed him back and told him to stop.

It didn't stop. It got worse and worse. I'd be sent to the basement to get tape or something stupid like that and sure as hell, this guy, this supervisor, would follow me in. I'd tell him to get the hell away, but he'd keep trying to get his hands all over me. One day, Moe goaded the guys, my coworkers, to mess with me. They took a huge roll of plastic wrap that we used to secure stacks of cases and the whole fucking gang grabbed my arms and started wrapping my upper body, arms at my sides. I told them to stop, that there wasn't anything funny about it. I tried to reason with the guys who up until then, I had no problems with. I tried to keep my shit together, but I couldn't. Talk about a wild animal. I was trapped, I was vulnerable, and I knew there was a predator nearby. I went into survival mode. I fucking lost my mind. I yelled and gnashed my teeth ready to tear out flesh if I could. I kicked at anyone who came close and I had on steel-toed boots so more than one went home with bruises. I don't know if it was actually me or just my mind that screamed over and over again. They finally stopped. Nobody helped. Nobody asked if I was okay. They just left me alone, even Moe, my supervisor. Alone was good. Once they were gone, I was able to tear through the wrap a tiny bit at a time until I was finally free. But I wasn't free because it didn't stop.

As I mentioned, there were many times in my career I've told myself I don't want to be "that girl." I didn't want to be the girl that whined and cried because the guys talked dirty (I obviously do that with the best of them). I didn't want to be the girl that turned someone in for a pat on the butt or because of other stupid, insignificant shit like that. You know, the stuff the guys try just to see what you'll do. I always wondered why those girls would work in such a place. I heard the guys talk many times about "those girls" and how they would never trust them. How they never wanted to work with or even around them. I finally admitted to myself that my situation had gone beyond that insignificant stuff that you could brush off. You know the stuff that would stop if you just told them to fuck off. This was bad, and I'd just found out how savage my own reaction could be. I worried that I would lose my job because of it.

Let me repeat this because it is extremely important and I know many, many women (and men) have thought the same thing. **I was worried that I would lose my job** because of it! Damn it! I worried myself sick that I would lose my job because I was being sexually harassed—by a supervisor.

In spite of all that had happened, I just wanted it to stop. I didn't want anyone to get in trouble. I didn't want anyone to lose their job. I just wanted it to stop.

I finally approached one of the other supervisors, we'll call him Larry. He was on the same hierarchical level as Moe so I thought that would be the best way to handle it. Larry listened, looked at me, and shrugged his shoulders, explained he didn't like Moe anyway so screw him. It seemed Larry the supervisor obviously didn't give a shit about me either and he obviously didn't care if anyone got fired, including me. It took some time to work my nerve up but then I went to a third supervisor. Of course, we'll call him Curly, and told him. He pretty much shrugged his shoulders, said he didn't like the guy, and walked off.

Eventually, Larry and Curly got their heads together and realized that maybe this shouldn't be ignored. Together, they decided to take it to the area manager, Mr. Tubbs. I was then given a time to meet with Mr. Tubbs along with strict instructions not to discuss the matter with anyone. I was not to speak about the situation, not to my friends, not to HR, not to the union, not to anyone. Well, that's enough to make you think you're going to need to clean out your locker. Again, I was afraid I was going to lose my job for turning in my abuser, my supervisor. It was a couple of days before the scheduled meeting, so I had a lot of time to think, and plan.

The time finally came for me to meet with Mr. Tubbs. I walked into his office at the designated time and watched as he and the supervisor, Moe, sat joking and laughing together. They ignored my presence easily enough and continued their banter, but then the union president walked in behind me. You could have heard the proverbial pin hit the old concrete floor, along with Mr. Tubbs' jaw. Neither supervisor spoke a word. Instead, the union president started the meeting. He explained that, against his will, all we were asking for was the harassment to stop and stop now.

He explained that if it was his decision, he would fight to see the supervisor terminated. The union president instructed me to leave the meeting at that point.

My union rep eventually told me that Moe had other reports against him for sexual harassment. I don't know what punishment, if any, Moe was given, but he did continue to work for the company for several years after our experience. Involving the union president was the smartest thing I'd done.

I would later become a union steward. I believed in the need for unions and appreciated what they had accomplished. They had, after all, helped me. The union instructed me that as a steward, my job was to defend the workers—no matter what. Unfortunately, for my union career anyway, I also believed in doing the right thing. We had one worker, Dandy, that had already taken a lot of sick days. It seemed a little odd to me seeing as this guy was the epitome of good health. Dandy was muscular, like a fitness instructor. He was always full of pep and energy, never dragging his ass around bone tired like many of the rest of us. But, I'm not a doctor, and health issues were not for me to question. That is until the day Dandy told me he needed more time off sick. I didn't realize sick was something you planned (short of scheduled surgery of course). I thought it just happened. He chuckled and told me to, "Watch this."

He then slammed his finger in a car door, breaking the aforementioned digit. I was supposed to go to the company and fight for this guy's right to have paid sick leave? After I had witnessed him injuring himself? Nope, my union career came to an end as I firmly believed folks should do the right thing, company or union, didn't matter.

Let's go back to the sexual harassment. The company has rules about retaliation. If an employee reports something in good faith, the company can't retaliate against said employee. That sounds good but more than once I found out it was just pretty words on paper because after all, in the famous words of one of the company's biggest assholes, "Prove it."

There was something equally bad as company retaliation, which was coworker retaliation. I never heard anything directly about the fallout of that sexual harassment meeting, but I did get the cold shoulder from my coworkers. It seems like a lot of guys really liked ole Moe. Even though not one of them ever asked my side of the story, they were pissed at me for getting the dude in trouble. A few of the snubs hurt. One guy in particular, Kent, who I'd always liked, always gotten along with, turned his back on me. He was one of those nice guys, always talking about his wife and kids. He seemed genuinely concerned about other people and was always willing to help. Kent mentioned once that one of his daughters liked skunks and I sketched a cute little picture of a pair of comic-like skunks and gave it to him for his daughter. Losing his friendship at work really hurt. Kent would later apologize to me after his wife found out what was going on. I guess she gave him something to think about and he said he was sorry. I told him it had hurt because he judged me without knowing my side of the story and I asked if he wanted to hear it. He said no, but that everything was okay. Again, nobody seemed to care what I had gone through.

There was one more incident at the loading docks that I'd like to mention. The company frowned on horseplay although it was a regular thing in the olden days. I was still working on the docks and had just finished loading a truck. Once complete, we would take a car seal—a thin, flexible metal strap that has numbers stamped on it, and seal the truck's doors. The seals were hanging by the supervisor's desk. Supervisor Larry was working that day, and he and I had actually developed a good relationship. That day he was wound up and joking around. He was another one of those athletic, high-energy guys. I took a car seal and turned to go back to the dock to finish up so the driver could get on the road. Just joking around, Larry reached out and jerked the car seal from my hand, slicing my finger to the bone. Damn it hurt. I cussed and bled all over. Wrapping the finger in paper towels, I got the truck sealed then went and washed my finger. you could literally see the bone. I wrapped it up again and went to tell Larry I needed to go to medical for stitches. Larry, however, didn't want me to go to medical because I'd have to report how it happened. He was pretty stressed about it and like I said, we did have a decent relationship, so I didn't want to rock the boat. I didn't go to medical, and that was a mistake. The gash took forever to heal. It kept breaking open for a long time afterwards. Fortunately, it never became infected or did any lasting damage other than a scar and I had enough of those that it really didn't matter. There was some nerve damage, but it was just on one part of the finger so, not a big deal. I think Larry and I both made a bad decision that day, but as pissed off as I was, I didn't hold it against him. In fact, I later introduced him to a family friend, and they ended up getting married.

Things weren't the same for me at the docks after the sexual harassment incident. The guys went back to joking amongst themselves, but I never really fit in again. We did have a bunch of gals working there and they were great, but I still felt a loss. A loss of not belonging, of not being wanted, of not fitting in. Thankfully, I still had Nancy and on our off days we rode horses, drank coffee, and hung out. She really was a life saver for me.

CHAPTER 12
THE HEALING POWER OF HORSES, FRIENDS, AND FUCKING FRITOS

Maybe I should discuss the Fritos now. Although this episode had nothing to do with my career, it was a monumental turning point in my life. It was one of the best and worst things that has ever happened to me. I believe that this had to happen for me to grow, to become the person I had buried down deep inside of me that cried desperately to be free. Here's how it happened.

I mentioned that Nancy got me back into horses. I hadn't ridden since New Mexico. We would go on trail rides with a local group, people on horseback, wagons, the whole bit. I can't express how amazing, how soul lifting, how therapeutic this was for me. I loved everything about it. I found my peace in the sights of nature, the rugged landscape, the horses, and the wildlife. I found my peace in the sounds, the squeak of the leather, the jingle of the bits and spurs, the rumble of the wagons, the braying of donkeys, the repetitive clomping of a multitude of hooves. I found my peace in the smells, the fresh air, the hot summer dust, the horse's sweat, even the manure. I really was happy there. Happy as long as I didn't have to actually be too close to anyone, or worse yet, carry on a conversation.

Figure 28 Lunchtime.

Figure 29 *Trail ride through trees, (Left) Jake last in line, (Right) Jake & Josh at the end crossing the bridge.*

Figure 30 *All-important wagon carrying the drinks! Diana on the front right.*

Figure 31 *Front wagon pulled by a team of Percheron horses. Wagons carry folks who prefer not to ride horseback along with food and drink supplies.*

On one particular trail ride, our evening dinner was provided, so we all got into line and helped ourselves to the food. I tended to hang back and wait for the crowd to thin. If people were around, I would constantly worry that I would do something wrong, worry that I might do something to draw attention to me. I was horribly afraid of making a mistake, a mistake someone would see. In fact, it was very rare for me to eat in front of other people. Yes, I was skinny back then.

I was looking the food over, trying to decide what was safest for me to eat. I sure wouldn't pick something like corn on the cob because you really couldn't eat that without potentially making a mess, drawing attention. Then I saw the Fritos. I love Fritos. Fritos and iced tea. I scooped some Fritos onto my plate and moved down the line. Someone behind me said something, and I panicked. I was immediately afraid I'd done something wrong. Did I take too many Fritos? Was I in the wrong line? Was I even supposed to be here? I had been reaching for something on the table but jerked my hand back. I somehow managed to catch the paper plate with my thumb and flip the plate. I watched in horror as the Fritos somersaulted into the air, then tumbled to the ground. I was mortified. Not only had I made a mistake, but someone had witnessed it. I heard the man talking again but couldn't make out his words over the roaring in my ears, my mind screaming at me to go hide, drowning out the outside world. I stared at the Fritos on the ground then saw a pair of cowboy boots next to the traitorous corn chips. I'm not sure how long it took, but I finally looked up. I heard a soft chuckle but somehow, I knew it wasn't a laugh at my expense. I looked into the face of the most gorgeous man I'd ever seen. Not pretty, not male model gorgeous, but rugged good looks, Kevin Costner good looks, with a sense of calm self-assurance. I don't remember what he said. I just remember my mind running through one of those death scene montages. I had a serious talk with myself. I realized in that split second that I had a choice to make. I could hide in shame. I could run away and never again be seen at one of these gatherings. On the other hand, I could realize it was just a bunch of fucking Fritos, and the world had not, in fact, come to an end. It was possible I might even become friends with this incredible man beside me.

I had so many moments of social panic in my life that at times could be crippling. I taught myself to stop, breathe, and think. Think honestly. So, I made a mistake—I made a mistake. I am not the only person in the world who has ever made a mistake. Then I would ask myself how bad it really was. Was someone going to physically eat me alive? No. Was I going to make Channel Five news for being a dumbass? No. Was the world going to end? No. Or was it just a bunch of fucking Fritos?

As powerful as this time was, I'm going to wrap it up quickly. A relationship did evolve with this magnificent specimen of a man. Sadly, he was married. I have no idea why that fact didn't penetrate my overwhelming need to be appreciated, to be wanted, but it didn't. I'd run from this type of thing before, but now, this fact didn't penetrate my brain fog. Of course, I didn't realize in the beginning that a personal relationship would develop. Hell, it was months before I even realized he was married. I never asked, and he never offered. Looking back, I equally wish it had never happened, and I also appreciate how much that relationship did to help me mature, to accept myself, my own inner beauty, my strength, my kindness, and my ability to love, along with my many flaws and stupid mistakes. I appreciated how he challenged me to grow. I appreciate how he made me realize I deserved better. I'm sorry for any pain I may have caused his family, and I'm proud of him that in the end, he chose them. I'm proud of myself for never asking him to do otherwise. From then on, I didn't look back. I looked forward with an idea in mind of who I wanted to be and what it would take to get me there.

Now that I was on the road to self-healing, I continued to grow through my love of horseback riding, sometimes in wild ways. The first was when I bought a horse, Mully, that came off the Mullendore ranch. (If you don't recognize that name, be sure and do a search for the Mullendore Murders—but that's someone else's story.) Old Mully was a great horse and one of the quirkiest I ever owned. He would look like he was one hundred years old when riding down the ditch beside a busy highway, but put him in a parade or a roping ring and he would rear up and paw the air. Sure, it was cool looking but could be a bit unnerving the first dozen or so times.

Figure 32 Me & Mully—Josh & Mully.

You might have noticed in the earlier pictures that I forced my sons to go on a couple of trail rides with me. Old Mully was great for that, very calm on the trail. I also had a young mare, Lady; a gelding, Walking On Clouds (Cloud); and a Shetland pony, Dolly. One year, we went on a trail ride in Tahlequah, Oklahoma. We arrived and set up camp, the three of us in one small tent. Word of caution here. Do NOT feed kids that canned cheese stuff if you are going to be confined in a tent, in the rain. Josh and Jake got to farting until the air got so thick you could cut it with a knife. I couldn't open the tent flap because of the pouring rain and was afraid none of us would live to see the morning. It was seriously so bad that it made my eyes water. I think the boys were proud of themselves. Definitely one of my fondest memories.

Figure 33 Jake & Dolly; Josh & Cloud, camping in a tent with the dreaded canned cheese fumes.

The Tahlequah trail ride takes you through beautiful trees and crosses the Tahlequah River several times. The trail is sometimes rough with steep hills. This was Jake's first ride and after one particularly steep decline, I could tell he was scared. I couldn't get him to talk to me. He appeared vapor locked. I always carried medical supplies for horses and humans in my saddlebags and knew immediately what he needed. I whipped out a small Snickers candy bar and gave it to him. Two candy bars later and Jake was racing his little Shetland pony up and down the line of riders, all fear forgotten. I was surprised to find out there was a young girl he was flirting with. Yep, Jake flirted with girls back then. He grew up having a crush on Reba McEntire too. As a grown man he even got the opportunity to sing with Shania Twain (as an audience member). In the end, not even Shania could turn his head from his true love and husband, John. I wouldn't have it any other way. I'm so proud of Jake for being true to himself, for being happy.

Figure 34 *Crossing the Tahlequah River.*

Figure 35 *Back across the Tahlequah River.*

It was my friend, Nancy, who conned me into another one of those—waaaay out of my comfort zone—moments. A group approached Nancy looking for a horse to use during a photo contest that would take place at the local Marland Mansion. She didn't volunteer herself, but she gave them my name. I quickly let them know that I couldn't allow my horse to be handled by strangers. They said no problem. Nancy shoved an English riding outfit, complete with boots and helmet, into my arms and told me to get dressed. Oh, crap.

The photo shoot was unbelievable. They had models that posed around the mansion, in old vehicles, the gazebo, etc. They even had one woman try to pose with me. The photographers would shout out directions and we tried to respond accordingly. However, I could not do a side-by-side, face-to-face, close-up with the real model. I kept cracking up, and she did not appreciate it. Thankfully, they quickly gave up on having me pose with another human being and just let me pose with my Arabian mare, Sara. They got some amazing photos and the one that actually won the contest was a photo of me sitting against a tree looking lovingly at my beautiful horse. People, no. Horse, yes, that I can do.

Figure 36 Photography contest, taken at Marland Mansion in Ponca City, OK. That's me in the foxhunting attire with Dotti and Mom observing.

Figure 37 *Photography contest, Me and my Arabian mare, Sara, at Marland Mansion, Ponca City, OK.*

Figure 38 Photography contest, taken at Marland Mansion, Ponca City, OK. I wish I had seen this when I looked in the mirror back then. I don't know that I ever thought of myself as pretty. I don't remember my mother ever telling me I was pretty. Surely, she did, and I probably just rolled my eyes.

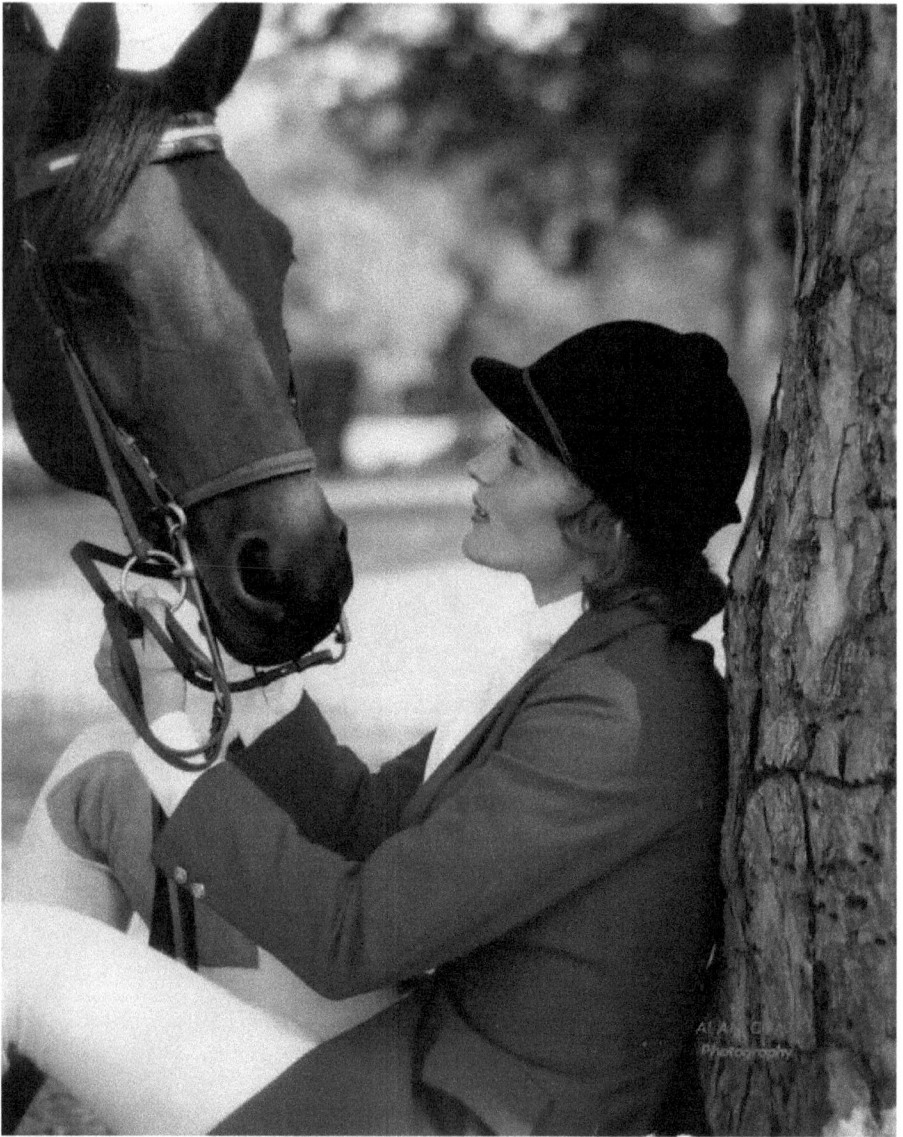

Figure 39 *This was the winning photo of photography contest. Me and my Arabian mare, Sara, taken at the Marland Mansion, Ponca City, OK. What a beauty she was (the horse of course).*

Sometime after the photography contest, Nancy and I took a fantastic vacation to New Mexico together. We dropped down to Artesia and saw Grandma and Grandpa then headed up to Albuquerque for an Arabian horse show. I was driving so Nancy was reading the map—you know one of those old paper maps that you can never refold. Nancy was in charge of getting us on the right road. The time came and went when I thought we should be nearing Albuquerque, but I never saw any signs. In fact, we should have been seeing mountains by then but all you could see was miles and miles of flat desert. It looked like even the cactus didn't want to grow there. Finally, I stopped for gas and directions. A young Native American woman came out and filled our tank (yes, full service, it was a long time ago). I stepped out of the car to pay and asked the young woman how to get to Albuquerque. She gave me a hard look, put her hand over her eyes to block the blazing sunlight and scanned the horizon. Finally, she looked back at me and said, "I don't think you can get there from here." Nancy had directed us out to the middle of the Indian Reservation. Today, I insist all my vehicles are equipped with a navigation system.

We eventually made it to Albuquerque and the Arabian Horse Show. One of the demonstrations they had was a woman who rode her horse without benefit of saddle or bridle. Instead, she used a single rope draped around the base of the horse's neck. With no control over the head, the rider directed her horse using only leg pressure and although it wasn't evident, possibly a little pressure with the rope. It was truly impressive, so of course I had to try it.

I had several horses I trained this way, but my favorite was my Appaloosa, Caddo. He was a beautifully marked gelding with a dark body and the classic white blanket with spots on his butt. I've heard it said that there are two kinds of Appaloosas. They are either the best horse you'll ever own, or the worst; presumably nothing in between. Caddo was in the best category. He was gentle, smart and willing to put up with all my nonsense. He was very easy to train. I could ride him without saddle or bridle, and he would respond to every command. He would even do a dramatic sliding stop.

Caddo and I were out on a weekend trail ride. We were camping in a pasture along with a herd of buffalo, which in itself was an amazing sight. I woke up early that morning and took Caddo down to the pond to get a drink—him not me—I had been warned about the dreaded beaver disease, after all. The dew was heavy that morning, so I had ridden Caddo to the pond bareback with just his halter and lead rope on. As I rode back to camp, I noticed that others were beginning to stir. I could smell the smoke from campfires and hear voices carrying across the still morning.

My inner extrovert decided to pop up and ask for attention. I decided to show off. I kicked Caddo into an easy lope and galloped into camp. At the last minute I shifted my weight back, stuck my feet forward, knees clamped hard and whispered the command to, "Whoa." Caddo immediately slammed on the brakes. Both front legs held stiffly out in front, he tucked his back legs under him and did his best to slide to a stop. Slide he did. We were on top of long, lush, native bluegrass, slick as snot with the heavy dew. Caddo's butt went closer and closer to the ground as he lost traction. I was already off balance since I'd been leaning back to give the command, and now I was in danger of falling off. I came to the conclusion that this wouldn't be the most impressive dismount I'd ever done. Why the hell had I even thought about showing off? I threw my body forward trying to hang on. Of course, that's when Caddo's hooves finally bit into the dirt and he jolted to a stop, got his back legs under him and lunged to a stand. Momentum is not a fickle thing, it demands action. I flew forward over Caddo's head and amazingly landed on my feet. I stood for a moment, shocked at my new position. Then very casually reached back and patted Caddo on the neck, pretending for all the world that we'd just performed a well-planned trick. As nonchalantly as possible, I strolled back to my campsite with a "yeah, I meant to do that" attitude.

I really loved that horse. I had named him after my Grandpa Juckes. I'd better explain that. Grandpa loved to tell stories. He would tell these amazing tales of the old west, all the cowboys and Indians stuff. I heard all about the adventures of Jessie James and his gang, along with stories about the great Indian chiefs. One of his favorites was Caddo George. The stories got interesting as Grandpa got older and went a little off the trail. He began believing he was actually the subject of his stories. The last time I saw Grandpa, he believed he was Caddo George. I sat for hours and listened as he told firsthand the struggles he and his tribe endured.

Figure 40 *Me & Caddo with Diana & Sonny, riding Caddo with a rope around his nose.*

I want to take a moment and discuss this picture. Diana and I rode in a parade, and I got it into my head to dress up as an Indian. After all, I'd been told all my life I had Native American blood. Not to mention Grandpa thought he was Caddo George. I wanted to try to be authentic and make my own costume. I bought some leather chamois, like you dry your car with, to make the top and loin cloth. I really thought I was being unique and true to my alleged heritage. I was wrong. So, damn wrong. Diana and I rode to the starting point for the parade. We passed a wagon with actual Native Americans. One elderly gentleman sat ramrod straight at the front of the wagon. As we rode past, his eyes locked on mine. I was shocked at the intense look of pride on his heavily lined face. He sat in his full native regalia, so quiet, never speaking, just staring at me. His eyes bore into me like an eagle contemplating his prey. I felt shame clear down to my bones. I had not meant to offend. I didn't think. I felt like the most hypocritical white girl ever. It didn't matter what stories I'd been told growing up. I had no proof, no claim to any Native American heritage.

I miss my grandpa and his stories. I miss my grandmother even more. I wish I had realized how much I would miss her and how much I didn't know about her. I wish I had sat and listened to more of her stories. I wish I had asked questions. Where are you from? What about your family? What was life like growing up? I know she didn't take any crap off of Grandpa. He chastised her once for saying "shit" in front of us kids. Her response was, "Shit, shit, shit, shit, shit."

Figure 41 Grandma Juckes.

Grandma had several jobs she really enjoyed. She worked for the gas company and enjoyed that, but she got to show her personality when she worked for Butt's Moving & Storage. Seriously. My grandma was a good-sized woman with the best deadpan expression. People would love to crack jokes about the company name and Grandma would just stare at them until they wanted to go hide. As soon as they left, she would crack up. She also worked at the pharmacy for a while. The days she enjoyed most were when men would come in to buy condoms. Back then, you had to get them from the pharmacist. She would get that deadpan, granny look on her face and question them at length (pun intended) about what size they would need. I hope Grandma wasn't responsible for a baby boom back in the day.

Grandma did have some stories to tell. She told me she was born in "The Osage" so she could be considered Osage Indian. I asked why her name wasn't on the Osage tribe rolls so that she could get head rights. She told me that she didn't want money, a handout, from the government. She told me that if she decided she wanted what was rightly hers, she would pick up her tomahawk and take it back!

Lake Mary Ronan

Figure 42 *These are from a vacation we took at Lake Mary Ronan. Grandma loved fishing and yes, she went fishing in her dress. That's my dad helping her into the boat, and me in my life jacket ready to fish. It's also the trip where one of the boys pushed me into the water as I was standing at the end of the dock watching the crawdads in the crystal-clear water. I was afraid of crawdads.*

Grandma also told me she was a dream walker. Mind blown. She didn't give me many details, just told me that she could appear in my dreams and hopefully help me. Even as a kid, I thought it was a grand story even though I didn't really believe it. It was Grandma that encouraged me to find my spirit animal. My grandmother's spirit animal was, unsurprisingly to me, a bear. Still, I didn't really believe it was real until I saw her in my dreams as a bear. She talked to me as a bear and guided me along a path that helped me find my way, the way of the white hawk.

I woke up the next morning and remembered the dream. I also remembered the calmness and strength I felt from the dream. I assumed that our prior discussions had prompted the content of the dream. But I was "intelligent" enough to know it was all just a dream. I went to the kitchen smelling the wonderful aroma of coffee. Grandma poured me a cup and asked if I felt better now. I lifted my warm mug, took a big sip and smiled. "I'm not talking about the coffee," she said. "You finally walk the right path." I spewed coffee everywhere. I still didn't believe it until I asked her what my spirit animal was. "A white hawk," she said without hesitation. She knew. She had been in my dream. I believe that in my heart and soul. Some things just can't be explained. However, I was upset that she was a bear, and I was a white hawk. Then Grandma explained the meaning of the hawk. There are two principal meanings. One, the hawk's vision encompasses all sides, seeing the big picture. The hawk is also known as a messenger from one group to another. That's a powerful, important job. I would later wonder if the significance of being a "white" hawk was due to a DNA test that proved I did not inherit a single drop of Indian blood. That was a shock.

I do miss her terribly, but I know she will be waiting for me when my time comes, and boy do I have a lot of questions.

CHAPTER 13
SABER-TOOTH JACK RABBITS AND OTHER FUN IN THE SNOW

Back to work. I was still low enough in seniority that on occasion, I would spend time out in the yards working as a laborer. I should explain the refinery layout a bit. We were actually three refineries in the beginning. Once combined, our refinery covered a lot of ground with operating units, tank farms, laboratories, research and development and office buildings. When I worked in the yards as part of a labor crew, we would be sent all over to do whatever needed done. I have to even laugh a little when I think back on my various times in the yards. I have literally been assigned to the farthest reaches of the refinery and told to move a pile of gravel from one spot to another. Not spread gravel out, just shovel it from one pile to another. It was busy work, but I grabbed my shovel and heaved gravel all damn day because it paid the same as worthwhile work.

One winter we were assigned to clean out an empty, decommissioned tank that was being used for storage. Snow was in the forecast, so we were happy to work out of the biting wind even if the tank wasn't heated. Supplies inside the tank were in total chaos. Rubber suits were strewn about in unorganized piles. Bags of cottonseed hulls had split open making a mess on the floor. Trash had accumulated from workers hiding out for breaks. We even found a couple of comfy looking pallets where I'm sure nobody ever caught a quick snooze. As we were cleaning, someone got the bright idea to use the cottonseed hulls to stuff the rubber boots, pants, jacket, and gloves to make a laborer dummy. Once completed, we dragged our life-size dummy outside and propped him against the tank as if he was sitting there taking a nap. We also used a hard hat and pulled it down a bit on his little dummy head to make it look even more realistic. Then we went back to work and finished cleaning up the tank. We soon forgot about our little dummy sitting outside. Snow did come that night. It drifted gently around Mr. Dummy as he snoozed peacefully. What we did not count on was the production supt stopping at the tank to look for some tools. Fortunately, he didn't hurt himself after he spotted Mr. Dummy and raced to save the poor worker he thought might be frozen to death in the snow beside the tank. The next day, we were made to understand that the production supt did not think it was nearly as funny as we had.

We spent part of that winter insulating the drain valves on the product tanks (large tanks that held gasoline, kerosene, diesel, etc.). The tank farm was an unpleasant place to be in the winter when the cold wind was blowing. You can't get out of the wind when hiding behind a cylindrical tank—it just follows the curved sides right on around and freezes your butt off. An earthen dike surrounds each tank. The purpose of the dike is to confine any liquid spill should the tank develop a leak. We would trundle bags of cottonseed hulls over the dikes to place in the drain valve compartments. This would provide insulation so the valves wouldn't freeze up if there happened to be water settling out at the low points. We drove from site to site, working our way through the tank farm. During these short rides, a seasoned hand, Randy, started telling us about the wildlife that was often seen out there in the boonies. We had plenty of coyotes, foxes, skunks, rabbits, even the occasional jackrabbits. The most fearsome of them all was the dreaded saber-tooth jackrabbit. Honestly, Randy told this with a straight face. The saber-tooth jackrabbit, he said, was a vicious killer, tearing its prey to shreds with 6-inch fangs and razor-like claws. Best not to be caught out on the tank farm at night, in the winter, all alone. Yeah, we laughed. We laughed right up until we came over a tank dike and saw a large spattering of bright crimson blood staining the snow. Something had definitely died there. Logically, we knew that it was probably a fox or coyote that had killed a smaller animal, a rabbit or a rat. A really big rat with a lot of blood capacity. But that didn't stop the mind from wandering. We walked around the bloodstain and set our tools down by the valve box. Randy, who was chuckling at our discomfort, yanked the partially frozen lid off the valve box. When he did, a jackrabbit leaped up from where it had hidden behind the box. Poor ole Randy flailed over backwards in the snow, shocked and surprised as the rest of us. As the long-eared bunny hightailed it out of sight, we tried hard not to laugh. Randy had totally lost his sense of humor. The story of the saber-tooth jackrabbit lives on.

Wintertime at the loading docks gave me a few laughs too. I was working stacking five-gallon buckets. The buckets came down a chute of rollers at a gradual decline. My job was to pull the buckets off and stack them on a pallet, four high, four wide and four deep. My work area was just outside of the lunchroom so I would sit inside, smoke a cigarette and watch the buckets back up on the chute. Once it looked like they would back nearly to the fillers, I would race out and start pulling them off the line and stacking them. I was pressing my luck doing it this way. The guys doing the filling would get pissed if I let the buckets back up too far and it slowed them down. Once I started, I had to hurry. I always stacked two at a time, one in each hand, to keep my balance and to work my muscles equally. I loved this kind of a workout, and it was a hell of a workout. Needless to say, I was pretty tough back in the day. Once the pallet was full, a forklift driver would pick it up and haul it to the warehouse leaving another empty pallet for me to fill.

It was on one of these days when a friend, Rob, decided to mess with me. He was my forklift driver that day. I say he was a friend, but he was a work friend, nothing more. Still, a great guy.

It seems so odd to have to explain my thoughts on the word "friend." However, a coworker once told me a story of his "friend." I didn't understand his use of the word in the story he was telling so I asked how "friend" could apply in his situation. He said something along the lines of, "Well, he wasn't so much of a friend, I suppose. I just called him that because I slept with his wife."

I cannot get this out of my head. Every time I hear someone talk about "friend" my mind goes straight to: Oh, are you sleeping with their spouse?

On this day, Rob was bundled up due to the cold in the warehouse. Snow was blowing in any open door or crack. There was even snow on some of the empty pallets he would bring me. Rob waited until I started stacking the buckets and then he began pelting me with snowballs. I wasn't wearing a jacket because I was working so hard and fast, I didn't need it. At least I hadn't before I got smacked in the back with a wet snowball.

It was a perfect setup because I couldn't stop my work. I couldn't stop to fight back. I had to keep stacking those damn buckets. It didn't, however, stop me from calling Rob every name I could think of, but I did it while I was laughing. I do have a sense of humor though for some reason most people don't know that. One of the dock supervisors, Curly I think, walked through about that time and almost got hit with one of the snowballs, but he didn't say anything. Hell, for all I knew he might have helped build the snowballs. This was what I considered good horseplay (as long as nobody got hurt, well, not too bad). Eventually, I caught up and had all the buckets stacked while the fillers were changing product. It was almost break time. I headed towards the docks to find Rob and caught him by the blender floor. The great thing about being in that one spot was the protective handrail that was set in concrete to protect the blending equipment. It was a heavy pipe railing about waist high. When Rob came sauntering by, we were both laughing about the snowballs. As he stepped past me, I grabbed him by the jacket and shoved him forward against the handrail. I pushed down on his shoulders bending him over double on the handrail and his feet shot up in the air. I kept pressure on his head with one hand so he couldn't catch his balance and get his feet on the floor. Unfortunately, that's when the damn supervisor, Curly, walked by again. He paused and asked me what the hell I was doing. I looked at Rob hanging upside down, feet still flailing in the air, my hand still on his head holding him down. With total solemnity, I told Curly, "I'm teaching him not to pick on defenseless women." He was satisfied with my answer and left. Ah, the good old days.

CHAPTER 14
(1987) LOSING MY SENSE OF SELF

My days at the loading docks were numbered. The company had plans to shut down C&P and let another plant do all of the canning/packaging, etc. The company gave us the option to go to the new, out-of-state location, or bid on another job. I know this sounds ridiculous, but I decided to go back into operations, shift work. I made this decision because I was in what I thought was a serious relationship with someone I have not previously discussed here. The first time I got married, I left shift work, took a pay cut and then ended up being the sole breadwinner. Logically, if I ended up getting married again, I needed to prepare. Leave it to say, it was a whirlwind, short-lived relationship. I fell for a guy that I didn't know who, I found out, was just using my money to pay off his debts—including an engagement ring for another woman he had run out on. Not the woman I would catch him cheating on me with but another woman from a town where he used to live. As I was packing my things, he said my leaving was for the best because, "I didn't need him." Food for thought. Then something happened that I still don't know whether it was real or totally in my vivid imagination. He asked if I would go squirrel hunting with him before I left. I told him no; I would not go out with him to kill some innocent squirrels. He begged me to go, saying that he really wanted to use my dog (a Chow—seriously?) because he was a great squirrel dog, but he didn't think the dog would go without me.

Now, listen closely because this is how fucked up my brain was at the time. I immediately thought, "This guy is going to take me out in the woods and kill me." What did I do? I agreed to go, picked up my shotgun, and went with him. The dog took off into the trees ahead of us and my, soon to be ex, told me to go ahead of him. I could see the newspaper story in my head. "Woman killed in tragic hunting accident." I even believed he would get away with it since he was in law enforcement. I stopped in my tracks and told him he would go first. After all, he was the one that planned to shoot squirrels, not me. I had been carrying my shotgun safely, loaded but broke open. I snapped it shut and insisted he walk in front of me. It was a short hunting trip. He tried repeatedly to get me to shoot at the squirrels, but I refused. I wasn't going to waste my shells. He eventually fired off a couple of wild shots and said he'd had enough. We made it safely back to the house. I loaded up my dog with the rest of my belongings and left, glad to be alive, and free of him.

What the fuck was I thinking? NEVER go into a situation where you think you will be in danger. It doesn't matter if it's all in your imagination. So many women go missing and are never found, or sadly, their bodies turn up. I have no damned idea why I felt the need to show him he couldn't get one over on me. Whatever his motive was, I wasn't going to let him best me. Stupid, stupid, stupid. I was lucky. Bad things do happen more than we know. Don't risk your life to prove how tough you are. Prove how tough you are by listening to your inner voice and staying out of the woods with gun toting, egotistical, maniacal assholes.

By the time I went back into operations, I had an attitude. Okay, more of an attitude. Along with the "don't fuck with me" attitude, I had gained an "I hate everyone attitude."

It makes me sad to realize I went through this episode. I remember Nancy saying that I was the kind of person who "saw the best in everyone." I eventually learned to ask myself who I wanted to be, a hater, or someone who at least looks for the good in others. It has been a very beneficial habit for me. Try it next time you're struggling over right or wrong, good or evil, gray or pink, up or down. Simply ask yourself, "Who do you want to be?"

First day back in operations I was introduced to my trainer, Curt, and I really didn't give a fuck. Little did I know, years later he would be my second husband. That day, I just wanted him to train me, and I didn't give a rat's ass about anyone. Just leave me the fuck alone and let me do my job. I was vocal about it too.

In spite of my horrendous attitude, even I had to admit we had a truly remarkable man as our area foreman, Danny. He told Curt to remind me that, as the new guy, it was my job to bring cinnamon rolls for the whole crew. By then Curt had spent more than five minutes with me and knew this was not going to go over well, but he did as instructed. Curt explained to me that we were "one big happy family" and we all got along. Then, as quickly as possible, he spat out, "Youneedtobringcinnamonrollsforeveryone." I told him this was the worst fucking excuse for a family I'd ever seen and there was nothing happy about it. And by the way, I didn't hire on to the refinery to be anyone's fucking waitress so go buy your own god damn cinnamon rolls. I was such a bitch.

I was obviously struggling and things kept happening that just spurred on my attitude. One day we had an anniversary celebration for one of the lead operators, Ray. The company provided cake and ice cream, and it was all nicey, nicey. That is until the bastard, Ray, turned to hand me the knife and said, "Since you're the only woman here you can cut the cake." I grabbed the knife in a white knuckled grip and promised I would indeed cut something. Other operators wrested the knife away from me and someone else volunteered to cut the cake. I don't know who, I didn't give a fuck. I just wanted to do my job, and this shit had absolutely nothing to do with my job and FUCK that guy for thinking I was here to serve him or anyone else.

I think I've made it clear that I was anything but perfect. I had a good work ethic, but my personal life was eating me up from the inside. Grief, depression, anxiety, stress, they can all eat you alive and it manifests physically as well as mentally. I didn't sleep well, and I had a lot of stomach issues including ulcers. But I always came to work. Many nights I'd spend some time hiding in the bathroom sick as a dog, but I always took my radio in case I was needed. The guys liked to screw with me then. Of course, they had no idea what I was going through because I sure as hell wouldn't tell them. They probably thought it was from partying because I was single. One week I was really struggling and barely made it to the bathroom in time. I tried to flip on the lights, but they didn't work. The guys had unscrewed the light bulbs or thrown the breaker. I didn't have time to figure it out. I groped my way into the stall just as I started throwing up. The next day there was a sign on the bathroom stall ripping whoever had made such a horrible mess in the bathroom. I have no idea how bad it had been. I'd tried to puke in the stool, but I guess I didn't totally succeed. I added my own comment to the note, "Thank you for your compassion." The note was gone the next day.

The worst thing you could do was to let anyone know what bothered you, whether you were sick, scared, angry, just didn't like something, the list goes on. Unfortunately, everyone knew I was a hornet's nest, and it was as if they just couldn't help themselves. Practical jokes were still the big thing even though the company was getting more vocal about stopping horseplay. All the guys knew I was a prime target with a really short fuse so they could get instant gratification from their pranks.

One of their favorite pranks was to put hand cream on the earpiece of the old rotary wall phone. You'd think they could only pull this trick on me once but if I had my mind on something else, I would grab up the phone and answer it because that was part of the job. I don't remember how many phones I broke. After being creamed, I would take the receiver and use it to beat the phone right off the wall and stomp it a few times once it was down just to for good measure. When I finally started becoming more wary of the phone, they got my hard hat instead. I put a good-sized dent in the metal cabinet when I threw my hat across the control room in a rage.

After giving me some time to cool down, they went back to the phone. I heard the phone ring and noticed that everyone had conveniently left the control room even though it was lunchtime. Hum, that's odd. Being the only one there, I had to answer the phone. Even a dumb dog learns a few tricks. I picked up the receiver and proactively looked, sure enough, hand cream on the earpiece. I unplugged the receiver from the phone and put it in my locker. One operator, Bill, had wandered back into the control room and sat at the picnic table near the sabotaged phone. Bill ate his lunch casting surreptitious glances at the receiverless phone.

I waited for the boss to return from lunch. Once he did, I went to my locker, retrieved the creamed handset and followed Danny into his office, closing the door quietly behind me. Danny looked at me, looked at the phone piece, and asked if he needed to buy yet another phone and I told him no. I waited. He asked if there was anything he could do for me. I told him no and waited. He waited. Once I decided enough time had passed, I asked Danny if he had any wipes (he always kept some in his desk). He pulled one out of his desk and I reached for it, pulled back and instead handed him the handset. I explained to him that I really needed to get outside and make my rounds and would he mind taking care of this for me. I turned and left his office.

As I was grabbing my tools, radio, and hard hat I watched the look on Bill's face as he sat at the lunch table. He knew I had been in Danny's office long enough to spill the beans. His look of nervous terror was enjoyable for me. Danny wandered out of his office, looked around, saw the same look of terror and then called Bill into his office. I was told later that Bill spilled his guts before Danny could tell him that I hadn't said a word, hadn't accused anyone. Later that day, Danny explained to me that if they didn't like me, they wouldn't pull these tricks on me. I told him I wasn't there to be liked. I was there to work, and I wanted them to leave me the hell alone so I could do my job.

It was becoming much more evident that I couldn't tolerate horseplay. One day as I came on shift a coworker took me aside and warned me that a trap had been set for me in a small shed where we caught cooling tower samples. I went about my duties but avoided the trap until after Danny came to work. I asked him to come with me to see something. Once we got to the shed, I motioned him to go in ahead of me. He pulled the door open, and a large bucket of water dumped on him. Fortunately, he stayed back from the doorway and the water hit him on the lower legs. It apparently filled his shoes as he made this loud, squishy sound all the way back to the control room. He appeared to be pissed. I think the horseplay pretty much quit that day. Besides, the company was putting more emphasis on safety and since horseplay could often lead to injury, there was less tolerance.

In spite of my bad attitude, I really did enjoy my job, being an operator. It had a tremendous amount of flexibility even though a specific amount of work had to be done each shift. Still, I liked the conditions. I got to work outside and inside. I didn't have any set break time so I could usually appease my horrible smoking habit almost anytime I needed to, as often as I needed to. Eventually, I started volunteering for all the shutdowns and turnarounds. The work was hard, but it was satisfying.

Quick explanation of the difference between a unit shutdown and a turnaround: a shutdown is normally a short-term affair and done to perform maintenance on a minimal amount of equipment. For instance, a pump or exchanger needs to come out of service, but the block valves are leaking (or don't exist) and the equipment can't be safely blinded and repaired until the unit is shut down. Once the unit is down, the failed equipment, along with the pipes to/from the piece of equipment, can be cleared and repairs done.

160

This may include repairing or replacing those damn block valves that leak. I really hated leaking block valves as they could add a heightened level of danger to the job.

There are also emergency shutdowns if a piece of equipment fails catastrophically. Many single pieces of equipment can be bypassed, and an auxiliary put online in its stead. However, not all pumps or compressors have an auxiliary that can be used to keep the unit running. Furnaces are normally a solo act and should they fail, such as a tube rupture, it necessitates an immediate emergency shutdown.

Let me explain the furnace tube failure a bit more. Furnaces heat crude oil or other hydrocarbons so that they can be refined into multiple products. Furnaces are large, heavily insulated structures, normally rectangular or square boxes with large stacks but there are also some cylindrical furnaces. Product is pumped through the furnace tubes (pipes) in several passes located at different sections of the furnace to enhance the heating process. Burners, like a much larger version of the burners on a gas stove, provide heat to the furnace box. Mounted on the sidewalls or floors of the furnaces, burners blow open flames into the firebox.

I'm sure you're getting the picture. We pump flammable hydrocarbon through tubes inside of a big ole box full of fire. One tiny pinhole in a single tube and the results can be catastrophic. Rest assured, due to emergency training and regular inspection during turnarounds, tube failures are extremely rare. Operators are trained on how to swiftly and safely contain any such emergency. And yes, been there, done that.

Turnarounds are a much bigger story. As mentioned previously, turnarounds are a planned, scheduled shutdown of an entire unit(s). All the piping and equipment, drums, towers, exchangers, furnaces, are cleared of hydrocarbon and other contaminates in order for mechanical to inspect, repair and replace as needed. It's also an opportunity to recharge or replace catalyst in reactors. There is generally a lot of welding going on as equipment/piping is added or modified. A turnaround can last for several weeks, maybe even months, though the time is kept to the absolute minimum to complete the work as each day out of service costs the refinery a lot of money.

Shutting down or starting up units is considered the most dangerous time for operations. For scheduled, planned shutdowns or turnarounds, there isn't a big red button that you push and everything stops.

There are big red buttons for emergency use. These are the "oh shit" buttons, the ones you never want to have to use. They are a last line of defense and designed to shut a unit down in a safe mode—either opening or closing valves, etc., to bring the unit crashing down as quickly and safely as possible. Not the preferred method at all.

I mentioned that turnarounds were a lot of work. To prepare for the turnaround, depending on the type of unit, we might have to pull the feed and then circulate a lighter material through the unit at lower temperatures to try to clean all the internals. For instance, washing a crude tower's innards and associated piping with diesel. There are even some vessels that are washed inside with detergents, normally by a contractor company. After flushing, the units are then steamed to help remove any remaining hydrocarbons. Once that is completed, we would start testing the equipment for hydrocarbon and/or other contaminants such as benzene or H2S. Once clear, mechanical personnel were allowed to start opening the equipment in preparation for bodily entry. Opening up equipment that previously contained refining processes can be hazardous. First, you don't want anyone exposed to any type of toxic or hazardous material. Second, you don't want the environment contaminated with any spills, vapors or even contaminated sediment. Third, you don't want flammable mixtures opened up to oxygen and the potential for fire or explosions.

Working turnaround, I learned a lot about the units, and it helped me picture what was going on inside the equipment during normal operations. During one of these internal inspections, I had the added challenge of the dreaded rope ladder. For those of you that have never tried to climb up and down on one of these torture devices, you need to give it a try before you scoff and say, "That's no big deal". Depending on the construction of the rope ladder, it can have a hell of a lot of give to it. You take one step up and feel like you sink back two. It gives you the feeling that you've climbed three times further than the actual physical distance. Squirrel that I was, I thought it was fun. It reminded me of the obstacle course in the Army, the place where I used to love to go for exercise. Others, however, such as my future husband, Curt, didn't see any entertainment value in entering a huge metal drum and then having to fight so damn hard to get out. That's fine, I didn't mind doing all the rope ladders.

FLASHBACK – There was this one time when I was working in the yards that a rope ladder made things worse. My job that day was to sandblast the inside of the drum to remove any scale. Sandblasting is exactly what it sounds like. Pressurized air is used to shoot sand through a hose, similar to but smaller than a firefighter's hose, and the abrasive sand beats off any accumulation of gunk until you reach clean metal. In order to have the maximum surface area open for cleaning, we installed a rope ladder instead of building a scaffold or even a solid ladder. When sandblasting, along with normal PPE, you wear a hood much like the fresh air hood I wore on the flare drum. The hood protects you from the abrasive ricochet as the pressurized sand/air stream bounces off the equipment surface. It also provides the worker with a constant flow of much-needed fresh air. Sandblasting was one of my favorite jobs. The repetitive sweep of the sandblast hose removes years of sediment and scale, leaving a clean surface. I appreciated being able to see the immediate result of my hard work.

Sandblasting inside a drum is noisy, even with the required hearing protection. In my imagination, the constant whoosh and shifting of sand was almost like being inside of an hourglass. On this day, I was happily blasting away, keeping my attention focused on the walls, not wanting to miss a single spec that might later clog a pump or foul a tower tray. I did not notice the sand building up around my feet, my ankles, my calves. It really just felt like a support, after all, I had to brace myself against the pressure of the hose. I don't know how long I had been blasting, what time it was, or if it was close to lunch time. I did after all, have a standby on the outside of the drum who would inform me of any breaks, changes, or emergencies. A standby whose job it was to look out for my safety. At least I thought I did.

The first thing I noticed was the air blowing into my hood about forehead level felt moist. Although it felt good after the dusty atmosphere, the air was never supposed to be moist, let alone wet. Sure enough, a moment later water started pouring in through the airline in my hood, blurring my vision. Before I could take my hood off, I had to shut down the sandblast hose. I pulled at the lever, but nothing happened. I could feel the difference in the hose, in the noise inside the drum. I was now blowing water full force out of the hose instead of sand. I felt the water mixing with the sand that was now nearly knee deep, turning it into quicksand. I assume the pressure made it difficult to close the valve. That and possibly the panic of being inside a hood that was blowing water into my face instead of air. I knew I had to get out of the hood to be able to see what I needed to do. I laid the hose down, bracing it against my legs, and struggled out of the hood, glad to get the water out of my face. I shouted repeatedly for my standby, but nobody heard me. I tried the hose again and was finally able to wrestle it closed. The water and sand mixture now had me mired knee deep in quicksand. It wasn't like it was sucking me down or anything as dramatic as that. It just made it harder to pull my legs free. Water was still pumping in through the hood, I wouldn't be able to shut that off but at least it wasn't a big stream. I would have to get out of the sand and make my way up the rope ladder. It took some time, wiggling and working my legs free. I continued to shout at the standby, but still no answer. You can probably imagine that my shouts became more and more colorful as I struggled.

I made my way out of the drum, and sure enough, no standby. Then I made my way to the breakroom. I found the rest of my crew eating lunch, chatting about their hamburger helper with "special herbs." I was furious.

It was soon discovered that water had inadvertently been tied into the air lines. It took hours to get all the water from the air system and back to normal. I seethed the whole time. But I never said anything. Not one damn word. I wanted to. I wanted to tell someone my standby had abandoned me, left me inside a drum full of sand and water. I wanted to tell someone to check out the special-made hamburger helper. Oh, and whatever you do, don't try the brownies. But I didn't. I didn't want my crew to turn against me for ratting them out. I didn't want to be "that girl." So, I said nothing.

Later, I was called in to the supervisor shack. I assumed they would question me, and I would have to tell them the truth. What did happen though was so far from the truth it still shocks me. My yard foreman, with another supervisor as witness, said he had been informed that I was telling everyone that he had been making passes at me. I was stunned. What the hell? What the fucking hell? Again, my mind raced. Why would my coworkers say this? Never, had I said anything like this to anyone. The mere idea repulsed me, physically made me want to puke. What were they doing? Was this a test? Why would they do this to me? As I remember this, my mind screams at me for not denying all of this at the top of my lungs, for staying mute, for not defending myself. I had been in a situation where my life could have been on the line. I stuttered as the foreman screamed at me, telling me he had a wife and a reputation. One thing is for sure, my reputation was never the same after that. Still, I didn't rat out my crew, the fucking bastards. I assumed any rebuttal would make matters worse, so I kept silent.

Times like those haunted me for years. Never knowing why people hated me so much to try and destroy my career. They haunted me until I finally realized what I was doing to myself. They weren't torturing me. I was. They had no power over me. I did.

Let it go. Let it be. Laugh at the motherfuckers. I do now. But I also feel sorry for them, the rat bastards.

CHAPTER 15
(1989/90) SEEKING THE WILD LIFE

As much as I enjoyed the work in operations, I seriously wanted out of shift work. I also had it in my mind that maybe I'd just be happier, maybe even accepted in another position. I wanted a normal schedule where I could spend more time with my kids. I hated being exhausted all the time. I applied for quite a few jobs within the company but only a couple that mattered. The first was a safety job. I didn't have the preferred college degree in safety, but by then I'd had a lot of experience. I had written a tremendous amount of work permits during turnarounds and shutdowns. Each permit listed the safety requirements of the job. I had a passion for safety. I was also good with computers and software and had already done some training for other operators. I asked different folks for recommendations for a safety position and here are some of the things they said:

Debbie can pickup new information quickly and applies it consistently. She stands for what she believes. She will not be a "yes" person.

Please call at ext   or reply if you have questions.

Advanced Control Engr.
West Plant

This is an opportunity to place the "right" person in the "right" position that will benefit the whole organization and develop the individual at the same time. If we really believe in diversity and valuing all people then we have a chance to do the right thing, at the right time for the right reasons and that in my mind is the true definition of empowerment.

Jim
B.I. Facilitator

I was Debbie's supervisor for a period of approximately 10 years. During that time I found her to have a good work ethic and wanted to do more than just show up and get by. She volunteered on numerous occasions for work assignments on shutdowns, procedure writing, making of blind lists, ect.. She was thorough in her work and often went beyond what was expected for the task she was assigned. I believe she would be good in this position because of her work ethic, her ability to research items, as she is extremely computer literate, and a curiosity she would bring with her about things. If selected for this position I believe her coworkers would come to respect her work ethic and thoroughness in her research and presentations.

Danny

Figure 43 *Job recommendations.*

I bid on the safety job and even made it to the interviews, which I totally sucked at given my fear of face-to-face interactions with people. I was surprised when I interviewed with Kay, a senior woman in upper management. It actually looked like I might get the job, but then at the last minute the job was given to a guy, Jarod. He had just completed his college degree and happened to be married to another woman in management. I was disappointed, but I also believed that Jarod was deserving of the job based on his background. I didn't necessarily think he should have been given the job over my experience, but I wasn't disgruntled about it.

I talked with one manager, Mack, about how young engineers or college grads, without familiarity in refinery operations were favored over long-time employees with years and years of experience. Mack explained to me that his job was to grow engineers. He asked how he was supposed to do that if he didn't put them in charge and give them the opportunity to learn. I pointed out that people like me hired on with the idea that we would spend our entire careers working at just this one refinery. That we would be here as all the engineers come and go. My argument of having a good foundation went unheeded. After all, people like me don't grow up to run the company.

I finally reached the point where I wasn't entirely sure I wanted to continue my career at the Ponca City Refinery. I made a trip back to Artesia and applied for a couple of jobs there, one in the oil field and one at the Cherokee Refinery. I was told at the refinery that they had just had a hiring spree and didn't have any more openings. He was, however, excited about my resume and asked to keep it. I did get an offer later, but I'd already landed a new position at the Ponca City Refinery (that story is coming up).

I applied for another job outside of the refinery, and had things worked out differently, I would have gone down in history. I studied and applied to be a game warden. I spent hours and hours poring over material and questioning our game warden buddies, John and Joe, until they were ready to run me off with a stick. Actually, they were absolutely great and taught me a lot. I studied and studied. I didn't want to be a game warden because I loved to hunt and fish (although I do like fishing). I wanted to be a game warden to enforce game conservation. Conservation doesn't mean preventing people from hunting. Most people don't realize that if hunting wasn't allowed in a controlled manner, that the wildlife suffers. They can overpopulate and starve. Wild deer are even subject to fatal levels of stress during times of overpopulation.

Testing for the game warden position happens once a year. If there are two openings in the state, they will interview the four highest scores from the written test. The first time I tested I earned an interview along with five other people. The next year I tested and earned an interview with three other people. It didn't seem to matter that a female could consistently score high enough to be in the top percent. No females were hired as game wardens.

I was so good at taking the written test that a game warden's son, Tony, contacted me and asked if he could borrow my notes to study for the test. I had compiled a considerable amount of notes, especially since I'd seen the tests and knew what types of questions were asked. I liked the guy well enough, but I figured if he didn't have enough gumption to study with his father and do the work himself, well, that was on him. I wouldn't just hand over my years of hard work. I did, however, tell him he could make the two-hour ride with me to take the test and we would study on the way.

I quizzed him as I drove, asking him questions I had seen on previous tests. One question in particular comes to mind. "What does an adult bobwhite quail weigh?" The correct answer is six to seven ounces. Now, you won't be able to tell it from reading this story, but I have been accused of having a mild accent; this is relevant. As I continued my review, Tony never asked any questions, just kept nodding his head.

We both took the test with hundreds of other candidates. On the drive home, Tony just shook his head, admitting the test was tough. He said he wasn't so sure how he had done because I seemed to have misled him. I was shocked and demanded he explain before I kicked his ass out to walk the hundred miles back home. He said that my answer about the bobwhite quail, sixty-seven ounces (danged accent), was not on the test so he just picked the largest number instead. Ole Tony never did make it to the interviews as far as I knew. Probably for the best.

I truthfully don't recall how many times I tested, interviewed, and wasn't hired. I have no idea how many other women did either. Eventually I decided to pursue the matter further. I contacted a state representative, and he took over. I was contacted by the Wildlife Commission soon after. I was told that I would have to test again the next time they were hiring and if I could pass the test, I would be given due consideration. After all, they didn't want to "violate someone else's civil rights" and there was a "limit to what we can do without getting into reverse discrimination."

Wildlife agency's hiring practices under attack

By BOB BLEDSOE
Tribune Outdoor Editor

A Tulsa lawmaker says he will vote for a fellow House member's bill even though he is not sure of its purpose.

Rep. Don Ross, D-Tulsa, unhappy with what he considered a personal attack on fellow House member Tommy Thomas, D-Atoka, said in a letter Wednesday he will vote for Thomas' bill to give the Legislature control of the state Department of Wildlife Conservation's budget.

The letter was to Steve Lewis, director of the Wildlife Department. In it, Ross also complained about the department's poor record for hiring minorities, to which Lewis replied that he is hampered by anti-discrimination laws.

Lewis, in attempts last week to muster public opposition to the bill, was quoted as saying that Thomas had been "deceitful" in substituting House Bill 2013 for another at the last minute and giving the Wildlife Department inadequate time to respond before a House Wildlife Committee vote was taken. The bill passed 5-1.

In the letter, Ross said the comments of Lewis were a "public and personal attack" against Thomas. He said he would vote for the Thomas bill, even though Thomas has "not told me of the bill and I'm still not sure what it attempts to correct."

"However, I have committed my vote with him and have talked with others who will do the same — whatever 'he' decides, we intend to vote with him."

Ross was one of a group of House members who summoned Lewis into a closed meeting Monday at the House lounge to chastise him for his remarks to the media.

"I have restated my position on the Thomas question," Ross says in his letter, "first because I wanted you to know that while I have other concerns with the commission — your historically discriminatory hiring practices, particularly of blacks — I do not take kindly to what was done and that is the central issue to be addressed first in this correspondence."

"On your record of hiring minorities, he continued, "at best, your record is awful; at worst, its outrageous."

Ross quoted the department's affirmative action report that said of 314 employees (Lewis says 313), only three were black. All three were office-clerical workers. Of 28 "new hires," none was black.

The report, Ross said, noted that compared to the civilian labor force there should be 14 blacks on staff.

Lewis said Thursday that the department has continually searched for minority employees but has had little success and has been hampered by laws meant to deter discrimination.

"Our job application forms cannot legally contain questions about racial or ethnic backgrounds, so until we see applicants face-to-face, we don't know if they are a racial minority or not," Lewis said.

The Oklahoma Office of Personnel Management approves our forms and inspects them to make sure they are not discriminatory. Of the applicants they do see face-to-face, few are blacks or other minorities, he added.

son," Lewis said. "The test scores don't know who is who."

"There is a bill in the Oklahoma Senate right now that would give agency heads leeway to hire minority applicants in the top 10 percent of the application group instead of the top 10 individuals. But even if the bill passes, a minority applicant has to get to the top 10 percent before we could do anything more. Beyond that, we may be violating someone else's civil rights," Lewis said.

Lewis said the department is sending representatives to a "career days" program at Langston University to try and recruit minority applicants.

"Historically, this agency has tried to find minority employees. But there is a limit to what we can do without getting into reverse discrimination," Lewis said.

Figure 44 Wildlife Agency hiring practices come under fire.

March 27, 1990

Mr. Steven Alan Lewis
Director
Department of Wildlife
P. O. Box 53456
Oklahoma City, Oklahoma 73105

Dear Steve,

This is a follow up to our telephone conversation regarding
Deborah Sioux Savage. It is my hope that you will ask her
to reapply for employment with the Department and at least
let her attempt to qualify again.

However, the larger problem is that the agency needs to implement a stronger minority hiring program for women, blacks,
etc. without lowering its standards.

If you were to expand your efforts to hire such minorities,
I am sure that a number of legislators such as myself would
endeavor to find you additional funding for such positions.
It is a problem that will not go away.

Sincerely,

James D. Holt

JDH/aj

CC: Carl Pierceall
          Jimmy Harrel
          H.B. Atkinson
          John D. Groendyke
          K. E. Pennington
          John Gibbs
          John S. (Jack) Zink

Figure 45 Letter from state rep (I briefly changed my name from Juckes, to Savage, an old family name, but soon regretted the change and would go back to Juckes).

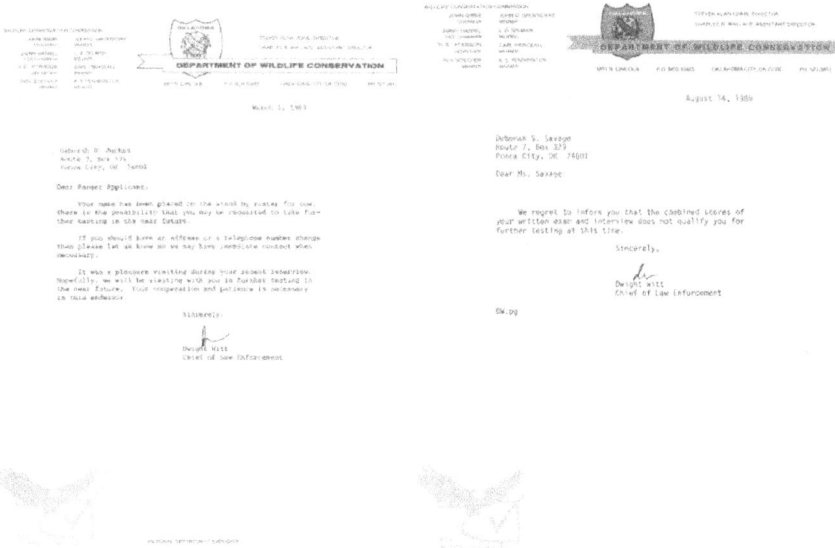

Figure 46 Letters from Wildlife Commission (note—I briefly changed my name from Juckes to Savage, an old family name, but soon after regretted that and would go back to Juckes).

I brushed up on my studies, took the two-hour trip, and went through the entire testing process. Again, I scored high enough to make it to the interviews. By now, I was much better at the face-to-face. I could also read the resentment of several of my interviewers. One guy in particular, Warden Butthead, was pretty arrogant and disparaging in his remarks and questions. One question was, "What would you do, going up against a number of hunters, all of them armed, of course, and having to arrest them?" I reminded him that I was an expert marksman and well qualified to handle a weapon. Warden Butthead kept pushing the question, pointing out that these would be big ole Oklahoma boys that don't take shit off of anyone—especially a woman.

I got really quiet, but I know I had that gleam in my eye and a little smirk on my face. I leaned towards Warden Butthead and said, "If they're not smart enough to be afraid of a woman with a gun, then they deserve to be shot." Then for the sake of the other interviewers, I explained that I would do just as any sane game warden would and call for backup. After all, who is dumb enough to go off in the woods with someone who wants to shoot you?

It was some time after the interviews when I was informed that I was one of two women that were up for the game warden's position. They didn't tell me the other woman's name, but they did say she was an avid fisher and hunter. This was the one area where I was weak. I also knew how badly I had pissed them off. This triggered another fast action, mental montage, of what the future might bring. I saw them being forced to give me the job. I then pictured myself in a damp, dark basement, confined to filing paperwork for the rest of my life. I had forced their hand, and they were obviously pissed, but something good could come out of it. I pulled my name from consideration, asking them to give the other woman the job. I saw a news piece about her just the other day. I wondered if she had any idea that I might have actually helped her get her job. Of course, I don't know if she'd been through the same type of fight herself. I do know she was fully qualified, or she wouldn't be there. I'm happy for her. Maybe a little jealous, but definitely happy for her.

CHAPTER 16
(1990/91) THE BLUE MOON, FIRE AND ICE

I was not on shift the night of the massive Crude Unit fire, but this is my understanding of what happened that New Year's Eve, 1990, the night of the Blue Moon.

Crude Units distill raw crude oil into various products including gasoline, naphtha, kerosene, diesel, gas oils and residuum (which is the heavy junk that's left over).

An experienced operator, Kent, went out on normal rounds to drain water from an overhead (gasoline) drum, a normal shift activity.

Water in the hydrocarbon processes can come from several sources. Raw crude oil can have small amounts but then we actually "wash" other contaminants from the oil by adding more water to the crude (many contaminants, including salt, prefer to play in the water instead of the oil). Once the water sucks up all the yucky stuff, the crude/water mixture is sent to a desalter, a round, ball-like drum that contains electric plates. The mixture is exposed to an electrical current and the gunk-laden water separates from the crude.

The company no longer allows this type of waste water to be drained to an open sewer (the initial cause of this accident). Soon after this incident, they went to an enclosed system to prevent any type of auto ignition event and to protect workers from hazardous gases. The waste water generally has amounts of H2S, deadly hydrogen sulfide, entrained in the water. Small amounts of H2S smell like rotten eggs. At higher levels, your senses become overwhelmed, and you don't smell it. You can also stop breathing, like, drop dead not breathing. I drained a lot of rotten egg smelling water back in the early years. We eventually went to wearing

SCBA (self-contained breathing apparatus—like fire fighters use) when we drained water until they completed the enclosed system.

The overhead product was primarily gasoline. The drum itself was several feet off the ground, and a drainpipe ran to the sewer (this was not a storm sewer but a refinery sewer that runs to a contained system that is gathered and treated/rerun downstream). Normally, you open the valve to the sewer and watch as it drains. You can't always see the difference between the water and hydrocarbon product, so you'd try to get a little splashing on the concrete. Then, you could see if it's water because it will bead up, hydrocarbon won't. You could also stick the end of your pipe wrench in the stream and look for the same thing, waiting until it no longer beads up, so you know you've flushed the water and hit gasoline. As soon as the water was drained, you'd close the valve. That's exactly what Kent did; he opened the valve to the sewer and began draining water.

Thankfully, the explosion that occurred did not result in injuries. It was also the day we learned about auto ignition. If the right hydrocarbon (fuel) is drained to the atmosphere (air) from a large enough pipe at a fast enough speed, it can auto ignite (spark), just as it did on that day.

The company was great at analyzing the root cause failure of accidents and sharing that information to prevent future occurrences. I greatly admired that about the company. During my career, most safety incidents provided a learning experience, more focused on education than punishment. There were times, however, if an employee was deemed to have intentionally bypassed known safety protocol, punishment would occur. In most cases, I totally agreed. In other cases, I wondered if a person who made a mistake, a head up their ass, mistake, if they might not be a better, safer employee because of it. I also wondered if the threat of punishment would lead to employees covering up mistakes. It's a really tough call to make and I believe that, for the most part, the company did a good job of making those really tough decisions. I will note that on the cases I did not agree, I understood that I was not privy to ALL the information that management used to reach their decision.

That night, as Kent drained water from the drum, it went to gasoline before Kent noticed. Without any kind of warning, the stream ignited. Fire would have immediately encompassed the drain pipe and the block valve. There was no way that Kent could reach it to close the block valve and shut off the gasoline feeding the fire. This was one of the times when you hit the big red, "oh shit," emergency shutdown button.

As Kent radioed for help, the gasoline began to spray upward from the sewer, carrying the fire higher until it engulfed the structure around the overhead drum. The drum temperature increased and pressurized the gasoline within, blowing it even harder to the sewer (the path of least resistance) and out towards the operating unit. A huge fire began melting everything it touched. Insulation was scorched off the nearby towers. Pneumatic tubing that operated control instruments ruptured. Electrical conduit and wiring were consumed. As the heat increased, huge steel "I" beams on the structure around the drum and tower began warping and twisting as metal catwalks buckled. The fire climbed higher and higher.

Inside the control room was organized pandemonium. The operators began crashing the unit down, diverting feed, shutting down the furnace, blocking in streams to other units. Nearby units were affected, and operators were forced to stay with their own units to either shut them down if they had been damaged or to divert any product going to/from the affected unit. Anyone who could, tried to help as the fire roared.

Now, imagine yourself being in the middle of multiple operating units that are processing highly flammable products while the largest unit has an out-of-control fire that is melting everything it touches and the heat from the flames is radiating out. A unit very near the fire processes propane and butane. Imagine what it is like to realize that your life and the lives of all the people around you are in imminent danger. Imagine that you have family living relatively close to the refinery. Imagine just how big of a blast could occur and how far the damage could reach—they have pictures of it you know, the estimated blast range of all the units.

Now imagine all the people, operators, mechanical, craftsmen, supervisors, that held their ground and figured out how to stop the fire, control the damage, protect the workers, the community, and the environment with as little impact as possible. Those folks didn't have time to stop and call loved ones to warn them or say, "I love you." They had a job to do, and they did it well. These folks acted heroically before the trained fire fighters even arrived on scene. Fortunately, it didn't take long for the fire brigade and local fire departments to respond to assist, and their arrival was not only heartily appreciated, but absolutely necessary for success.

Not one person was injured that day. It was actually our foreman, Danny, that figured out how to stop the fire without just waiting for all the gasoline to dump out of the drum. He instructed workers to attach a fire hose to piping outside of the fire's perimeter and they pumped water into the drum. Water is heavier than gasoline. Once the fuel was floated above the drain line, the main fire was extinguished. The remaining fires were eventually knocked down.

New Year's Day, 1991, I was part of the crew selected to work the rebuild. As much shutdown and turnaround work as I had done in the past, nothing prepared me for this kind of devastation. A lot of the work centered on and around a multilevel structure of steel beams, stairs and decking. I remember climbing those stairs on the first day to view the damage. It was freezing cold that January day. The water that had extinguished the fires had frozen to ice on every surface. Enormous ice stalactites hung from the upper levels. The concrete and gratings were thick sheets of ice. Climbing the ice coated, metal stairs was made even more dangerous by the fact that they were twisted and warped. One operator said it looked like a funhouse the way everything lay at odd angles. For some reason I thought of the movie *The Poseidon Adventure* and how, in the movie, nothing looked familiar because everything was upside down after the ship sank.

We worked two shifts during the rebuild. I was lucky to work days although the downside was there were more management/engineer folks to get in the way. Each shift had a lead operator and at least a couple of us "working" operators to help. I say it like that because the lead operator mostly sat in the permit shack and directed traffic, attended meetings, and worked on the planning/paperwork aspect. On day shift, the lead happened to be Curt, the guy who had trained me when I bid back into the unit and who would, as mentioned, eventually become husband number two. At the time however, I was a bit disgruntled that he sat on his butt while I did all the physical work.

Which position I worked was definitely a mixed bag of emotions. On the one hand, I have discovered that I love being in charge. I like using my own thoughts, my knowledge, my common sense to guide and direct, especially when I see things going down shit creek. I always thought that if I was in charge I could help, I could make things better. Over the years, I did learn how to step back and teach others how to make those decisions. Being in charge also meant you had to do all the face-to-face with management and take the ass eatings if such ass eatings were on the agenda from supervisors or management. There was a tremendous amount of stress in being the lead, making the right decisions, making sure the underlings follow directions and most importantly, making sure that nobody got hurt—nobody, company or contractor. Lots of pressure. That kind of stuff can lead to sleepless nights or nights filled with dreams of, "Did I do the right thing? Did I miss anything?" Dreams, however, helped me many times to figure out solutions to problems that had eluded me during the day. Sometimes we get so stuck in the rut that we can't see the cornfield.

On the flip side of the lead is plain ole unit operator. Now that is a peachy spot. If you see management coming you just slip on out to the smoker and let the lead take the heat. You don't have to answer tough questions or argue with assholes that want to circumvent the process. No scheduling, rescheduling, and running full speed ahead just to hit a brick wall, veer, hit another brick wall, veer and wobble on down the road. Nope, unit operators can go outside and smell the fresh air, enjoy the great outdoors. Then put on ten to twenty pounds of PPE and tools and climb ladders till their shoulders scream (I had surgery on both shoulders years later). While outside enjoying the winter weather you could taste the bitter cold on your cracked lips, feel the tingling in your frostbitten fingers and especially the pain of your frozen toes inside those wonderful steel-toed boots. This was almost as much fun as the summer when you would have one-hundred-degree days where you enjoyed the scorching Oklahoma sun. Add to that the warm, cozy heat from the furnaces and other heat exchangers. Luckily, you have your long sleeve, fire retardant clothes to keep you from being sunburned. Yep, sarcasm is my middle name.

No matter what I just said, I am a total supporter of wearing fire resistant clothes in the refinery. My father was adamant about that after losing friends in flash fires. The material itself just makes life a little tougher. It is designed so that the fibers open and allow air to flow through on the cold days. It is also designed so that the fibers close when exposed to heat, providing protections from burns. That's good. That's also damn hot in the summer. It's also not perfect and I would lose a coworker to a flash fire in spite of his protective clothing.

Yes, there was sheer physical exhaustion and extremes in weather to deal with as a unit operator. More than once, I cussed Curt sitting in the heated permit shack drinking coffee. Not that I knew he was drinking coffee at the time, but it seemed to justify my righteous indignation.

In order to allow mechanical work to begin, trained personnel first tested the area for contaminants. Results showed the asbestos insulation had been damaged and fibers were found everywhere within the fire zone. The entire area would need to be encapsulated with plastic to begin asbestos mitigation. However, it first had to be determined that it was safe for workers to enter the area. Remember, this was a different work situation. There had been no time to clear the equipment and soon after the fire began, they lost control to do so. There had been a lot of flammable material put down the contained sewer system and although it was designed to catch hydrocarbons, you could still get some vapors if the system lost its water seal. There was also hydrocarbon that went to the ground and ended up in the storm sewers. Testing had to be done for hydrocarbon presence before asbestos mitigation could begin. That testing fell to me on the day shift.

I would get to work at least thirty minutes early for my twelve-hour shift. In addition to my normal PPE of fire-resistant coveralls, leather boots, leather gloves, and hard hat, I also wore a white Tyvek suit and half face respirator any time I entered the "hot zone." You've probably seen similar apparel worn by the health care workers during the COVID-19 pandemic. I removed and disposed of my Tyvek after exiting the hot zone. I was not, however, instructed to shower afterwards like the folks who were actually removing the asbestos. I assume that's because I wasn't intentionally stirring up the fibers.

It wasn't the first time I was exposed to asbestos since I'd went to work at the refinery. The very first time was when I was

181

working as a pipefitter helper. He was cutting insulation with his saw and told me to step back because it was asbestos. I asked why he would sit right there unprotected, and he explained that it takes about fifty years for it to show up and kill you so he wasn't worried about himself; he was just worried about me because I was a pup. That day has never left my mind, and I still wonder if it's going to show up on my chest x-rays some day in the not-too-distant future. For someone who smoked as much as I did, the danger from asbestos frightened me even more.

I was rightly afraid of the asbestos and every time I wore my respirator, I cinched it down as tight as I could to my face. I always did the check to make sure the respirator wasn't leaking either. I would hold my hand over the inlet valve and take a deep breath . If the seal was adequate, the respirator would be sucked down tight onto my face, and I wouldn't be able to pull more air in. As the days went by, the bump on my nose where the rubber mask rested became more and more tender. Each day I cinched it down just as tightly. I remember my face streaked with tears from the pain but making sure to hide it from all the guys.

I would gear up, take my gas tester, go into the shrouded area, and begin testing. It was amazing how many cracks in the concrete still emitted gas vapors. I would check the entire area from the ground to the uppermost level and everything in between. Labor crews would mitigate any problems I found, usually by covering a sewer or crack in the concrete with tarps and dirt or water to prevent any type of spark or ignition source from reaching the vapors. Afterwards, I would have to recheck for hydrocarbons.

The asbestos removal team finished their work, and we quickly got to the point that mechanical could start working. The amount of work required for the rebuild felt monumental. It was nearly incomprehensible to imagine ever getting all the work completed. One thing I had learned from working turnarounds—even an enormous amount of work is easily managed by breaking it down into sections and prioritizing. The work wasn't being done on the entire unit as a whole but by multiple crews working on individual pieces of equipment or piping. Once you looked at the pieces, you could prioritize the work based on multiple factors, time to completion, worker availability, parts availability, engineer input, etc. Of course, you had to rank things according to "this" has to be completed before "that." For instance, if you have to replace a valve that is twelve foot off the ground, you will first need to build a scaffold to be able to safely reach and work on said valve.

Many seemingly unsurmountable tasks can be accomplished the same way. Don't stay focused on the enormity of the situation. Break it down and prioritize into bite-sized chunks while keeping the final goal in mind.

Normally, the company puts a tremendous amount of planning into any unit shut down, especially for a critical crude distillation unit like this was. They have to figure out how to keep other affected units running, where to store any feed/product that isn't being run, all the economic and environmental impacts…there's just a lot of things that go into planning a productive turnaround. An emergency shutdown on the other hand, by definition, doesn't give you time for any of this. It was always in the forefront that this was costing the company a significant amount of money. It's really important that you understand I'm not saying the company pushed us too fast, cut corners, etc. They did give us reminders on time and money but remember, my goal was still retirement, and I wanted the company to make money. We all felt the pressure of getting the work done correctly and as efficiently as possible. We worked a twenty-four/seven schedule with two shifts which overlapped a bit. We also worked every day with no days off until complete. It was just over thirty days, I think. Back then, we didn't have a fatigue schedule like they do now that limits the number of days in a row that employees are allowed to work.

The rebuild work was extensive for all crafts, electricians, pipefitters, repairmen, welders, insulators, along with operators, inspectors, engineers and others. Ironworkers underwent a massive amount of work to rebuild the structure. That's when I met the guy we referred to as "The Great Bearded One." Ironworkers were a real special breed in my opinion. Ironworkers seemed to have absolutely no fear of heights or much else for that matter. They reminded me of my buddies back in EOD. They were a jovial bunch and made the day go a little faster. I loved watching the cutting, welding, and grinding that went on. Back then, we didn't do a lot of spark containment, so you'd see the glowing red sparks cascading down from the upper levels along with the bright white glow from the welders. The air carried the tang of that unmistakable smell of hot metal.

Each day I would do my gas testing before our shift started. I wanted to be prepared to sign off on the work permits when mechanical arrived. We also stayed after our shift to make sure that the night crew knew where we were on the work schedule. I would put in thirteen to fourteen hours a day before going home, showering, eating and barely sleeping.

I was glad to be free of the face respirator, but now that mechanical work had started, I had a lot more places that needed gas testing. The worst place was around the tall crude tower. Workers erected scaffolding around the tower to allow access for repair. Normally, climbing a tower seems secure. Ladders with cages around them, are built onto the towers and are generally only so high before reaching a landing. The thought here is that if you do fall, you'll only fall twenty feet or so. For example, you'd climb one ladder on the left side of the tower, cross a landing to the middle of the tower, climb another ladder, cross a landing to the right side of the tower and climb again. I think you get the picture.

Climbing scaffolding was NOT a secure feeling. Scaffolds were built with interconnecting poles and usually wooden (sometimes metal) boards that were wired down for decking. Scaffolds don't have enclosed ladders. Their ladders were usually on the outside of the scaffolding going from one level to the next. I had to climb several of these ladders to do my gas testing. I remember being so damn high that I couldn't stand to look down (normally heights don't bother me much as long as I feel secure). I was terrified every time I had to climb one of these outside ladders at a greatly elevated height. I would grab the rungs so tightly my hands would cramp. I would lean in as close as possible and force myself up the ladder usually moving just one limb at a time, one hand followed by one foot. Slow painful progress to be sure, but the best I could do with all the winter clothes, leather gloves, steel-toed leather boots, radio and pipe wrench cinched tight at my waist, gas tester slung over my shoulder. As soon as I'd reach secure footing, I'd take in a deep breath and immediately feel better. I always stopped to enjoy the view, whether it was the refinery with all the steam rising from different stacks, the unit lights glowing at night, or the many sunrises and sunsets. Even as the cold air stung my cheeks and nose, I would love the feel of it, all the sights and sounds of being outdoors. As much as I dreaded climbing those ladders, every day, at least twice a day, I was careful never to tell anyone of my fears. I also doubted that anyone wanted to hear about the sunsets.

The physical toll of those long hours and strenuous work began to tell on me. I reached the point where I didn't think I'd be able to do it anymore. I thought the time might have come when, for the first time, I was going to have to cry, "uncle," and tap out. But I didn't. I went to work the next day and the day after that. I think your body and mind tend to adapt. Even in the harshest of times, we can build habits that help us get through the day without even realizing it. We leave the familiarity of the mundane behind and the current environment becomes our new normal. It has to in order to survive.

I remember telling myself just that. I am a survivor. Go ahead. Say it. "I am a survivor." It doesn't have to be a catastrophic incident for you to feel like you are a survivor. Pass the math test? Survivor. Lost ten pounds? Survivor. Got out of a bad relationship? Survivor. Flew on an airplane and arrived safely? Survivor. Ate your mother-in-law's mystery meatloaf with a fake smile plastered on your face? Survivor. Take credit for your accomplishments whether they are deemed small and insignificant, or huge and life altering. You did it. You survived. Now, what can you do tomorrow? (I love this paragraph. Sorry, I had to take a moment and read it again.)

Once all the equipment was cleared and mechanical work commenced, the first rush was over and there was a slight lull in the workload for us operators. We still did all the safety checks, all the gas tests, and constantly monitored the work to see that safety protocols were followed. I enjoyed those times. It was crazy how much stupid shit went on when workers thought nobody was looking. I'd catch guys smoking in unauthorized areas and they would argue that it wasn't going to hurt anything. I'd have to remind them that just because one piece of equipment was clear of explosive material didn't mean the equipment right next to it wasn't in normal operation. Remember the propane and butane unit right next door? Idiots.

We've discussed tower standbys. Welders also have a helper, or a standby, to keep an eye out that they don't catch anything on fire. If a welder is working at height, there will be a helper on level with them and a standby on the ground watching for falling sparks. One day, I noticed sparks hitting the ground and a fire extinguisher sitting right under the falling embers. The only thing missing was the standby. I finally spotted him about twenty feet away watching his welders intently. I verified his work permit and then pointed out that if a fire did occur from the falling sparks, that he wouldn't be able to access his fire extinguisher. His eyes lit up in understanding and he thanked me, assuring me he'd fix the problem. After making my rounds, I passed by the same standby and literally bent over double laughing. He and the fire extinguisher were still in the very same places, twenty feet apart. Only now he had one end of a rope tied to the extinguisher and held the other end of the rope dutifully in his hand, fully prepared in case of fire. As much as I'd wanted to leave him like that for others to see, I had to tell him that it would be much safer if he would just move the extinguisher to sit beside him, away from the falling sparks. At least he tried.

Eventually, the work was completed, and we were ready to start the unit back up. Startups were extremely stressful. Had we forgotten to remove a blind? Had we missed any damaged gaskets that could cause a leak? If a blind remained in a line, it could be very difficult to figure out unless you actually spotted the thin metal handle of the blind poking out of the flange. I don't remember who first started it, but on every turnaround or shutdown I worked, Curt would tell me that there was one blind left in the unit, and I needed to find it. I would go out and climb every damn tower, every drum, check every pipe rack where work had occurred. I would search each flange on every pump, furnace, and exchanger all the time looking for that stinking blind handle. I was lucky enough that I never missed one. There were several ideas put into place in later years to keep track of blinds or at least make them easier to spot. Kind of like surgeons having to account for each piece of gauze. One tiny little thing can cause the biggest mayhem if overlooked.

After all the worklists had been checked off, we would start steam to the unit with the low point bleeders and drains opened. As steam enters the cold metal vessels, it will condense. The open bleeders allowed the steam condensate to drain out of the equipment until we'd get a good hot blow of steam at all the various locations. Once that occurred, we would start blocking in bleeders and drains and let the steam build pressure in the system. As the pressure built, we'd look for leaks, open valves, missing gaskets, loose heads, etc. Once we passed the pressure test, the steam would be shut off and we'd back gas into the unit. This enabled us to remove any oxygen from the system along with the steam condensation.

Next step was to start hydrocarbon feed to the unit and establish circulation. Some equipment might be charged with a lighter material to get a good flush before adding the heavier material that requires much higher temperatures. Heat would be slowly increased and as levels and pressures started to build instruments would be checked. Still more feed was brought in and as product began to fill the system, we'd line it up to slop to be rerun later (at this point the products are generally not yet on specification). The startup process is a delicate balancing act of temperatures, pressures and flows. Then the time finally comes to pour the coals to her. Feed in and product out. We'd catch a lot of samples and as quickly as possible, get all the streams lined up to normal operations.

Suddenly, we were done. I'd just spent an enormous amount of my life (albeit one measly month) living through a physically and mentally challenging period and now it seemed really strange to go back to normal. I guess I just felt lost. I had been a critical part of the rebuild. My gas testing kept people safe. I had found myself interacting more and more with all the workers during the rebuild. I was very comfortable in my work role. Hell, I actually enjoyed it. Then it was all gone, and I felt alone and invisible again. I was just an operator doing normal, everyday duties. Little did I realize this was the tiniest tastes of what it would be like later when I retired, the overwhelming sense of loss.

Before I go on, I need to tell another story of the dangers of steam condensation. It was normal in the old days to steam out equipment in preparation for putting it back into service. On this day, Curt was working with a well-seasoned lead operator, Benny, to put a temporary gasoline treating drum in service. They hooked up a couple of steam hoses to the large, horizontal drum (approximately twelve-foot diameter by forty-foot long) and opened the steam valves wide open. As the steam and heat built in the drum, Curt went on top to check for leaks while Benny watched from below. The drum was warming to the touch but hadn't built up much pressure. As they waited, it started to rain. Curt yelled down to Benny and told him the drum had begun to suck air through the vent. Benny screamed at Curt to come down off the drum, "NOW." Curt scurried down, and they both headed into a nearby electrical building to get out of the weather. They had barely gotten inside when they heard a horrendous booming sound like thunder combined with the deafening screech of metal. Both men ran outside to see the drum sucked in and crumpled like an aluminum can, a twelve-foot by forty-foot aluminum can. Engineers later calculated that they couldn't have attached enough steam hoses to build pressure fast enough to counter the effects of the cold rain. The steam had condensed and pulled a vacuum on the drum. It's a good thing that day that Benny was smart enough to get Curt to come in out of the rain.

CHAPTER 17
MY BAD ATTITUDE AND PEOPLE'S PERCEPTIONS

This chapter covers a lengthy period as I, and anyone around me, struggled with my attitude. Although the timing was sporadic over many years, I decided to lump the highlights together to give you a good sense of what I suffered through during many personality clashes...or maybe I should say, crashes.

I continued in operations, but I never really figured out how to fit in. On the one hand, I never wanted my peers or supervisors to see me as "the female operator." In one sense, I wanted to be one of the guys, to be treated just the same, to be appreciated for my work. As I look back, I wonder if that was a mistake. I should have been proud of being a female and doing the work that I did. Back then, it could be volatile with men and women working together. The way I was treated was so drastically different from one guy to the next. My coworkers either respected me, ignored me, flirted with me, treated me like trash, or raged against me for "taking a man's job who had a family to feed." I had to figure out how to gauge and handle each situation, each person differently. I still loved being an operator, I loved my job, but it was actually getting more difficult to fit in, to get along. Part of this was because I refused to play the weaker female that needed help. Well, that and my propensity to tell people to fuck off.

One tool the company began using should have been useful, should have helped, but it twisted a knife into me for years. At first, I raged about it, then I tried to understand it, and then I raged again. It was a wonderful little tool called 360-degree feedback. It is an exercise where you get feedback to/from your peers, supervisors, managers, etc., on what they think of you, and you of them. I will admit that it can be beneficial to see how others perceive you. For instance, if everyone perceives you as not being a team player, maybe you can offer to help others more often. If you want to be a good team player, you let others help you occasionally—gasp, choke, cough (obviously not one of my strengths). If everyone perceives you as being a control freak, you can learn to step back and instruct and encourage others rather than just shouldering them aside and doing it yourself because it is so much easier and sure as hell will get done right the first time… but I digress. That I could understand. That I could handle. Then some rat bastard says something so utterly stupid, so fucking incomprehensible, so totally "what the fuck does this have to do with my job?" that you just can't believe it and can't do anything but rage. The limp dick, son of a bitch coworker says, "She needs to smile more."

FUCK YOU…… FUCK YOU…… FUCK…YOU.

All I could see in that one comment was that I had to be more presentable to the men. I needed to be friendlier and more feminine. I needed to be more compliant. I needed to smile prettily and maybe flutter my eyelashes. I needed to be weaker. I needed to be the waitress the men thought they had a right to fondle. I needed to drop to my knees and suck dick as ordered. Who the hell did this guy think he was? What the fuck did this have to do with me performing my duties as an operator? Would smiling get my work done faster? Fuck no. Would smiling get me promoted? Fuck no. Would smiling get me appreciated for all my hard work? Fuck no.

I struggled with this for a long time. It is true that I wasn't friendly to everyone, especially assholes like that guy. I was, however, friendly to most people. I even liked to make people laugh. Not everyone saw that part of me. Instead, they developed a perception of me, a perception built on impressions or worse yet, gossip, without knowing me. In my reality, I truly liked to make people laugh. I loved to tell stories. I loved to talk, chat, and laugh. If I didn't like someone, I would be respectful but not friendly. I never saw it as part of my job to make others comfortable to be around me. My physical face is my mother's face (aka resting bitch face). It has conformed over the years to a constant frown. I suppose those are the muscles I exercised the most. I look pissed even when I'm smiling. Sad, but true. I don't consider myself ugly, but it does take some effort for me to appear less ugly, less intimidating maybe. I never worried about improving other people's perception of me. Back then, intimidation was something I had spent years cultivating. My, "don't fuck with me" attitude.

(2022) I just had a conversation with my son, Jake, and his husband, John. I went to visit for my birthday weekend and did the usual touristy selfie pics. Jake laughed at my facial expressions (I was trying to smile). He told me I looked a whole lot like my mother. Humph. After a few more pics I decided it is probably best if I don't try to show my teeth when I smile but instead, just do my normal smirk. Smirking seems to fit my face.

I continued to analyze this on occasion over the years. At one time I wanted to believe that what the "smile more" meant was maybe just being happier, not being depressed and pissed off all the time. I know that when you're in a group, family, team, that just one member can bring the whole group's attitude or behavior down. A strong, upbeat personality can inspire the group and make the work so much easier. I know this. I admit this. I wish I hadn't wasted so much of my life being depressed, being angry, being hurt. I wish I hadn't allowed things to happen. I wish I had made better choices. I wish I had been stronger. I even, I will admit, wish I had smiled more, been happier. I wish I had simply kicked that asshole in the balls. Okay, that's where I might have slipped back on the attitude thing, but that guy deserved it, he started it.

This type of attitude can be extremely detrimental to your career. When I finally started caring that people had this perception, I found it nearly impossible to fix. I had a supervisor tell me that the production supts didn't like me and that prevented me from getting certain jobs or promotions. I asked what I had done wrong. What could I do to correct the perception? Here's the big problem. Time and time again, I had supervisors that failed to give me proper feedback. It's actually helpful to know there is a problem, but you have to know what the problem is beyond someone just pointing a finger and saying, "You." A good leader would never say, "Well, they don't like you." "You're a square peg." "Make lemonade." A good leader would say, "People don't like being told to fuck off." "People feel shaded when you refuse to join in." "Some production supts don't like it when the new girl tells them there are better ways to do their job." Then, a good leader would find ways to help. Maybe suggest a training course in, "Difficult Conversations." By the way, I voluntarily attended that course.

I still believe in the flip side of the coin. A leader could tell you that, "People are intimidated because you ride a Harley and wear leather." That is not a "me" problem. That is a "them" problem. Nobody should have to dress or look a specific way to please others. A good leader would instead ask the dudes why they are intimidated. Are they afraid I'm gonna kick their ass? Are they jealous because their wife won't let them own a Harley? A balance can be found. Communication is the key.

This "soft stuff" really is the hard stuff. Leaders need to be able to have respectful, difficult, honest conversations with their underlings. I cannot say this enough. Moreover, if I cry during the conversation—ignore it! I cry because I'm passionate. I cry because I care. I cry because it's just who I am and how I'm made. It is not a sign of weakness. It's not contagious. See the passion.

Feel the passion. Recognize the passion. Then, a good leader would figure out how to harness the passion.

The most difficult thing in all of this attitude platitude bullshit is when we realize that it is nobody's fault but our own. Huh, you say? We choose our attitude. We choose how we respond to all the shit that is thrown at us. We stress ourselves out. We build walls around ourselves. We begin to seethe and hate and retaliate. We begin to blame—them.

"I wouldn't be so upset if they would just…"

"I could be happy if they would…"

"If they didn't treat me so bad…"

"If life was fucking FAIR..."

You choose. You respond. You define yourself and your path.

I have found myself drowning in all these emotions, all these evils that others were inflicting on me. I railed against these unfair treatments. I began to search for the key to happiness. How did other people do it? I remember getting so pissed off when I read that it is all up to me to choose my attitude. My first response? Fuck that! I didn't do this. This happened TO me. One day, I looked around, and nobody was there but me. Nobody was forcing me to be depressed. Nobody was forcing me to be angry, or hurt, or forlorn. Just me. For some stupid reason, I had chosen to punish myself with all those negative emotions. I finally accepted that my attitude was all on me.

Now, I needed someone to tell me how to fix it. Yes, I wanted to slap the bitch that sang, "Let it go, let it go, let it go, let it go...." I wanted to know HOW to "let it go." Teach me! Ain't gonna happen, baby. This is something you have to experience for yourself to be able to recognize and repeat it. For you it could be meditation, yoga, religion, counseling or just believing in yourself. If just once, you can banish a bad feeling, a bad attitude, let it slide off your shoulders with a simple sigh of relief. If you ever feel that, the weight lifted from you, you'll instantly

195

recognize it. Then teach yourself to repeat it. If you've ever forgiven someone—truly forgiven them—you've felt it. Maybe that is why so many powerful people say that forgiving others is the road to healing. HEALING. Think about it.

My brother Steve saw me on the verge of an anxiety attack one day. He shook his head and said, "Just let it go." Somehow, I did. I felt it. I felt the tension release. I felt the weight come off. I felt my gut unclench. I felt my heartbeat slow. It works. I did it and you can too, but it takes practice.

Major note here. I believe that letting go is the second step. The first step is to acknowledge your emotion and do whatever you need to do (as long as you do not harm yourself or others)—scream, cry, roll on the ground in agony, hide in the dark with your favorite stuffed animal, hug your dog, your friend, your lover. Feel the emotion; acknowledge it, then, when you can breathe again, just let it go.

CHAPTER 18
CREATIVITY AND THE PAIN OF
CONSTRUCTIVE CRITICISM

Not long after I married Curt, we went on a weekend trip to Branson, Missouri, a favorite vacation spot of mine. I love the arts and craft stuff. One little store had a wall covered with the coolest wooden Intarsia projects.

Intarsia is a method of creating a three-dimensional picture with different types of wood using the natural wood color and grain to enhance the picture. Each piece is cut out individually, shaped, sanded and a natural finish applied (generally three coats on each individual piece), then glued to a backboard to complete the final picture. A medium sized project can have around seventy to eighty individual pieces. My biggest project had over 300 pieces.

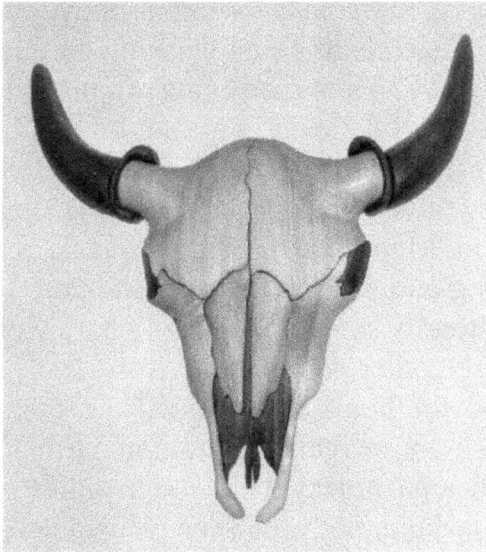

Figure 47 Intarsia skull, poplar, walnut & oak.

The finished artwork the store had on display was beautiful, but they also sold patterns and instructional books. The books and patterns I like the most were designs by Judy Gale Roberts. Her work is amazing. Humph, I can do that I thought. I went home with a bunch of patterns, borrowed Curt's old scroll saw, and got to work.

I knocked out a bunch of smaller projects, maybe twenty to thirty pieces each and then did my first big project, a pheasant. Each feather of the wings and tail was cut out individually with special attention to the grain to make it appear feather-like. I spent hours shaping and sanding, carefully rounding over the edge of each piece, then making sure they all fit together snuggly in preparation for the final gluing. I was happy with my efforts and couldn't wait to show Curt. He looked at my work and admitted it was good...but...it could be better. He suggested that instead of just rounding the edges of each piece, I should shape them further to be more realistic and lifelike. For instance, taper the feathers down as they came out from the wing or body.

I was pissed. I had spent hours working on this. What the hell did he know anyway? How many Intarsia projects had he done? How many hours had he spent working on this? He sure as hell couldn't do anything like this. In a fit of anger, I picked up a wing feather and began sanding it aggressively, taking off large amounts of wood. I tapered it so that it was thick on the end that tied into the wing and thin on the opposite end. I almost cried. I thought I'd just totally screwed up all my hard work. Nothing left to do but make the other pieces match.

Sawdust flew for hours as I sanded the once blocky figure down to a much more realistic looking bird. Once finished I stepped back in amazement. Curt, who didn't have an artistic bone in his whole damn body, had seen what I had not. Had I been an even bigger dumbass, I would have thrown his suggestion out the window and done adequate work, but nothing special. Nothing you'd really want hanging on your wall. Instead, I'd followed his suggestion, albeit in a fit of anger, and taken my artwork from nice, to beautiful.

Figure 48 Intarsia pheasant made from oak, walnut, and poplar.

That's the day I really, truly learned how valuable it is to tuck your pride away and be open to possibilities. Major Life Improvement Alert: Creative criticism is a good thing. Seek it out. Be open to it. If you're able to do that the opportunities are endless. That's also the day Curt bought me a nice scroll saw, drum sander, belt sander, and vacuum system. I couldn't wait to do more work.

Figure 49 *Example of how using different types of wood changes the finished Intarsia.*

Figure 50 *Intarsia clown, walnut, cedar, red oak, white oak, & poplar.*

As my expertise grew, thanks to being open to constructive criticism, my work was becoming more and more popular. Eventually, the company listed me (Dragon Art) as a vendor in the Female Owned Small Business category. When high-level managers left the refinery, the company commissioned me to produce Intarsia works of art for them. I realized that at one time, my artwork had been hanging in the US, UK, Germany, and Malaysia. There was only one time I was asked to create a project and refused; that was for Lance, a manager I will talk about in Chapter Twenty.

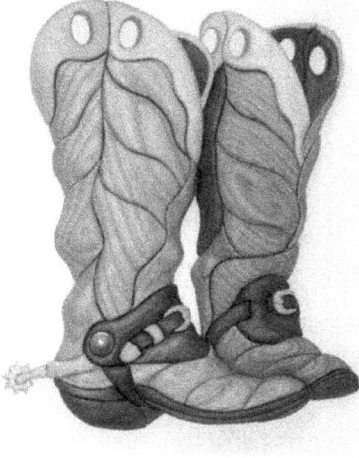

Debbie,

I want to thank you again for the great "Boots" and the very kind email. I really appreciate the feedback. I have very much enjoyed working with you. I really like your fresh and innovative approach to problems. Please take care and best wishes

Tom

Figure 51 Intarsia cowboy boots, made from oak, walnut & poplar.

Figure 52 *Intarsia, corvette for Nick Spenser, made from cherry, poplar, & walnut. Indian Chief head for Mike Fretwell, made from cherry, poplar, oak, walnut, & heartwood.*

Figure 53 *Intarsia motorcycle made for George Paczkowski.*
Yep, this was the 300+ piece project.

Debbie,

Thank you so much for the "Harley" art! It is truly awesome and I'll treasure it forever. Best wishes in your career and in your life! You're terrific

George

My very favorite work, however, still hangs above my fireplace.

Figure 54 *Intarsia, Indian and horse, made from cherry, walnut, poplar, oak, and ebony.*

Figure 55 *Indian close-up to show shaping detail.*

CHAPTER 19
(1998) WHEN PASSION DROWNS PERCEPTIONS

The perfect job, Operator Excellence Resource, opened up at the refinery. I interviewed for the position, and I think I did well. By then I'd had a lot of practice with interviewing. There was one strange thing that happened. Kay interviewed me again, and she made a comment about, "I owe you a job." Humph. Now, what do you suppose she meant by that? One might suppose she had given the previous safety job to the inexperienced but educated college kid, Jarod, because he was married to another management person. Seriously, it didn't matter to me. By now I knew a little of Jarod, of his work ethic and knowledge, and I liked him. I believed he was great in the safety job. As luck would have it, I'd just landed a job that was great for me. Strange how things work out.

I was thrilled with the new job. First, it was daylights with weekends and holidays off, which did not suck. It was also a job where I was free to think outside the box. I was no longer in a union represented job but a salaried position. One of the biggest things that really impressed me was how not one salaried person said, "It's not my job." Salaried was a completely different world. I thought I had freedom being an operator, but this side of the world was crazy. I couldn't wrap my head around the idea of leniency in so many things. Come in five minutes late, no problem, work five minutes late. There were definite boundaries I had to operate within but there was so much room to maneuver within those set boundaries. Oh, and I had an office. I was so out of my element I really had no idea what to put in my office. I was thrilled that I had a window that looked out onto a very small interior courtyard. The narrow courtyard had grass and a couple of small decorative trees. It didn't matter to me that the tiny space was surrounded by brick walls. I could look out my window and get a glimpse of the sunlight, rain, or whatever weather Oklahoma brought us. My very first office. I loved it.

The first snag I immediately ran into was setting goals. Um, what? Okay, now I understand goals but back then, I knew nothing…and not just any goals…goals following the company format. Holy crap. It was an extremely structured process. Management has certain goals; your goals are to support those goals. Then you pick some personal goals. Then you put it all in the specified program using proper format, font and… ugh, there were so many crazy rules about goals and goal's structure. Then you realize that your pay raise next year could depend on whether you reach all those goals. As the years went on, it seemed like the company adopted more and more difficult programs just to enter goals.

I caught an enormous break when my new counterpart, Darren, said not to sweat the goals. He handed me his goals for the year, told me to put the same thing down since we had the same job and turn it in, no big deal. I did as Darren suggested and came up with my very first, very official-looking company document. I was so proud.

The next step was to discuss the goals with my new boss, Rolfe. He wasn't just new to me; he was new to the refinery. I don't know if this was a boon for me, if he knew nothing about me, or, if he was told anything about me and my dour past. Maybe, he was just the kind of leader that didn't put weight in hearsay but decided to let my work speak for me. I didn't know anything except that I was terrified. I also didn't know at the time that this was the man who would give me one of my greatest rewards and one of my greatest betrayals in the days ahead.

Rolfe came to my sparsely furnished office. I sat nervously at my desk while Rolfe sat back in a chair across from me as if for a

208

casual conversation. Not what I expected. I know now that this is a practice common with good leaders. He made me more comfortable, more relaxed by coming onto my turf. He took my goals, my carefully worded, properly formatted goals, scanned them ever so briefly and then literally tossed them aside. He looked me in the eye and said, "Fine, but what do you really want to do?"

I just stared mutely, one traitorous eyebrow cocked.

Rolfe gently prompted me, "What are you passionate about?"

"Um, what?" I was so confused. I know it had to show on my face. I was dumbfounded. "Um, what?"

Rolfe repeated himself, "What are you passionate about?"

I tried to remember one single thing I had written down on that stupid goal sheet and nothing came to mind. My head was one big, buzzing empty shell. I was not going to embarrass myself further by asking what the hell he meant, so I just tumbled that thought around in my empty skull. What was I passionate about?

"Helping people." I finally squeaked. "I want to help people, to make things easier and better for them." Mind you, this had absolutely nothing to do with my current job, but it was from the heart. Rolfe nodded his head and told me he would open doors for me, remove barriers for me to enable me to do those things. That my dear friends, is what leaders do.

I think it's fair to say that I had a major attitude shift after getting this job, after getting this boss. I had developed a bad attitude over the years. Suddenly, like overnight suddenly, I had a good attitude. Seriously, just that fast. The whole culture was so different from what I had been exposed to thus far in my career. I loved the outdoors and the work itself in my old job. I struggled a little moving to an indoor, desk position, but still, I reveled in my new job. I actually started smiling. Me, smiling. I know what you're thinking but I still say, "Fuck that guy."

I would walk down the hallway making eye contact with every person I passed, and I didn't fail to say good morning. If someone asked me how I was doing, a question nobody really wants an answer too, I would smile and say, "Marvelous!" I would put money on the fact that people thought I had been abducted by aliens and replaced with a pod person. I was happy; how weird. I didn't realize it at the time, but my change in attitude was entirely due to feeling appreciated, believed in, rewarded, and valued.

The new job included mundane regulatory procedure validation and review. I also researched new ideas for training and set up the first pilot using hand-held devices to enter/share maintenance data in the refinery. Eventually the hand-held devices were put into extensive use. The first pilot run, however, had mixed reviews for various reasons. First, I had just left a union represented job and was now on the company side. Some of the union folks believed it was their duty to give me shit about being a traitor but not all of them did it to my face. Second, change is often difficult. It wasn't like our mechanical folks didn't have enough work to do and now I was adding a technical aspect to their job that some weren't exactly thrilled with. The craftsmen were highly technical folks, and some did appreciate it. Keep in mind, this was back before there was widespread computer use by frontline refinery workers. It was a big shift for many of them. Fortunately, there were those techy folks that appreciated the advantage of having data easily stored/retrieved from a central database To improve maintenance. The idea, while not popular at the time, was revisited later with different people involved and had better success.

A huge project I participated in was moving operators to a centralized control room, or CCR. Although some of our sister refineries had already made this move, it was new and very controversial for us. Since our combined refinery spanned a very large acreage, there was a lot of traveling involved just to get folks together for daily meetings. Two groups had to cross the train tracks to get to meetings so that could cause a delay. There was also a cultural issue as the different areas were very possessive about their operating and management styles. This is why the areas were often referred to as "little kingdoms".

The premise of the CCR is that it would improve communication between the areas. For instance, when I was an operator, we didn't always fully know or appreciate how making moves on our unit affected the upstream/downstream units. If we had a problem in our area and had to shut off feed to protect ourselves, we didn't always think to let the other areas know immediately, let alone before making the move. We would make changes beneficial to us that could possibly upset another area if they weren't made aware so they could make their own lineup changes. I don't believe anyone ever intentionally delayed these type of emergency communications but sometimes when things got to rocking and rolling you acted on instinct and that instinct was usually self-preservation. On the other hand, if the other areas were made aware of upcoming changes they could plan and react, and it would be a non-event. To enable this enhanced communication, the plan was to take one or two operators from each area (per shift) and move them to the CCR. Their job would be to monitor and handle all the operational changes that were made using the computer system and if they needed to communicate to the other areas all they had to do was walk (or yell) across the room. The operators left in the areas would then handle all the hands-on work.

Some operators liked the idea that they would no longer have to do the technical part of operating on the computer systems. Now, they could take care of their equipment, catch samples, monitor the area, and it did reduce stress for them. The operators in the CCR however, were now going to move from taking care of one unit to being responsible for multiple units. It was a lot to take on. Not only was there the added stress of multiple units but now they would be confined to a windowless, blast proof room and no longer have the comradery of their fellow operators. Many of these folks had worked together for years and even enjoyed their time off together, hunting, fishing, eating, and of course partying. Now they were going to be separated from friends and isolated with folks they generally had never worked with before. One upside, however, was the controlled temperature indoors. Weather can really suck in Oklahoma. Another boon was being safely away from the physical hazards of the refinery jobs.

There were many thoughts on how to staff the CCR. One idea was to put the lead operator in the CCR as they were used to monitoring all the units in their areas. They were also used to being in charge and telling people what to do. However, it would cause a problem when the lead operators attended multiple meetings, as the CCR must be manned at all times. Therefore, it was decided that the operators would be tested to see who would be best suited to the dramatic change in their job.

I won't go into details here. I just want to say that this testing was not appreciated by many operators. I remember grading one guy's test and soon realized that he missed every single question. I also realized he missed every question by one. If A was the correct answer, he marked B. I loved that he let us know he actually knew every correct answer, that he had intentionally marked them wrong. The dude was brilliant.

I had actually started taking this testing myself, just before I got my job as Operator Excellence Resource. One test was the "Career Assessment Inventory Profile." I ranked high in these career choices: firefighter, Navy enlisted, police officer, veterinary technician, chiropractor, respiratory therapist, counselor for chemical dependency, athletic trainer, park ranger, carpenter, painter, pipefitter/plumber, teacher, data entry operator.

I scored very low on: cosmetologist, barber/hairstylist, card/gift shop manager and real estate agent. Oddly enough, I scored "dissimilar" on author/writer. But then the testing was several years before I would write my first book, *Meesha Guardian of Grand Mountain*.

CHAPTER 20
(1999) THE WORLD OPENS UP TO ME

As the CCR project was unfolding, I started one of the most important projects of my life. It was important to me because of what I learned through the process, about life, leadership and people. I was asked to join a team being formed to benchmark operating practices. Benchmarking is comparing how we do our business at the refinery, in comparison to similar businesses. This included everything from how the business was run: management styles and processes/procedures, to employee satisfaction. We benchmarked to try to establish what could be considered "best practices."

An engineer, Les, from a sister refinery put a diverse group together for this exercise. Les made a tremendous impact on my career. He exposed me to material, people, and situations where I learned so much about what leadership is and what it is not. He was responsible for expanding my vision beyond what I could have imagined.

I was the only peon on the benchmarking team and essentially represented the hourly operators. We also had a tech guy, Mike, an HR guy, Bob, and supervisors and managers at different levels of the organization. Seriously, I was way, way below these guys in everything. Everything except frontline, union represented experience. Before we began interviewing others, we spent some time covering material of reported best practices. Les talked about teams and teamwork, and I have to confess, I was stumped at first as I looked at our group. This was my first exposure to diversity. I'll expand on that to say, diversity of thought, knowledge, experiences, attitudes, and backgrounds. I believe it took a lot of courage back then to put this kind of team together instead of just a herd of managers or a gaggle of engineers. In the beginning, I couldn't see this. I saw Mike, who was allergic to everything and probably the only one who suffered physically during all the travel as much as I did. He was the stereotypical nerd. He was also a kind, genuine, caring individual whom I was proud to work with. One manager, Paul, was a salt of the earth kind of guy. We had more than one of those guys, actually. Then there was this one management dude, Alec. He didn't really participate in a lot of our meetings. He came off as arrogant and holier than thou, and at one point, just sat in the corner and picked his nose. I don't know how many times I asked myself what the hell Alec was doing on our team. What the hell could he offer? Was he even paying attention? It seemed like we were working our butts off, and he really didn't give a shit. Until the day he did. Alec stood face-to-face with high-ranking managers and shocked the hell out of me by giving a professional, detailed presentation of all our months of work using all the fancy words that managers at that level seem to like. Never broke a sweat. The guy was brilliant.

You might wonder what I contributed. The guys on our team really did intimidate me but I also had my own super power. We sat down and met with many frontline workers. Not just refinery operators but frontline production workers at an automobile manufacturing plant and even a badass Harley-Davidson assembly plant. No matter what, I was able to connect with them. I understood their daily work issues. I had a lot of shift work hours behind me. I had been on strike. Even the angry union president at one refinery tried to give us the cold shoulder and trip us up but I got him to talking. And yes, I owned and rode a Harley-Davidson Fat Boy. In case you were wondering, Fat Boy is an actual Harley model. My husband, Curt, was a fairly big guy and I think he liked to hear me tell people I rode a Fat Boy. My favorite Harley, however, was the Springer Classic. I loved riding that bike. There was just something different in the feel of the springs in the front fork that somehow made me feel like I was riding a horse at the same time. I loved the rumble of the dual pipes. It just has to sound like a Harley, "loud and proud." Another safety factor —"loud pipes save lives." So many people don't see a motorcycle, but it's hard not to hear a Harley. Sweet memories, but back to business.

We went to each of our Conoco sister refineries in the states and then went to England. I had always known that my great grandfather, James Juckes, had come from England (born in Rowton, Shropshire). He worked on a sheep ranch until leaving the UK to come to America where he married my great grandmother. It was interesting to be in England, but I had no time to try to trace my roots; we had work to do.

We stayed at the Habrough Hotel, built in the 1600s by the Pelham Family, whose head was later given the title Earl of Yarborough. It was unlike anything I'd ever seen…especially the plumbing. I found out later that I was the only one of our group that had a room without a shower. I was also the only one in our group that had hair down to the middle of my thigh. I looked at the old tub and wondered how in the hell I was going to manage to wash my hair.

The hotel also had an internal kitchen, called "The Slut's Kitchen," although we usually dined outside on the patio.

The Slut's Kitchen!

The Habrough Hotel's World famous Slut's Kitchen, is unique to the area and has become something of a talking point.

The main feature of this 60 seater dining room is the large black-leaded grate used in the 1800's to provide meals for the guests of the local Gentry, and still used by the Hotel's Chef who cooks in full view of the diners.

On arrival at the Hotel, serving wenches will usher you into the comfortable bar of the Horse and Hounds pub where you can enjoy a fine range of traditional ales while awaiting your call to the Kitchen.

The pub is included in the British Good Beer Guide, reflecting the high standards to be found in all services supplied by the Habrough Hotel.

Once at your table, which is yours for the evening, the wenches will provide an abundance of superb food in a restaurant where the atmosphere is conducive to relaxation and enjoyment.

Figure 56 *Hotel we stayed at while visiting the Humber Refinery.*

I enjoyed watching television in the evenings while I was compiling my notes from the day's interviews. I especially enjoyed the commercials where they were recruiting women for law enforcement. They talked about the percentage of women already employed and I was impressed thinking that this would be a theme while in the UK. It was not.

Surprisingly, I hadn't run into any issues around what I perceived to be sex discrimination until we went to our own Conoco Humber Refinery in England.

We began our interviews at the UK refineries, and I was dismayed to find out how few women worked for Humber even though they were in good number at other plants we visited. I was shocked even further when the women in their starched uniform dresses brought in tea and biscuits for tea time. I didn't challenge any of this during the interviews as we had a pretty tight schedule, and I didn't want to rock the boat. I also understood that this was most likely a cultural issue and far be it for me to challenge a time-old tradition. But I sure didn't like it. These ladies were hired to wear a servant's attire and serve the managers/guests. And you know how I feel about having to serve the men. I did understand that was my hang up, and I had no idea how these women felt about it. I wish I had asked.

After passing the afternoon tea test, I was tested further that evening. Lance, a fellow American and upper-level manager at the Humber refinery, treated our team to dinner. We also had the added privilege of having my boss, Rolfe, present. As dinner progressed, I started asking questions about the lack of female employees. Lance's immediate response was, "Do you know how much it would cost me just to build bathrooms?" I was pissed. I flashed back to how many times I'd used men's restrooms in the refinery. I remembered how many times I had to leave the building and walk across the road in bad weather while I was pregnant just to use a women's restroom. I damn near choked on my food. I asked Lance how that could possibly even be a concern in the big picture and... I believe Rolfe knew I was fixing to explode. He subtly managed to get me to stand down and not cause a scene, something I'm sure would not be good for my career. Little did I know I'd already stuck my foot over one of those damned invisible lines you're not supposed to cross.

From England, we split into two groups, and I had the privilege of going to Ireland while the other group went to Germany. I'm sorry I missed Germany. I have more than a small amount of German ancestry also, but I absolutely fell in love with Ireland.

Ireland, what an absolutely beautiful place. How the hell did I ever get so lucky? We landed at the Belfast airport after being coached on what to expect and how to conduct ourselves. I was told it wasn't uncommon to see security with automatic weapons. There was actually a travel restriction at the time, but the company had cleared us for the benchmarking exercise. Because of the increased security, I did decide to make a change to one of my

220

personal habits and I am so glad I did. Um, fellas, if you don't like personal "girl" talk, turn away now.

One thing I don't think is discussed often in the refinery setting is feminine hygiene. Back in the day, there were quite a few guys that blamed every damn thing on menstrual cycles. I can't believe all the derogatory names and put downs they had for women in relation to their periods. One trip to the bathroom carrying a purse or bag and you had to listen to non-stop teasing from the guys about it. I remember a dude who used to ask me if I was on my period, and I adamantly informed him he would never know if I was or wasn't and to mind his own damn business. To that end, I reverted to a trick I used when riding horses on long trail rides and would carry tampons stuffed into my socks. I never had to worry about them falling out of my pockets, etc. Wearing my cowboy boots would doubly ensure that nobody would be able to see any bumps in my socks and wonder what "gross" female items I might be carting around.

So, there I was in the Belfast Airport and who do you suppose was pulled out of line for a pat down? Of course it was me. As the very nice security woman patted down my leg, I silently thanked myself for taking my tampons out of my sock and putting them in my purse…in a brown paper bag. Can you imagine what it could have been like if she had felt a pair of tubular objects hidden in my socks? As it turned out, the pat down was a non-issue, even for an introvert like me. It was professional, clinical, and non-intrusive. No big deal at all. Then the nice lady searched my purse. Thoroughly. There was a pause when she got to the brown paper bag. She had already removed all my other items from my purse and laid them out on the table. I was pretty sure the tampons would soon be out of their plain brown wrapper and sitting beside my other items. Fortunately, that did not happen. The nice, compassionate, worldly woman peeked inside the bag, moved the contents within the bag slightly to see everything, rolled it closed again and stuck it back in my purse. She had done her job expertly and thoroughly and allowed me to retain my dignity. What a wonderful woman. (It shocks me today, to read how embarrassed I was about this back then.)

Okay fellas, you can look again.

Our team split up into two groups as we took cabs from the airport to our next destination. The trip was long but not nearly long enough. I could have driven around the entire country and wanted more. Our cab driver was an extremely chatty fellow and regaled us with Ireland's history. I was sitting up front with him and the guys rode in the back, so I assumed that is why he asked me so many questions. He told us about the Protestant/Catholic issues in Ireland and how dangerous it could be for him to even talk about some things. It was all fascinating.

I couldn't get enough of the countryside, and I felt a connection to Ireland in some way that I just couldn't explain. Something in Ireland spoke to me, way down deep in my soul. It broke my heart when I had to leave. I had been amazed by what I saw of England but as much as I thought there should be a personal connection because of my ancestors, I only felt like a tourist. Ireland was different for me.

I personally attracted a lot of attention in Ireland. I stood out by being a female with really long hair at a time when most women were sporting the Princess Diana cuts. I was also tall for a female by Irish standards. I hadn't thought much about that until an operator was telling me that they had to make revisions to their unit because the tallest person in their operating crew was 5' 4". I was actually surprised by this because most of the management folks we'd spoken to were as tall or taller than me.

Once we left Ireland, we had the same two cab drivers, but we switched so the other half of our group could enjoy the monologue given by our original cab driver. That's when he told our guys that he had enjoyed asking me questions so he could listen to my accent. He said I sounded like Granny on Beverly Hillbillies. Egad. So even back when I was young, I wasn't an Ellie Mae, I was a Granny. Humph. That's a wee blow to the old ego.

I am still in awe of how much knowledge I gained through the benchmarking process. We learned what worked and why and even how long it worked or why it stopped working. It was amazing how much centered on the simple fact of how you treat people. That doesn't mean you have to be touchy-feely, heart-on-your-sleeve type of stuff. It is all about treating people fairly, consistently, and doing the right thing for the right reasons. People matter. People make all the difference, and it takes great leaders to see that and even greater ones to put their people first.

One plant we visited really resonated with me. I questioned the fact that their robots got regular time off for medical (mechanical) checkups, but their human employees did not. On the flip side, the humans did on-shift stretches/exercises before beginning each shift to make sure they were acclimated to the repetitive motions they would be performing. Kudos for that. The biggest thing for me, however, was that management rewarded employees for finding mistakes. Not only for finding them but also for shutting down work if needed to investigate or correct an issue. Mind blown.

As much as this experience changed my life, it was also extremely hard on me physically. I love traveling but I've always had stomach issues, and the stress of traveling made it worse. Most days I was struggling not to throw up, or worse. I had terrible bouts of diarrhea but wouldn't drink water to rehydrate. I was afraid I'd have to pee on the plane at a time it wasn't allowed. (I recently learned they were much stricter back then than they are today.) I remember running through the Denver airport to make a connection and thinking I'd never make it, that I might have to consider giving up this dream adventure and just go back home. I remember thinking that I couldn't do it anymore, that I had to quit.

But I just couldn't. I couldn't quit. I couldn't tell anyone how sick I was. That day nearly did me in.

As you've seen, I've been at this stage more than once in my life. I'm sure many of you have had that feeling…that, I just can't take anymore, feeling. But you can. Keep breathing. Keep putting one foot in front of the other. Keep showing up.

Although I wouldn't tell anyone about my medical issues, I was worried about something else and discussed it with Rolfe. I was considering getting a divorce from Curt, and I was afraid it would affect my chances of being allowed to continue getting assignments where I would be traveling with the guys. I was worried that management would frown on having a "single" woman going on out of town business trips. He did ask why I was asking him this and I explained my fears. He assured me that this shouldn't be a factor.

I discussed many things with Rolfe that I'd never discussed with anyone before. I felt I was able to do this because he had initiated such a relaxed relationship between us. It never once occurred to me at the time, but in later reflection of some of his responses, I wondered if he ever thought I was verbally flirting with him. As soon as the thought occurred to me, I wanted to disappear. I was mortified to think I might have come across this way. I don't even know how to flirt! Of course, without asking him, I'll never know what he thought. I can only hope he realized I never meant anything but the greatest, professional respect. Seriously, thinking about it makes me want to put a paper bag over my head. Rolfe was one person I would never want to think poorly of me. It did, however, make me cautious in verbal discussions with future supervisors or managers. I still spoke my mind, way too much probably, but I intentionally gave no reason for words or actions to be misinterpreted. It's possible some folks may have seen this as being unsociable. For me, however, it was a form of respect. I never wanted someone to think I didn't respect them first and foremost. Well, unless I didn't. But if that was the case, I simply did my best to ignore them, never spoke their name, and never looked directly at them.

CHAPTER 21
PASSIONATE WORK, VALUING ALL PEOPLE

Between all of our traveling, I was able to start my "passionate" work. Rolfe mentioned a project around diversity and Valuing All People, (VAP), that was being used at our sister plant, Lake Charles Refinery. He suggested I look into developing something similar for our refinery and to let him know whatever I wanted/needed. After giving me the information, he stepped aside and gave me free rein (understanding that I still had wide boundaries that I must operate/perform within). He was there if I needed advice or assistance but allowed me to proceed without hindrance. That is what leaders do.

NOTE: There are very few instances where we don't need set boundaries or limitations. Companies all have rules, regs, and standards they must follow. Having boundaries is a good thing. When you're a young person wanting to stretch your boundaries, you may chafe under the restrictions. When you're responsible for that young person, you are grateful for the restrictions that are put in place for their safety and wellbeing. The same goes for employee/employer. Boundaries can, however, be tested and challenged—carefully and respectfully.

I reviewed Lake Charles Refinery's VAP program and absolutely loved it. Soon after, we started a similar diversity program, Diversity University, at our Ponca City Refinery. The program rewarded individuals who spent time/effort learning about diversity. Employees received credits for a wide variety of things from reading books/watching movies (on their own time) or participating in diversity events. I built a library of diversity books, and my door was always open for people to walk in and borrow whatever they wanted.

We even awarded degrees, associate's, bachelor's, etc., based on the number of credits earned. The final degree of course, was a Doctorate in Diversity which employees earned by writing a thesis. These papers were often profound and heart wrenching as the individuals delved into their own diverse backgrounds.

We had numerous diversity presentations, and I even developed a PowerPoint slideshow based on the popular TV program, *Who Wants To Be A Millionaire*. We had a great MC for the event, a comical character fondly referred to by many as Carlos. Talk about brilliant, this guy had a great speaking voice, and comedic timing with a classic deadpan delivery. He was funny, articulate, and totally entertaining. He was also a wonderful artist and had rendered many sketches around safety.

Another program I came across, borrowed and adapted for our plant, was the Peer Pat on the Back. Simple enough basis—just say something nice about someone else. All participants had to do was name the person and tell what they had done to deserve a pat on the back. Employees sent their peer pats to me, and I published it in a monthly paper called *The Leading Edge*. We also gave small rewards to folks for sending in their Peer Pats. I did hear some negative grumbling that it was all nonsense, that people were just making stuff up so they could earn a pocketknife, or some other small prize. My thought was that it didn't matter to me if they were just wanting the reward because the damage, so to speak, was already done. They had said something good about someone else, how it had helped, and the words were published— no take backs. There were also many Peer Pats from supervisors and management. I personally believe those went a long way with frontline folks even if some of those hard asses would never admit it.

During my career, management was also great about sending out letters or cards of congratulations and thanks. What a small thing, but it gives a big return. I now have a display cabinet (my forty-year service anniversary award from the company) in my living room with my company mementoes in it. I don't have all my letters/cards in there, but I have several. I don't care that the CEO doesn't personally know me. I know the cards are rubber stamped "thank you" or "congratulations" with their automated signature. I care about the thought that went behind it. I care that it is there in black and white and maybe one day my children or grandchildren will look at them (and the dozens in my storage boxes), and say, "Wow, that's cool." I do, however, have extra appreciation for the notes that were written or even just signed by hand. Those are treasures to me.

Debbie   28 May 96

I would like to express my appreciation for your help during the #5HPr explosion and fire. Your assistance with Matt; the notification of his wife were very thoughtful. Taking notice that we were short H2S monitors and making arrangements for more as your own initiative - the fact the willingness on your part to come over and help on your own initiative to begin with really tells *a great deal about your character and the folks in the West Plant.*

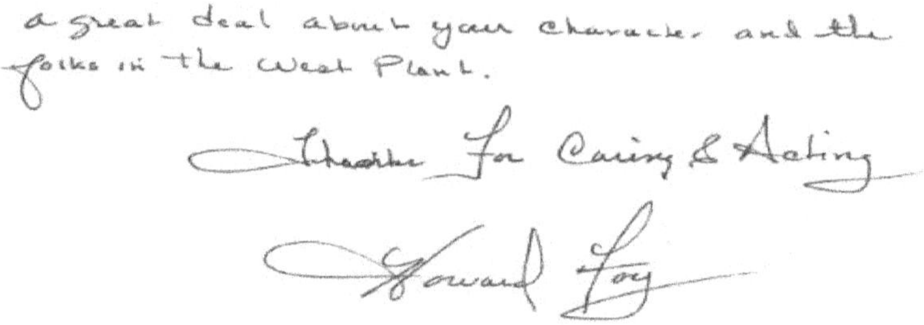

Thanks For Caring & Acting

Howard Foy

***Figure** 57 Thank you note from Howard Foy after I assisted another area during an emergency. It reads: 28 Mar 96 Debbie, I would like to express my appreciation for your help during the #5HDT explosion and fire. Your assistance with Matt; the notification of his wife were very thoughtful. Taking notice that we were short H2S monitors and making arrangements for more ... In fact the willingness on your part to come over and help on your own initiative to begin with really tells a great deal about your character and the folks in the West Plant.*

Signed, "Thanks for Caring & Acting Howard Foy"

CHAPTER 22
THE VALUE OF BEING VALUED

Part of my job involved interviewing new-hire candidates. I went through a training process that ensured we followed company standards. Multiple company people interviewed each new-hire candidate one-on-one. We asked specific questions laid out by our process and monitored by HR. At the end of the routine questions, HR allowed us to ask, "Is there anything else you'd like to tell me?" I have no idea why, but people would confess the craziest things to me. I would ask them questions about how they got along with female coworkers or supervisors. They would tell me something about how a supervisor helped them cover up their harassment of a female coworker. Did you really just tell me that? I would ask them about their work ethic, and they would tell me about how many times they fell asleep at work and how good they were at finding hiding places. You really don't want a job, do you? Why the hell would they tell me these things? Was it my "Granny-like" accent? I didn't even have gray hair…yet.

Three interviews really stood out. HR called me on a Saturday, which was not normal. They explained there was just something about the guy they couldn't put their finger on. Since I'd developed a reputation for uncovering issues, they asked if I would mind doing an interview. I was curious. I came in without any further information about the candidate. I met him in the conference room, introduced myself along with a firm handshake, then indicated we should take a seat. Normally, I would explain the process in an effort to make the candidate more comfortable. This tends to unwind a person that's all jacked up and prevents them from undermining themselves.

This guy, however, was already sending odd signals. I decided to let him. I began shuffling and rearranging my papers and didn't say a word. His agitation increased. After a moment, he pulled out his cigarettes and asked if I minded if he smoked. I explained that smoking was only allowed in designated areas outside of the building. I continued to silently read through my list of questions. He asked if he could go outside to smoke. I told him no; we were getting ready to begin. I have total compassion for the overwhelming desire for a smoke. I was up to about four packs a day when I quit cold turkey. I also knew the guy had just been out for a smoke minutes before I got there. I ran through my papers one more time, stacked them neatly, laid my pen down on top of them, looked the guy in the eye and... he bolted out of the room, never to be seen again. I wasn't totally surprised; I'd had that effect on men for years. This was, however, the first time it ever happened during a hiring interview.

The second wasn't an official Interview. I was asked to pick up an engineer candidate, take him to breakfast, tell him a little history, and generally just try to make him feel welcome and comfortable. This was something I'd never been asked to do before, and I was surprised. But, in everything that we do, there is a lesson if you look for it, and I jumped at the opportunity. The young man was an African-American, which shouldn't have mattered, but there was a lesson in it for me. We went to breakfast, and he asked about our town and the current population. Admittedly, I didn't know. "Bigger than the town I was born in," didn't seem like a good reply. He explained the things that would go into his consideration for taking a job and making a place his home. He said that he would like to meet a woman and marry someday soon and that the percentages of black, educated women in a town our size would be limited. I didn't know what to say. I did tell him that our company had attracted many highly educated young female engineers and that I hoped he would be happy here.

This young man's goals for his personal life were something I'd never thought about. How would I feel to be a minority somewhere looking for a similar person to share my life with? I had never mentally put myself in that position and I tried to feel what he must have been feeling. I don't believe he took the job.

The third interview came much later, but I wanted to document it here so that you can see a pattern to my perceived bad attitude development. It changed things for me, my life, my attitude, my career. After multiple company people interviewed the new hires, we would get together and rate them as a group. During our assessment, one of the company interviewers, Erick, made racist remarks about one applicant. He wondered why a black person wanted to know about different neighborhoods in Ponca when everyone knew that the black people all lived in "Dixie." Dixie referred to a lower income area on the south end of our town. I immediately stopped the process and pointed out the inappropriate discussion. I also asked him what he supposed one of our top managers, Nathan, would think of this discussion given that Nathan was a person of color and undoubtedly made more money and lived in a nicer place than Erick and I combined. When the applicant didn't get the job, I wondered how much racism played a part in the decision. I took my concerns to HR and was told that the racist behavior was overlooked because Erick was from a nearby small town. I don't know if that meant he supposedly didn't know better or because it was common behavior in that town or just what the hell it meant. The guy in HR even admitted this was not the first complaint of this nature he'd had on Erick.

After my complaint to HR about Erick's inappropriate behavior, I was no longer invited to participate in the new-hire interviews. Erick, however, did continue to interview and later received a job that directly influenced hiring. I personally felt this was a major failing in HR practices and became more than a little disenchanted with the company.

I did continue with my "passionate" work and was nominated for the company's "President's Award for Valuing All People." It was indeed an honor to be nominated. Even here, things did get a little hinky though. A supervisor told me that they had a friend that was on the selection committee. You know those times in your life when you wish you'd never heard something but there's just no way you can un-hear it? The insider claimed that I was the most popular choice to win the award but that an upper-level manager needed this honor on his resume. I suppose I can understand how this would benefit a manager going on to bigger and better positions. I did wonder if his VAP values would trickle down to the frontline workers where I felt the need was the greatest. Selfishly, however, I was disappointed to have not won the award. I believed that the winner would have an opportunity to speak to and possibly influence the company on diversity and inclusion principles, of basically, you know—valuing people. I can talk all day about this stuff, but people look at me like, "Okay, but who the hell are you?" We had a previous winner come to our plant, and I watched as others listened intently and asked multiple questions. The thing is, it was essentially the same things we had already been trying to teach. Not that we can't always learn something new and find new avenues to engage people and get our message across. It's just odd to me how it takes a title or award associated with one's name to garner enough attention for some folks to even care about the message. That had been my hope, that the award would help me get people to listen just a little bit harder. It didn't stop me from constantly promoting VAP to my smaller audience. What I really desired was to be an intermediary between frontline workers and management. I wanted to take workers needs and desires and get management to appreciate and help them. At the same time, I could try to help frontline workers understand the essential boundaries the company had in place for safe, effective, and profitable operation. As much as I tried not to let it happen, my disenchantment increased.

I continued in my job, doing both the required work, which I enjoyed, and my passionate work around VAP. I was eager to get to work each and every day. I still answered the ritual, "How are you," with totally out of character remarks of, "magnificent," "fantastic," and other exaggerated expressions because that is how I truly felt. I was still a bit intimidated and getting used to being around management, but I enjoyed the challenge. I loved my job.

Another thing very different in salaried versus union positions was the pay structure. Union wages are set in negotiations. Salaried pay is, in my opinion, a total crapshoot. So many things were calculated into what ranking you received for next year's wages. I'll expand more on that later.

The first year in my salaried position, with my—unnatural for me, upbeat attitude, I received an extremely high rating, which was then used to determine my salary for the next year. My boss, Rolfe, explained that normally, this never happened for a person their first year, but it was my hard work and outstanding attitude that convinced him to push for me receiving such a high grade. I was beyond shocked. I felt like the most valued employee ever in the history of our company. To say I felt appreciative was an understatement. It wasn't about the money. It was about being VALUED.

CHAPTER 23
CATTLE, A WICKED VAGINA, AND BETRAYAL

Since life at work had become so fulfilling, my husband, Curt, decided to muck things up. He was born and raised on a farm in Kansas and grew up working cattle with his father. Unfortunately, his father died too young from health complications, some of which may have been brought on after being a POW during WWII. Curt was devastated and left the farm, which is how he eventually ended up at the refinery.

We had a little patch of land just outside of town and he decided we should raise cattle in our spare time. I didn't know we had spare time. Our yard alone was five acres and at the time, we were mowing with push mowers. His solution was to add some cows.

Figure 58 Turned the cows out to help mow the lawn around the house. Curious little ladies.

Figure 59 *Life at the old place.*

I didn't know anything about cattle and how to take care of them. Curt was working out of town more and more often and I found myself doing things I never imagined I would have to do in his absence.

On one rare occasion, Curt was home at feeding time. He chastised me after I explained to him that I whistle to call the cattle in for feeding. He insisted you don't whistle at cows; you have to call them. He let out some weird, cow-calling holler. We waited but nothing happened. I asked if I should go ahead and whistle but he still insisted cows won't come to a whistle. Oh, yeah? Watch this. I whistled and in just a few seconds, we heard the thundering of hooves. Our little herd came charging over the hill and into the pens. Curt never learned how to whistle, but the cows always came when they heard me.

It seemed like Curt was always out of town when the big events happened, like the pond freezing over or calves being born. We did have a heated water tank, but the cows would naturally go to the pond. If it was lightly frozen, they would easily break through the ice. Sometimes when the ice was thick in the shallow water, they would wander further out until reaching a place where the ice would be thin enough to break. I was always afraid we would lose a cow or calf to drowning that way. Each winter I would take my ax and bust ice to prevent losing any of my babies. Yes, I had gotten attached, way too attached. I even made the mistake of naming all the cows and calves after family members.

Figure 60 *Feeding time. Rain, sleet or snow, cows gotta eat.*

It really isn't a good idea to name your cows after loved ones. We had one cow, Carol, who injured her leg. The vet said it would be best to put her down, as her leg would never heal properly.

That was my first and only experience with taking a cow to the butcher. I cried as we loaded her up and took her to the meat market. We went inside and I did my best to hide my tears. The butcher asked Curt how he wanted her cut up and I'll be damned if that asshole didn't turn to me and tell me I'd have to decide. I stared at the meat in the display cabinets and the butcher diagram on the wall. I couldn't talk. They both kept pushing me for answers and finally the butcher started offering suggestions so all I had to do was nod. I flinched as I heard a cow bellow from somewhere in the back. My heart almost stopped as I tried not to imagine what was happening.

The butcher worked his way down his checklist and looked at me expectantly again. He had asked a question and once he finally got my attention, he repeated it. "What name do you want on this?" he asked.

I started bawling, not pretty tears but those gut-wrenching sobs that wrack your whole body. The ones that start down in the pit of your stomach and end up ripping your heart and soul in half. I imagined all those white, butcher paper wrapped chunks of meat in the freezer, each of them with a name in bold black print. "Carol." I said. "Her name was Carol."

It was the butcher's turn to look stunned. He turned to Curt in confusion. Curt shook his head and in a low voice, gave the butcher our last name… not the cow's name.

After the first year of working calves, I decided I no longer wanted to cut (castrate) the bull calves. By this time, we had registered Beefmaster cattle and could sell the bull calves for breeding. I spent a lot of time with the bull calves. I fed them by hand, brushed them, and constantly talked to them. They really were my babies. When a prospective buyer would come to look, Curt would stand outside the pen and do the negotiating. The "little woman," me, would go into the pen and whistle for the bulls. They would charge into the pen then come up and snuffle

240

all over me looking for treats. I could lead any bull past the buyer without a rope. One day, a buyer bought my favorite, Baby Huey. As he backed his trailer up to the gate, I moved all the other bull calves out and then said my goodbyes to my baby bull. As you can imagine from his name, he was huge, as Beefmasters tend to be. The buyer opened his trailer gate, and I stepped back crying, gave Baby Huey one last pat on the shoulder, and told him to get into the trailer. The huge bull calf amazed us all and walked straight into the trailer. The buyer remarked that he would come back to buy all his bulls from us.

Figure 61 Beefmaster Bull, Baby Huey.

Selling my babies was tough, but birthing time was tougher. Beefmasters are supposed to be born small then have huge gains in size and weight. It doesn't always work that way. Sometimes the calves are just too big, and the cows need help. If you've never had to help birth a calf let me tell you, it's the scariest thing I've ever seen. There are tools used that would normally be used to tow a car. Big, scary tools. I was always a nervous wreck when the cow's time got near. When it's their time, the silly old things will hide from you too.

We had one cow, Annie, that taught me more than I ever wanted to know about birthing. I knew she would be calving soon, so I kept an eye on her. Sure enough, one morning when the other cows came in to eat, Annie was missing. I found her in the trees behind the back pond and she looked bad. I've heard about cows that throw their uterus when birthing. I think the proper term is a prolapsed uterus. I'd never seen it before, so, in a panic, I called the vet. Doc Taylor asked me to describe what I was seeing. It looked like a deflated basketball hanging out all the way around her lady parts. Doc calmly reassured me that it wasn't her uterus, it was just her vagina.

I stared at the phone for a minute and then shouted, "Do you think that's supposed to make me feel better? What the hell am I supposed to do with it?"

As calmly as before, Doc Taylor said to wash it off and "stuff it back in." Definitely an OMG moment.

I wasn't even sure whether this had happened when Annie had calved or if the calf had yet to be born. Was the calf in trouble? Was it still alive? Would Annie survive? I searched the area but didn't find any sign of a calf or afterbirth.

I slowly herded Annie back up to the pens and into the chute. I happened to spot my neighbor's (grown) son, Troy, in the pasture next door. I whistled and waved, and my panic must have shown because he hotfooted it over. I told Troy what Doc Taylor had said, and he stared at me much like I'd stared at the phone. Seems he'd never experienced this either.

We hooked up the water hose and stood behind the cow. I tried to hand the hose to Troy, but he just looked at me aghast and said,

"It's your cow!" He was right, of course, but I figured it didn't hurt to try.

I washed Annie's lady parts as gently and thoroughly as possible. Ugh, if felt like a deflated basketball too. Now came the hard part. Again, I stared at Troy...again he said, "Your cow."

Humph. I worked as gently as possible but soon discovered it was going to take a whole lot of force to get the job done. The poor cow had put a lot of effort into pushing her vagina out and it was going back the same way. I finally figured out to start at one spot, fold a handful of flesh back into the cow and continue working my way around the opening in the same fashion.

Troy stood at Annie's head and talked to her, doing his best to try to get her to relax. As I worked, we discussed whether we thought she had calved but she did still look enormous. It soon became obvious that she was still having contractions. We called Doc Taylor again and were reassured we were doing the right thing and to keep it up.

I would stop working during Annie's contractions, holding my hand against her partially reinserted vagina until she relaxed again. I had all but one last handful to go and stopped for another contraction, thankful for the break. Sweat was streaming down my face, and my clothes were soaked with sweat, water, and whatever else was coming out of the cow. Troy looked almost as wrung out. Annie relaxed again, and we all three took a deep breath.

It took one hell of a push to get that last roll of vagina back into poor old Annie. Once it started moving into place however, it was like it all sucked back in like a vacuum, literally sucking my hand with it. So, there I stood, elbow deep in a cow. I started to pull my arm back, but Annie contracted again and Troy suggested I wait for it to pass. The good news was I hadn't felt the calf so maybe she wasn't too far along. Eventually, I was able to withdraw my arm without upsetting Annie any further.

I looked triumphantly at Troy, and we were about to congratulate one another when Annie bawled and her sides rippled. All I could think about was her having another contraction and blowing her vagina back out. I did what any sane person would do that didn't want to ever see anything like that again. I put both my hands flat over the opening and pushed hard against her trying to hold everything in.

Have you ever heard the expression "peeing on a flat rock"? Same thing happened here. That dang Annie started pissing, and I stood there pushing against it for all I was worth. Pee sprayed up and out in a huge, hot, smelly golden fan, raining down on everything, especially me. She peed, and peed, and peed. I stood there through the whole damn thing. When she finally stopped, I dropped my arms, exhausted and disgusted. I couldn't even wipe my face off because my hands were—well, there's just no telling what all I had on my hands. Troy turned his back politely and although I didn't hear anything, I grumbled as his shoulders shook from barely suppressed laughter.

We turned the poor cow out into the lot and then my good neighbor Troy took the water hose to me. I stayed with Annie until after dark and she never showed any signs of birthing. I should have stayed with her that night, but I had to work the next day. I dragged my tired, filthy ass to the house, showered, and fell into bed for a couple of hours. I rose early the next morning to check on Annie and found her and a sweet little calf. Both looked normal and healthy.

I recounted the story to Curt when he returned from his work trip. I asked him if he planned to raise cattle after he retired. He shook his head and said no, they were too much work. I could have gotten pissed but instead, I went shopping. We sold the farm and moved to a house with a swimming pool. Sure, pools are work too, but I think I can handle that work when compared to cattle.

I guess this is as good a place as any to talk about betrayal. Before we got out of the cattle business, I ordered a big red pickup truck. I negotiated the deal with a local salesman and for some reason I got one hell of a deal. It was for a ¾ ton, 4x4, crew cab pickup with a full-sized bed. It was the first red vehicle I had ever ordered. There was a problem with the deal when the dealership changed hands before the truck was delivered. The owner of the new dealership reviewed my order and eventually decided he would honor the original commitment even though he thought he was getting screwed. I told him damn right he would, since I had a signed contract and they had already cashed my deposit check.

It took forever for the truck to finally be delivered. It was roughly the size of a firetruck. Okay, that's an exaggeration, but this truck was huge, and red. Two days after I got the truck someone keyed it on the passenger side from one end to the other. I have no idea why people do this. Have they never had to work for something? Curt insisted that red vehicles attract that kind of attention.

My big red truck was a work truck, after all, so as much as the scratch pained me, I didn't spend a fortune to repair it. I used it on the farm and drove it to work. One day, I needed to drive across the plant for a meeting. Before I left my office, an operator I knew and respected came by my office. He wanted to warn me to watch out, that someone was out to get me. He refused to give any more details, just told me to watch my back. I took this kind of thing seriously. I went to the parking lot to get my truck. I was hyper sensitive about the vehicle previously being keyed so before I left, I checked the truck out on all sides. No new damage. I then drove across the tracks, parked in the middle of an empty lot, and went to my meeting.

When I came back to my truck, I was devastated to see new scrapes. It wasn't as if it had been keyed. This was something else. These shorter, deeper scrapes peeled the paint down to bare metal in crescent moon sweeps. It was as if something had gone back and forth across the metal. This was something I would have to pay to fix to prevent rust.

I reported the damage to security. They asked about the scratch from front to back. I explained that was previous damage and had not happened on this day, just the crescent moon scrapes. After I returned to my office, I talked to my boss, Rolfe. Again, I explained the old damage from keying, the warning I had received from the operator, and the new damage. Rolfe said that if someone was caught and found to be responsible, he would have their job. He would not tolerate this type of behavior. Later, we were able to watch the security video of the parking lot. During the time period I had indicated, another vehicle clearly pulled up beside my big red truck. The camera angle was such that it caught the vehicles from the side, my truck behind his vehicle. As the driver exited, the wind caught his door and blew it open wide. The video clearly showed the driver closing his door then looking closely at my vehicle where the damage had occurred.

I immediately felt two things: vindicated that I had proof, and I even felt better knowing it was entirely an accident. It all looked so apparent to me. I felt good for about two seconds. Then, Rolfe explained to me that he talked to the man in the video, a young, church-going engineer, Bangor. Rolfe said that Bangor had sworn that he had not damaged my truck. I couldn't believe my ears. We had just watched the video. We had both watched as Bangor went to the exact spot where my truck was damaged after his door flew open. Then my heart dropped. The angle was such that the video couldn't catch the actual damage as it happened. It came down to whom my boss wanted to believe, me, or the church-going Bangor. I knew the damage had happened then, but the gutless Bangor wouldn't admit he'd made a mistake, that an accident had happened. If the truth were known, it would have all been forgiven as a mistake and nobody's job would have been in jeopardy. Unfortunately, Rolfe had now taken sides. He had chosen to believe the engineer, Bangor, over me, despite the video evidence. How was I supposed to fight that? I did try, once, saying I'm sure it happened then and that at least it appeared to be an accident. Rolfe reminded me that Bangor, who, he repeated, was a good, church-going man, said he didn't do it. What reason would an upstanding young man like Bangor have to lie? I stopped arguing. What reason did I have to lie? Rolfe's mind was made up. It didn't matter that we'd had what I thought was a great working relationship. It didn't matter that I once thought Rolfe respected me. None of it mattered when I was judged side by side with the good, church-going, male engineer, Bangor. Again, I convinced myself that if I continued to fight and argue, to demand action, that I would slip even further down the ladder. I did respect Rolfe. I did believe he made good decisions and was a great leader. If the video wasn't enough proof, I couldn't say anything to change his mind. I gave up.

To make matters worse, I discovered that one of the senior production supts was telling everyone that my truck wasn't damaged that day. He told folks that it was already damaged (keyed) and that I was just trying to cause trouble and should be fired. I understand he petitioned for some time to get me fired but of course was unsuccessful. Instead, he just spread lies to the operators and anyone else who would listen. Maybe this is why Rolfe lost respect for me over his fine, good, church-going, male engineer, AKA—the lying motherfucker who albeit accidentally damaged my truck.

I never did willingly speak to Bangor again. Every damn time I passed him in the hallway the guilt was evident on his face, as evident as the hate on mine. I still can't believe Rolfe would have so easily dismissed my claim and sided with this guy.

CHAPTER 24
(2000) WHEN ONE DOOR CLOSES ANOTHER ONE OPENS – RIGHT INTO THE DAMN SWAMP

Despite the drama, I was happy in my job. I loved my job. Then, as many things do, my little world changed overnight. Rolfe left the refinery with very little notice. We ended up with the manager, Lance, that didn't like to spend money on restrooms for women. He was upper management, not my direct boss, but shit does roll downhill.

When management changes, goals change to match. People are repositioned, practices are revised. What one person may have seen as value adding, another may see as an unnecessary expense. We fought to save them, but some of the first things to go under Lance's management were my passions, our diversity and VAP programs.

Soon after, we had goal review and yearly evaluations. My new supervisor asked what job I wanted to go to next. I loved my job but felt I had learned what successful operations looked like and I wanted to be able to get back into operations and share my learnings. To do that however, I needed to be in a position that would allow me to influence change. I wanted a job, Operations Lead Maintenance Coordinator (OLMC), supervising area operators. This was another daylight position with weekends/holidays off. My supervisor explained that the OLMC job was a good position to shoot for. However, no "uneducated" person would get that job without first working the production supt job…as in shift work.

I was adamant I did not want to work shift work again. My supervisor reminded me that no one gets the OLMC job without first working the production supt job. By the way, I had until

Monday to decide. The pièce de resistance—they were doing away with my current job. It was Friday with a long, emotionally fraught weekend ahead. In just a few days, I went through all the stages of grief and then circled back to anger.

One thing I finally learned about anger, much after this happened, unfortunately; it is okay to be angry. Then pull your head out of your ass and get over it. Don't lose yourself to anger. Yell, scream, cry, and then get the hell over it so you can enjoy life. Otherwise, you are just killing yourself.

Monday morning, I accepted the production supt job. I would be working for a senior production supt, Doug, who I knew and respected so at least that helped. I told Doug how glad I was to be on his shift. He said there wasn't any other choice because the other senior production supts had refused to work with me. Damn, kick me again.

I had barely dug out my old work boots, fire resistant coveralls, etc., when I heard that management moved two male operators directly into the OLMC position. The same position that I had applied for and been denied. Neither of these two had previously worked a salaried position. Nor had they worked the production supt job that was supposedly a necessary prequalification. How do you reconcile that kind of betrayal? How do you make yourself come to work on hoot shift and not wonder what could possibly have justified this type of treatment? What had the two males done to skip the "required" work to get them to the better job? Why, when I asked these questions, would nobody (management/supervisors) tell me why? Instead, I just heard the fucking lemonade story over and over. They also told me to be happy I had a job. This, my friends, was not an incentive to bolster a good attitude.

I struggled to make sense of what had happened. In the meantime, I had a job to do. One great thing about the production supt job was getting to work a larger area of the refinery. There were several production supts so we might work the West Plant, South Plant, etc. It was fun to go to units I'd never worked at and meet the folks, learning more about their operations. My operating background was mostly around distillation, but I'd also operated a unit with a reactor, so I had some basic knowledge of reacting/reforming units (reshapes the molecules). I did not have any experience with cracking units (cracks the big molecules into smaller pieces). Right away, I was asked how I expected to be the supervisor when I didn't know all the answers. I explained I didn't have to know all the answers. I just needed to know where to find the answers. There was a wealth of knowledge in the operators working the units and I would rely on their expertise. I would give them guidance, set boundaries, and help them make the right decisions. I wasn't foolish enough to think that just because I was a supervisor that I knew more than any of them. What I could do was help them. I could bring messages from management, explain "why" as well as I could and, in turn, take their thoughts and concerns back to management. I sincerely wanted to make things better and began a difficult balancing act trying to be supportive of both sides.

Operators seemed to enjoy challenging me in numerous ways as I began visiting the areas. Some would ask technical questions to test my knowledge, and some would be surprised that I had the background experience to help me answer their questions. Others tested me in the old, familiar, disrespectful way.

One night, I was sent to an area I hadn't been to since receiving my supervisor status. Before I left, Doug told me to watch out for this one operator. It seems the dude believed himself to be a real lady's man. I walked into the area control room and as I came around the corner, I saw an operator that had been nodding off. He jerked upright when he saw me and immediately started yelling something about me being female. He scampered towards me ogling me up and down still yammering on about me being female. I never stopped walking. I looked down on him, literally, with my best, don't fuck with me face, and backed him right up. He stumbled backward as fast as he could, stopping only when he hit the wall. I just stood there, inches from his face, and stared. He never said another word. Finally, he slid down the wall a bit then slunk over to his chair and sat down. I introduced myself and asked for the info I'd been sent to retrieve. I asked if there was anything he needed then left telling him to have a good evening. Every time after that, he treated me respectfully despite his womanizing reputation.

There were things to like about the production supt job, but it definitely had its downsides too. Shift work was getting harder and harder for me, especially now that it was twelve-hour shifts. I didn't mind working nights; my body seemed to be attuned to nights. Switching from one schedule to another was killing me. I also struggled with one of our other production supts, Pettigrew, who had a total lack of people skills. He was very knowledgeable about the units/refinery, but he was a real asshole to people. I will say that Doug saw how much Pettigrew's behavior was a lot more "old school." He knew that times were changing and admitted Pettigrew needed to learn a little more about valuing people. The one mistake I felt that Doug made, was telling me Pettigrew was just that way because he was from this familiar little town nearby. This was the second time I'd heard this small-town excuse for inappropriate behavior. I don't think being from a certain town, born in a certain country, having a certain color of skin, being born rich or poor, etc., is an excuse for treating people badly. What I didn't understand was that Doug was from the same town and didn't seem to suffer with the same affliction. So why was this being used as an excuse?

I did appreciate how Doug tried to improve the people issues and it was almost painful to watch Pettigrew try to modify his behavior though he did really try. The great thing for me was that

Doug appreciated my desire to improve relationships among all the workers. He allowed me to build training material on people development and even to purchase outside training material. My favorite was *The Power Dead Even Rule* by Dr. Pat Heim. The training addressed the differences between how men and women communicate.

Doug would also send me to the areas to handle personnel issues. You know, the ones that nobody wants to handle. As mentioned earlier, the "soft stuff" is the hard stuff. Referring, of course, to how difficult it can be to handle the personal issues.

For instance, Doug sent me to one area to mediate an argument between two operators. Operator A was pissed because Operator B would only call him by his first name. Operator B was pissed because Operator A would only call him by his last name. I talked to both guys separately and found out they both used the styles they believed were respectful. You might call someone by their first name to show you appreciate them enough to feel more casual and familiar with them, almost family. Inversely, you may call someone by their last name to show respect, such as in the military. Both guys had good intentions but when treated differently than what they perceived as respectful, they just got mad and didn't even try to work out their differences.

We focus on what we believe to be our own right way. We don't understand—or maybe just don't care, that the intention of others is meant to be good and right. Something I read long ago, in a mandatory HR training I believe, said, "It doesn't matter what our intentions are." It only matters what effect it has on the other person and how it makes them feel. I can appreciate that. Well-meaning people have made me feel belittled on many occasions. We should at least try to appreciate the intention. If we can understand and appreciate what they meant, what their intention was, maybe it wouldn't hurt so much. Maybe if we understood, we could teach them what we needed instead.

We are not born knowing what other people think/feel or how they want to be treated. Hell, many of us were raised by loving families that, nevertheless, intoned their own prejudices into our psyche. Where do you suppose racism comes from? Are we born that way? Is it how we are raised? Is it developed due to personal interactions? I am not the only person to ever feel fear of the unknown. We fear something different. The most important thing is what we do with that fear, discomfort, or wariness. Do we try to learn from it? Knowledge is the key to overcoming fear. How do we learn? Reading history and other books is a great tool, but it is just the beginning because things change daily. We have to communicate and that takes guts. Proper communications. You can't just listen to someone talk; you have to listen intently and question to understand. Too many times we think we might understand, but we taint what we see or hear with our prejudices whether we realize it or not. It takes a lot of honest communication to really understand and appreciate what is important to another person. Sadly, so many people don't want to communicate. Instead, they try to hammer their own beliefs over someone else's head and wonder why they do not understand. Alternatively, we erect a wall around our beliefs and think that the only truth hides behind a barrier that nobody is allowed to penetrate. We have to talk. We have to listen. We have to empathize. We have to be open. We have to be honest. We have to want to get along together, to work together, to live together. We have to see ourselves as equals. Listen people—that takes two. One person alone, no matter how badly they want it, cannot do this. WE, WE, WE, all the way home.

Another personnel issue Doug sent me to handle was based on one guy, Christopher, being a totally different type of duck in the pond. Christopher's coworkers were freaked out about his discussions on chemical warfare and what they believed to be a scary and excessive knowledge on the subject. You really have to take these kinds of things seriously when working in a hazardous environment. I believe Doug had already deduced that there was no real threat involved, rather, it was a case of fearing the odd duck, Christopher. To make matters worse, the odd duck was the team lead.

I went to the team first and listened to their concerns. Next, I went to Christopher and asked him if he knew he was freaking out his team. He chuckled and said yes; of course, he knew they'd gotten upset. Christopher and I had history as we'd gone to school together. He'd been an odd duck the whole time I knew him. That is what I liked about him. He had thoughts and views alien to mine, and it roused my curiosity. I'd never before explored the types of things that he believed in, and I found it interesting. Nothing that would ever sway me to be more like him, but I appreciated his passion.

Christopher told me about his recent study on chemical warfare. He was extremely interested in specifically how to PROTECT yourself against such a disaster. If you have any awareness of what's going on around us in this world, how can you not appreciate that? I told him so. I also questioned him to verify that he had no thoughts or intentions of using such knowledge for evil. You don't know if you don't ask.

I went back to the team and asked them if they understood the basis of the chemical warfare discussion by Christopher. They did not. I explained that this one individual they were supposedly frightened of, had more knowledge than anyone I personally knew on how to protect himself and others from the hazards of a chemical attack. I then asked the team if they would prefer Christopher to be with them, or against them. The all opted for "with them."

I want to paint in some details on the image of Christopher for you and why it's hard for people to look past differences when challenged with something so beyond their own beliefs.

I was working nights and went to the area control room to check in. I pushed open the blast-proof door and walked down a dimly lit hallway. This opened up to a large room that was completely dark except for the green, luminescent glow coming from a circle of two half-moon shaped banks of computer terminals. In the center of this glowing cauldron sat a solitary, very large man, wearing a fedora and a full black cape. Eerie, sinister music was playing in the background. I walked closer until the man, Christopher, turned to me and whispered, "Welcome to Hell." This was typical behavior for my buddy.

NOTE: I knew Christopher was doing his job. He was the only person in the control room at that time, so the choice of music was his and was permissible according to company practices. He was also monitoring the computer readouts and like many, found the screens easier to see with the lights dimmed or out. The really, really, important thing about this guy, was that he had a profound passion for doing his job as well as possible. He did everything in his power to make sure that work was performed safely, that units were fine-tuned, products were on test, and all direction from management followed. He was also a great communicator, in that he shared knowledge and kept folks updated on pertinent operating conditions. Undoubtedly, he was outspoken and unabashedly different. When we developed a dress code for the CCR, this is the guy that showed up wearing tights and a tunic just to mock us—we had excluded sweat pants from the dress code, but it had not occurred to us to exclude tights and tunics. He was/is truly unique.

I continued to work my production supt job and although Doug tried to help me, I was not happy. I hated shift work. I was also unhappy in the job because at that time, it was more of a babysitting job and not work that really made a difference. There was also that big damn burr under my saddle about the two guys that got the job I wanted without the same requirements that were put on me. Admittedly, that continued to chafe, and it wasn't just raw on the surface. It was deep, and the infection was spreading.

CHAPTER 25
(2002) MY NEW TEMPORARY PERMANENT JOB, MAKING LEMONADE

An opportunity arose for me to work a temporary daylight job as a yields analyst. The original plan was that the production supts would all rotate through this job and I was deemed a good fit to be next in line. I would replace another production supt, Laurel, who currently held the position and who wanted to get back on shift work, win-win. The job involved using an inventory software that attempted to balance the refinery purchases, internal inventories, and sales. I really enjoyed computer programs, and it almost seemed like playing video games to me. (Yes, egad, I am also a gamer. In World of Warcraft, my main is a Night Elf Hunter but my favorite character is a druid.) I sat down with Laurel and watched him work through a single day's balance. Laurel then let me take the controls and told me to drive. Minutes later, he was called away for some unknown (made up?) bullshit. Although I was able to ask Laurel a few questions after that, he pretty much skipped out never to be seen again—that is an exaggeration, he went back on shift.

I like to exaggerate when I'm joking or making a point. In real life, however, I caution against this as you can start believing your own words. Beware of using words like "never" or "always." Do those two things truly happen?

When I train, it helps me to see the task performed. Even if I don't remember exactly how it was done, I do recognize familiar steps, and I can figure it out on my own. I was able to fumble my way through most of my new job. Another thing that helped was that this guy, Rudy, who originally put the yields/inventory software into service, was working nearby. I knew Rudy from when we both worked on the loading docks. He was a hard worker and a good person.

Rudy also had an evil plan. He explained that he built software programs to ensure his own job security. He had extensive knowledge on different programs and coding. His Excel spreadsheets were truly impressive, but it was a hair puller to try to maintain—which was his intent. He called it "job security." He liked to be indispensable. This was a recipe for disaster. We relied on these spreadsheets to help us in many areas of planning. Rudy eventually left our company to work for a competitor. He did take one call for help when I needed to know his embedded passwords. He made it clear, however, that he would charge me for the next call. Oh, hell no! I came up with a plan of my own. I would replace every piece of software Rudy had built. This would admittedly be a challenge since I had minimal experience with spreadsheets. I bought training books, I googled, and I learned.

It is hard to write about Rudy now. Years after our time together, Rudy was murdered. Shot in cold blood, his body dumped in a ravine. How the hell can one human being do that to another? You just never know where life will take you. One trip to the airport, one tiny fork in the road, and life is never again the same. We've become so busy in living today and forget that tomorrow may never come. That is probably for the best. We can't live our lives in fear. We can't torture ourselves with "what ifs." But, if we stop now and then and think about it, we just might do better while we're still here. Tell them you love them. Tell them you miss them. Tell them you are proud of them. Tell them with your actions, your words, your hugs, and your smiles. Laugh with them, cry with them, celebrate with them, and grieve with them. Just as important, never pass up the opportunity to pet your dog, your cat, your hamster, hairless rat, snake, Iguana, or whatever animal it is that comforts you.

Rudy, you were unique. You were an inspiration and a pain in my ass. You were brilliant and problematic. You were funny, kind, and compassionate. Rudy, my friend, I hope you found your peace.

As stressful as it was to have so little training, I enjoyed figuring out the new (to me) yields software and maintaining the supporting Excel spreadsheets. I didn't have much experience with Excel coding, but I learned a lot while attempting to reverse engineer Rudy's spreadsheets. Generally, if everything was contained in one spreadsheet, I could figure it out. Unfortunately, Rudy never did things the easy way. One spreadsheet would reach out to a database for this, to another spreadsheet for that, then another database. Oh, and each spreadsheet and database had its own password. He didn't like the working spreadsheet to be slowed down doing calculations, so he always had files tucked here and there that were crunching data while we mere mortals slept. Users could then pull the compiled data into any spreadsheet. We even used the name "Rudyware" for any spreadsheet he had developed. His work was fascinating, incredible, and scary brilliant. That is, until a password changed somewhere, or a tag was updated or deleted. Oh, Rudy had error checkers that would keep the system working. What it couldn't do, however, was tell you if the data was still valid. For instance, a tag (nametag for a flow, pressure, temp, etc. reading) could be removed or decommissioned and may still carry the last value that it read instead of zero. As they say, there are ghosts in the machines.

My supervisor "allowed" me to attend the daily production supt meetings where they discussed lineups and upcoming changes that would help me validate my inventory data. I was even "allowed" to ask questions. It seemed strange to be "allowed" since technically, I was still a production supt.

Some information I needed wasn't normally discussed during these meetings. The operators and other production supts caught on to the types of data I needed and a few of them started updating me more often with phone calls or emails. This was extremely helpful. The one guy who was the best about notifying me of changes was Christopher, the dude who wore the fedora and cape, or tights and tunic, depending on the day.

FLASHBACK: I do remember a story of when Christopher finally pushed the limits on his dress code, but I have not verified if it was true. One day he supposedly showed up with a Bowie knife strapped to his waist as part of his "normal" attire. Weapons are prohibited anywhere on company property, and he was immediately sent home to disarm. It seems odd to me that he would pull something like that. After all, I thought he was much more of a sword type of guy than a Bowie knife type.

Another delicate issue around my new job was that a union represented employee, Lola, originally worked the job. Once management decided to keep the program going, they decided it should be performed by a salaried person. Management offered the job to Lola, but she refused to give up her union status and take a salaried job. That is why we started using production supts. That is also how we pissed off the union.

I was lucky to be in another office that looked out onto the same interior courtyard that my first office had. Even better than before, I had a tree right outside my window, a small ornamental tree with beautiful reddish leaves. I would end up spending several years in that office watching the leaves turn color then fall, always trying to spot the very last leaf before it dropped. The office was located directly across from a cubby that contained four interior offices where several clerks and the yields supervisor, Paul, were located. None of their offices had windows, and the area was so dismal we referred to it as The Cave. Seriously, we made a door plaque and everything. This office thing may seem like a little thing, but it was huge for the clerks and me, and it turned into a major issue in the years to come. As they say, location, location, location.

I think I worked the yields analyst job for about a year per the original plan. Then I was supposed to go back to shift work, and another production supt would take my place. However, management decided to offer me the job permanently. Once again, they gave me a choice. I could rotate back into shift work and resume my old production supt job, or I could take a pay cut and keep this new job. Um, what? Why would I receive less pay just for taking the job permanently? Why would the company decide to pay me less than Laurel, who had the job before me?

The reason given was that I would now be permanently working a daylight job, weekends and holidays off. Therefore, they were removing the extra pay that was given to production supts who worked rotating shifts. As much as I can understand that logical thinking, I, of course, disagreed. This was a brand-new permanent position, and it was entirely up to management what the pay scale would be. I, and Laurel before me, had just worked a year receiving full pay for the job. We both worked days with weekends and holidays off. Another important factor, little did I understand at the time how important, was that I would be the only person working this new position. There were numerous production supts to fill in for each other. There was only one of me. My reflecting self wants to stop here for a moment and kick my current self in the ass. You'll understand why if you keep reading.

Bitch and moan as much as I wanted to, I also had to give in to the logic (of removing shift differential pay). I signed the paper and took the pay cut to keep the daylight job, a job I had grown to love. Still, that burr under my saddle was getting a little more irksome.

Management almost screwed up later when they attempted to have me temporarily cover a production supt job—working nights of course. I pointed out to them that I wasn't paid enough to do the production supt job anymore. They stuttered and then chose not to stir that pot. Yep, it ended up being a win for me. My name remained on the production supt's schedule for quite some time after that, but I was not asked again to work the higher paid job for less money.

I was now part of the production group. My new boss, Harry, and the rest of the production group were located one hallway over in the same building. Harry thought it would be better if I stayed closer to the clerical group. I did work closely with a few of the clerks, Lola, Brittney, and Lucy. I also worked with their supervisor, Paul, for weekly, monthly or yearly reports. On one hand, it was convenient to remain where I was. On the other hand, it alienated me from my actual work group. I watched time and time again, as the group, sans me, would go to meetings or lunches. I was happy I didn't have to attend most of the meetings. Odds are I wouldn't have gone to the lunches had I been invited. It was just another one of those burr under the saddle, thorn in my side, straw on the camel's back kind of thing. I felt alienated from my work group. I began to wonder why my supervisor treated me so differently from the rest of the group. Each time, I just stayed in my office, beside my window with my little tree and I worked. Admittedly, I did get one or two invitations to join the group, but I'd given up trying to be a part of the team and didn't want to take advantage of their generosity to play with the odd kid.

I tried to tell myself I was happy about not being included. I'm no damn good at small talk and rubbing elbows anyway. I also hated to be taken away from my work. I didn't realize it at the time, but later, when someone described me as "driven," I realized that it was true. Put work in front of me and my fingers would itch to get busy. I wasn't comfortable until I had my work done.

Keeping a backlog of busy work was hard for me because I tended to knock it out as quickly as possible also.

The real problem came during the end of the year reviews. The company allots each manager a certain amount of money to award their direct reports for yearly raises. Therefore, if someone did a stellar job, making the company lots of money, they may get a high rating and more money. To balance that higher amount of money, someone has to take less money. My group consisted of people that had tremendous impact on the strategic planning of not only daily operations but also upcoming work, turnarounds, and so on. They handled how much crude we would buy, how much product we could sell, and to whom. Important stuff. They all had degrees and career paths. Then, there was me. I was essentially an uneducated bean counter. They were the filet mignons, I was the side salad, and I knew it. It really didn't matter how hard I worked because the work itself would never compare to the work they provided. At least that's what I thought in the beginning. It wasn't until later I learned how valuable the data that I provided was.

One of these reviews had a huge impact on my life but not like you might think. My boss, Harry, had reviewed my work and didn't have anything bad to say about it. He knew I did my job. Now he had the delicate task of explaining to me that I was the weird kid. He was extremely professional about it. He told me to my face that I was, "…a square peg that didn't fit into the company's round holes." He even went so far to say I might not be a square at all. I was possibly an even more unique shape. The problem was, however, I did not fit the company's standard. He politely sat quietly while I mulled that over.

I asked Harry if I did my work on time and accurately; he said yes. I asked if my attitude was adequate; he said yes. I asked if I did my share of the work; he said yes. I asked if I had met all expectations for work performance; he said yes. I asked if I reached all the goals handed down to me; he said yes. Then I asked what I could do to fit in. This is where he totally failed. A leader would have a development plan. A leader would be honest, even if he had to use words that weren't in normal corporate lingo. Harry just couldn't or wouldn't tell me anything other than I didn't fit. I mulled some more. Then I looked him in the eye and told him, "Thank you."

His lame ass response was, "It wasn't supposed to be a compliment." I didn't care. I was unique. I was proud of myself. I wasn't a square peg; I was actually something more. He wasn't enough of a leader to appreciate that my differences could bring value to his team (because I cared, I loved my job, and wanted to do good work). He wasn't enough of a leader to harness my passion and direct it in a way that would be beneficial for the team. He wasn't enough of a leader to help me, but I would take this and work with it. I would play to my strengths. I will say that Harry was probably a good leader to all the round pegs. You know, the ones just like him, the right school, the right education, the right church, and of course the proper attire.

Before I left that meeting, I did tell Harry that if the day came that I was required to wear a dress and makeup to work, that he could just bring my final paycheck. He didn't respond.

It wasn't like I was able to brush this off. My boss had just told me I didn't fit in and yet I still had my job, was still a member of his group. I still had to compete for the money he was given to divvy up amongst his team each year. I asked several supervisors and managers what I needed to do and guess what they told me? Yep, the fucking lemonade story. Not one single person was able to give me an idea of how to fit in. It's not like we didn't have other women either. Our group was the best at hiring female engineers. But I was the only one that rode a Harley to work, wore biker boots, jeans, and T-shirts. I rarely wore makeup. I'd grown my hair until it was down to my knees before I got fed up and got it all hacked off. While it was long, I usually wore it up or in a braid. If I let it down, it would get caught in everything. I've even had another biker pull up beside me and worry that my braid would get caught in the wheel, but it never got quite that long. Despite the wicked mass, I washed my hair every day. I wore clean clothes, and I constantly worried if I smelled bad because of the way people avoided me. I just didn't know what was so off-putting about my appearance or demeanor. One thing I was completely sure of, I was not going to start wearing makeup and feminine attire in an attempt to be accepted. I would do this on rare occasions for specific reasons, but I was generally uncomfortable. Not that I didn't like doing this occasionally, but it was always short-lived. I'd probably wear blouses more often if I wasn't such a square shape. Most women's blouses just don't look good on me. I am a tomboy. I love being a tomboy, and I am happy being a tomboy.

As I reread this, I do know one of my biggest failures that put people off, beyond my attire or choice of transportation. I just couldn't keep my damn mouth closed. If people were being disrespectful, if I disagreed, or just had an opinion to offer, I could not keep from saying what I thought. I tried to be respectful in my delivery but granted, I could lose my temper. Oh, and people really don't like being told they are wrong, not even if you smile when you're telling them. Come to think of it, especially if you smile when you tell them.

I remember one incident when I lost my temper big time. It was back when we still had our diversity and inclusion program. A coworker, Pratt, an older fellow and engineer, came into my office. He was discussing issues around granting diversity credits for some Native American events. I fully supported giving the credits but for some reason Pratt was against it. The discussion took a bad turn when he made a generic reference about all Native Americans being alcoholics. I tried to get Pratt to rethink what he had said, but he told me it was okay; he could say something like that because he had his "Indian card." I lost it. I firmly but politely told him to get out of my office, but he persisted on telling me why it was okay for him to slur Native Americans because he had a card that indicated he himself was Native American. I suppose it never occurred to him that according to his logic, he too would therefore be an alcoholic. I told Pratt several more times to leave my office, but he wouldn't quit talking. He was convinced he could make me see his side. I finally came around my desk and began yelling at him to get the hell out of my office. Unbelievably, Pratt still argued with me, but he did back away as I came at him, my face red with anger. I repeated my command to get the hell out of my office and as he finally stepped into the hallway, I slammed my office door right in his face. Then I had the audacity to wonder why I didn't fit into the company standards.

I continued to mull over what Harry had told me about not fitting in. Then I remembered what I have told other people—play to your strengths. So…what are my strengths…that was a real head scratcher. What was it about me that made me different, unique? Again, I went back to my passions. Diversity, inclusion, helping people, oh, and if you hadn't noticed, I love to tell and write stories. I am not much good at face-to-face, but I like to write. I got the idea to write a novel. I didn't want to write a non-fiction book. I wanted to get my mind as far away from what was going on in the real world as I could. I wrote a fantasy book, *Meesha Guardian of Grand Mountain*, for young adults. The story was about a diverse group of kids coming into adulthood and finding their own inner strengths. They then must learn to work together to overcome evil, an evil that hates them just because they are different. I made it a bit more entertaining by adding dragons, another passion of mine.

Writing was the easy part. I read Stephen King's book, *On Writing*, and he said you must know your characters. I looked at my family, took their individual traits, exaggerated them to fictional proportions and invented my characters. I knew them so well that my writing would take weird turns I wasn't expecting. I would sit down to write with a plan in mind of what would happen. As the story unfolded and the characters interacted in ways I thought fit their personalities, they often took off in a direction I hadn't anticipated. Many times, it was as if I was watching a movie in my head and my hands were just trying to type fast enough to get it all written down. I don't know how many times I was surprised to see typed words on the page instead of the full-blown movie I had just seen in my head.

After a year to write the book (I did have a real job after all), I then went through the process of getting it published. I received a lot of rejections but then one agent showed some interest. She wanted me to make one change. I had not included physical descriptions of the characters in the original manuscript. The agent said that most readers don't want to have to work that hard; they want the visuals all laid out for them. I wasn't sure I wanted to do this, especially after getting so many reviews where the readers didn't even realize I hadn't included that info as they had all pictured the characters as they wanted to see them. I did finally rewrite the book and included as few details as I could.

I waited for some time but never got a commitment from that publisher. I did get another publisher interested and was even offered a contract. I was still checking out the agency when they closed their doors. I still have the unsigned contract—but at least it wasn't a rejection.

It was important to me to get my novel printed. My father had read the story and loved it. He was dying of cancer at the time, and I wanted so badly to give him a copy of the book before he died. I did the only thing left to me. I started my own publishing company. I hired an amazing artist, Twila (who was married to my senior production supt, Doug), to do the book covers and interior sketches. I then found a printing company, bought ISBNs, and finally, in 2005, had my book in print. Sadly, it wasn't before my father died. I did make the trip back to New Mexico and gave my dad's widow a copy of the book as I had promised Dad.

I wanted the story to be a series and years later, in 2011, finished a second book, *Meesha and the Temple of the Jaguar Moon*. The print company I had used for the first book had gone out of business, so I decided to go entirely digital with the second book.

What I did not do was all the publicity and promotion needed to have a successful book sale. It did, however, make me feel good just to have the books out there. I had planned to have five books in the series and started the third, *Meesha and the Lost City of Atlantis*, but I keep getting distracted. I hope to finish those books someday.

You might ask what this has to do with my real job. How did this help me? It was an outlet for my passion. It was my emotional and physical release just as yoga or meditation is for so many. It was a distraction from my building resentments and irritation. It gave me a sense of accomplishment, pride, and value that I wasn't getting from my real job. Plus, the added satisfaction of building fictional characters. Piss me off at work and maybe a new character would show up in my books, briefly of course. Maybe it was also a way to win. I controlled the outcome. I controlled the wins and losses. Basically, writing my books kept me sane and happy. We all need a sane and happy place.

CHAPTER 26
(2003) FIRES YOU CAN'T EXTINGUISH

Sorry, I've jumped ahead of myself in time to tell my story-writing story. Now I need to go back to reality and tell the story of the worst fire we ever had during my career. We had fires where people were gravely injured, but this fire took the life of one coworker and affected so many, many others.

I was still working the yields job when we had another horrible fire back in my old operating area. It all started with a flash fire. A flash fire is self-explanatory in that it happens in a sudden flash. You may have seen this if you've used some type of lighter fluid to start a grill or campfire. Pour the fuel on then toss in a match. If you have excessive fumes or vapors, they ignite in a sudden flash of fire.

After the initial flash there was still a large fire burning at the source. During these types of rare events, anyone who can help does. I went to the CCR to see what I could do. Upper management had gone to the command center, so I monitored radio communications going on at the unit and passed on important details. Communication from the area was vague so we knew something bad had happened. We finally heard that someone was injured and that an ambulance had been requested. Still, we had no idea who it was or how extensive the injury. Radio communications could be picked up from outside sources, so they were doing their best to restrict how much was being shared. I wanted to suit up and go to the area but was told I was needed there in the CCR. I did as ordered and finally got one of the production supts to confirm the injured man was not my husband, Curt, who was on site that day.

We have TVs in the CCR to monitor the weather channel. Someone had turned on the news, which is how I figured out where the fire was. The news channel showed a brief, graphic, close-up of the injured operator, Tim, as he was loaded into the ambulance. Soon after the ambulance left, a senior manager, Marvin, came through the CCR discussing what they would do next. I asked if Tim's wife had been notified yet. Marvin said that he was going to the hospital, and he would decide if and when she needed to be notified. He saw no reason to cause a panic. I didn't lose my temper, but I think my voice conveyed my feelings. I told Marvin he could call her right now, or I would. He decided that making the call now might be the better option. I had just pissed off another manager who would have input on my yearly reviews and raises. Nevertheless, there are just some things that are far more important.

So many times, I have pushed the boundaries by "persistently arguing" with my superiors and voicing what I believed to be the right thing to do. Too many times, I have been punished for it. Never have I regretted it.

Our coworker, Tim, lived for several days before succumbing to his injuries. Curt had seen Tim on the day of the fire, lying on the ground. There was nothing Curt could do to help Tim, but it was hard to walk away and do his job.

After the incident, I was back in my office job and worried about the psychological effects the disaster would have on frontline workers like my husband. I can't speak for anyone else, but Curt still carries those mental scars. The fire still burns somewhere deep in his brain, and he just can't put it out.

Curt tells me that after the fire, the company did get all of the responders in one room together and asked them if they were okay mentally. Asking them in that group setting if anyone needed counseling or psychological help was about the stupidest thing I could imagine. How many of them do you suppose raised their hands? That's right, not one single person. I still wonder how many of them wanted to raise their hand.

I was finally able to get Curt into counseling (many years later). He went just long enough to convince me he needed to retire. I attended most of his sessions, at his request. Eventually, I agreed that retiring might be best for him—he still couldn't escape the fire. I assumed he would continue counseling but, once he had the green light, he left it all behind and never looked back.

For years after, Curt refused to look at the refinery when we drove past. Curt still suffers from PTSD from this incident. In the years that followed, I have seen what PTSD can do to a person. Curt still has nightmares from the refinery. I have memories, good and bad, and a big part of me wishes I were still there. I did love my job. I just didn't know how to help Curt, and he seemed unwilling, unable, to help himself. Living with a person with PTSD can be extremely difficult. You never know what will set them off or how they will react. There were times that I had to physically stop him from taking his anger out on strangers. There were also nights I locked my (separate) bedroom door and hugged my dogs close, worried for our safety.

NOTE: 2022—Curt did finally go to counseling once he understood we were again on the verge of divorce. He was treated for PTSD with a method called EMDR, Eye Movement Desensitization Reprocessing. The counselor told him she had no idea how it worked but that EMDR had a documented history for actually working. After just two EMDR sessions, Curt can talk about the incident without feeling the trauma of seeing Tim's injuries. He can watch fireworks without feeling the trauma of explosions and fire. He thinks it helped with his anger issues. He also admitted that he thinks it caused him some memory problems. Of course, once he believed himself to be cured, he immediately quit counseling.

I wish I had some words of wisdom about relationships to share here. It would take a whole other book to try to explain my own personal reasons for staying or leaving. Every person needs to make their own decision based on their own situation. The only help I might be able to give is this. First, make a decision, and then own your decision. You aren't a victim. You chose to follow this path. I don't blame Curt for my situation because I chose to be here. There may be one nugget of help I can offer. I reached a point where I knew I needed help. This coming from a person who HATES to ask for help. Yet the time came when I knew I couldn't do it on my own. I was lucky to find a great counselor, Kaye. The most important thing she taught me is that I wasn't responsible for Curt. I wasn't responsible for his happiness. I wasn't responsible for his mental well-being. This is not to say it wasn't important to try and help someone in need, to offer them a shoulder to cry on, a big bear hug. But his happiness was not my responsibility. His attitudes, his actions were his choice, just as mine were my choice. Not only did it free me of trying to own his pain and anger, but it also gave me a tool to help deal with him. When he would get angry, I would ask him, "Why are you choosing to be angry? Why are you choosing to react in this way?"

Another thing that Kaye taught me was art journaling. I love to write, draw, paint, etc. Kaye suggested I start art journaling. I struggled at first because I didn't want my art to be dark and depressed like I felt on occasion. I knew it was supposed to be an outlet but, in my mind, I didn't want to see those pictures come to life. I did finally put my feelings in words. I wrote the following poem, *The Lightening*. You may think I didn't know how to spell but trust me, lightening is spelled how it should be spelled in this case.

The Lightening

I feel the cold weight of the shackles, a heaviness that binds me.
I struggle under the confinement, longing to be free.
I search the darkness for something that eludes me, a light to ease my soul.
I listen intently, hoping to hear a sound, dreading to hear a sound.
I wait, longing for a rescue I know will never come.
I wait, looking for meaning in all the pain.
I wait, knowing I can't take much more, knowing the end must come soon.
I wait, and remind myself to breathe.

The rain begins to fall all around me, the thunder pounding inside my body, lightening blinding me with each strike.
I turn my head trying to hide from this new torture.
The rain streams through my hair, pours down my back and pools within my palms.
The thunder ignites a spark in my chest, my heart pounding with each crescendo.
The lightening illuminates the sky with brilliant intensity.
I bow my head, trying to hide from the deluge, trying to not hear the pounding, constant noise, to not see the bright, hot light.
I wait, and remind myself to breathe, just breathe.

The rain eases my aching muscles, washes the darkness from my eyes, my hands, my heart.
The thunder speaks to me, calls to me, demands me to raise my head and listen.
The lightening shows me brief glimpses, life beyond my confinement, beautiful in its freedom.
It all seems so far away, so unobtainable, so impossible.
I cannot break my bonds, I can only stay and suffer.

The rain relentlessly whispers to me, the thunder laughs at my self-pity, the lightening taunts me.

I jump to my feet to shout my agony, to cry out my grief, to deny my responsibility … my responsibility.

My chest is tight with pain, sobs racking my body as I fight to breathe.

I look at my wrists, my ankles, my body and see the shackles are gone.

What have I done?

Suddenly I'm afraid. I'm afraid of the torrential rain, the booming thunder, the deadly lightening.

I search for my bonds, but they are gone, washed away by the salty rain.

I listen for someone to tell me what to do but the thunder fades, leaving my ears ringing in its absence.

I look for a way out, but the lightening has blinded me.

I tremble in my effort to breathe, just breathe.

The sun slowly climbs in the east, bringing light, warmth, hope.

As I watch, I see the darkness give way to slivers of the soft, warm colors of life.

I marvel at the sight of golden sunbeams lancing through the dark thunderclouds, illuminating their crowns with brilliant light while their dark bellies still rumble and threaten.

I am awed once again with the beauty of life. I long to join the living, to share the beauty, to live ... to live.

My heart swells with possibilities. But then I remember … I am not alone.

My breath catches in my throat and for a moment, I forget to breathe.

I search the darkness until I find him, hunched and broken, bound by shackles and chains.

Darkness threatens to overtake me again as the sun fails to burn away the storm.

The wind whispers to me, "You cannot set him free."

My heart breaks.

Fight, I scream at him. Fight! But he turns from me in anger.

Fight, I plead to him, tears streaming. Fight! But he spits in my face.

Stunned and shamed, all I can do is breathe.

I realize in the impending gloom that I cannot help him.

I cannot break the dark bonds that tether him to this lonely place.

I cannot break the bonds he, himself, created.

The wind whispers to me, "Only he can set himself free."

Stay with me, he begs. Don't leave me here in the darkness, all alone.

I immediately move to sit next to him, to comfort him, but catch myself.

I remember now as I stop to breathe.

Each time I stoop down to comfort him, my shackles return, stronger than before.

The weight of the chains makes it nearly impossible to rise again.

It becomes easier to just stay down, stay confined, stay isolated … so easy.

But my head turns toward the rising sun. It hasn't moved any closer. So far away, yet it calls to me relentlessly. It would be such a long journey, a hard journey to reach that place.

Choose, White Hawk whispers as she soars overhead.

Choose, Grandmother Bear rumbles as she crosses the night sky.

Choose, echoes my heart as I struggle to breathe.

Years roll by as I stand frozen, unable to forsake one I once loved, one still in so much pain.
And yet, I am unable to stop looking towards the horizon at dreams of what might be.
I have broken my chains, yet the scars remain.
I am no longer bound to him, yet the tendrils of connection still reach out for me, clutching, grasping.
I am afraid. I know I want freedom over bondage, I want light over darkness, happiness over anger, but I'm afraid of what it will cost me to leave, of what it will cost me to stay.
I wait and I breathe, just breathe.

Deborah S Juckes

CHAPTER 27
(2008) NEW RESPONSIBILITIES AND THE SAME OLD GAME

My job changed when the yields supervisor, Paul, retired with very little notice. His job was split up. The inventory part went to one of the guys in finance, Abacus, and I became the clerical supervisor. Once again, I had to sign a sheet agreeing to take on the new job. I would now be doing my normal job and supervising thirteen clerks across the refinery. I also would NOT get any pay raise for the additional responsibility. Again, I signed the paper.

Things went along this way for a while. Eventually, Curt received a promotion to a salaried position (obviously before his retirement). We were the same pay grade, but he got significantly more money than I did. This didn't seem right, or fair to me. I had been salaried for years now, had received some higher ratings, and was a supervisor with direct reports. It seemed logical to me that I would make more money than someone just starting in the salaried ranks would. I went to HR and asked for an explanation. I was told that yearly wage increases had not kept up with entry wages and it wasn't just our refinery, it was a problem with a lot of companies. I reminded them that I now supervised thirteen employees and that I believed I should, at a minimum, be paid equal to my male counterpart, especially since he was not a supervisor. HR said they would look into it and get back with me.

I googled the problem and sure enough, several companies were struggling with the same problem. I waited patiently for over a month and then went back to HR. I was told they were still working on it. Several more trips to HR and I was finally told, sorry, that's the way it is. I would not get matching wages.

Although I knew I wasn't the only one to find myself in this position, according to Google, I wondered if I was the only woman in this position at our refinery. Surely not. I had no way of knowing because we're not allowed to discuss wages with other employees. I talked to my lawyer, and he suggested I carbon copy him on any future emails discussing my pay. I immediately sent another email to my HR contact, told him that his response to my wage discrepancy wasn't good enough, and of course added my lawyers email address that clearly had the law firm's name attached. Then I waited.

Eventually, I was summoned to HR along with my immediate supervisor. Well, shit, I'd done it now. There was no explanation, just come to HR. This is how they normally terminate an employee. I was glad to see that security wasn't waiting to escort me out. I sat down with my supervisor (Harry had moved on) and expected the worst. I was taken off guard, however, when they gave me a promotion. HR explained they couldn't just boost my wage, so they had to promote me to a higher pay grade to get me the money they thought I deserved. After all, they admitted, they hadn't given me any additional compensation for supervising the clerks. I told them again that I didn't want more, I just wanted equal. But, they said, this is how it had to be…sign the paper. It actually made sense. If I agreed to get the same amount as a male who wasn't a supervisor, I would still have grounds to bitch and moan. I signed the paper.

One thing that shocked me after this promotion was how much Curt would resent that I made more money than he did. What the hell?

I think forcing the pay issue was held against me for the rest of my career (by the management people in office at that time), preventing me from advancing. It is what the company calls retaliation but…. Prove it. That's just my belief. Nobody likes being forced to do something. In truth, I hadn't forced them, I was bluffing. I would never have gone so far as to take legal action. Not for this anyway. Why? I may not have been getting equal pay, but I was getting an amazing salary and I always appreciated that fact. Yet, I had hoped they would see an opportunity to do the right thing and act on it themselves. I also understood how this could turn into a huge financial issue for the company with the large number of people whose wages had slipped into those stinking cracks. They were trying to provide competitive wages to entice new people to the company at the cost of sacrificing the wages of their existing personnel. Since we weren't allowed to discuss wages with our peers, I would never have known of this discrepancy had it not been for my own husband getting his job. I wonder how many others were/are receiving below average wages simply because they've been in their positions for a long time. No wonder companies can't keep good help. It is financially beneficial to leave and go to work for a new company at competitive wages. It is sad because I would want to attract and keep people, by paying them for their loyalty of staying with the company. Admittedly, if the company had advanced my wages when I was given the job of supervising thirteen people (the right thing to do), we wouldn't have been in this situation and I would have been none the wiser.

Being a supervisor has one distinct responsibility. You have to be there to supervise. I still performed my yields analyst job, and I was the only person in the refinery that did this specific task. The data I provided was used for planning and several required government reports. The government reports were due at a specific time so I couldn't just take off a week and get caught up when I got back. I had previously started the bad habit of powering through my work to get caught up in four days, then I'd take a day of vacation on the fifth day. I did this because my supervisor would not designate a backup for me. Nobody covered my job when I was gone, even though the work had to be done. I also needed to burn vacation. Each week I'd bust my butt to get five days of work done in four days. At the time, I thought it was okay. I liked to be busy. I also liked the three-day weekend. Then I hit a snag. Once I became a supervisor, I couldn't just take off. I had to find someone to supervise the clerks when I was gone. It had to be someone familiar with the clerk's union contract and scheduling. They would only stand in as clerical supervisor; they would not perform any of my other normal work duties. Abacus normally filled in if he was available, but at times, it became a juggling act, as there was no designated backup for me. It was definitely an added weight on my shoulders.

Although I had my struggles, I was excited to hear I was getting yet another new supervisor and one that I knew. It was the manager I had done the benchmarking project with, Les. I carried on and on about how great this was going to be for our group until one of the clerks, Lola, got angry at hearing me rave. Let me tell you, ole Lola knew how to do angry.

Things didn't turn out exactly as I had expected. I was even more outspoken about standing up for others and had the belief that this boss of all the bosses would understand. After all, he was the one that had exposed me to all the best practices of how to treat people. Once we began working together, I realized we had different visions of leadership. For the most part, I was not included during non-work activities. To be clear, there were a lot of working lunches on site. However, the group took numerous off-site lunches. There were a few times I was invited to join in for lunch and had I thought any of the invitations were sincere I might have gone. I was beginning to see the advantages and disadvantages of not participating any chance I was given. I was also seeing that Les had a much different relationship with his engineers than he had with me. At least, that was my perception. I also understand now that my own anxiety of being around new people and public places could have done me harm. My immediate response was always "no" in my head. I tried to stop my mouth from speaking before I had time to mull it over and make a rational decision.

I had worked the yields analyst job for some time now and during all that time (years) there was the issue of me not having a backup for vacation coverage. Although (in the early years) the initial thought was that Rudy would help, he was always given first choice of vacation. Every year Rudy would take Christmas, even though his religion didn't celebrate Christmas. I did suggest we should maybe swap holidays each year, but he declined and I was not given a choice. Plus, he wasn't around much longer before leaving the company. His replacement, Kary, did train on my job but due to numerous technical difficulties, I'm not sure he ever successfully was able to work the job. As I mentioned, I had gotten into the habit of just taking off on Fridays to use up my vacation. With the extra workload of supervising the clerks, it had become more of a struggle to get five days of work done in just four days so I could take off on Friday again. Most of the time I did work at home to get caught up. I brought this up to my new boss, Les, several times and even pointed out that all the rest of the team had someone trained to replace them so they could go on vacation. Like real vacations, not just one day but also a whole week. This is how the repetitive conversation got started about how important my job was…or wasn't. As you know by now, my work supplied data for planning and reporting, including required government reporting. Every time I tried to justify my job and its importance, Les said we needed to look and see if we could do away with my job. Just to twist the knife a little, he put me in charge of figuring out how to do away with my own job. Every discussion, every belittlement from my supervisor, added to the weight of the proverbial straws building up on my back.

There was no doubt that a glowing ember of resentment began burning brightly that day. One of my many failings was my inability to hide my feelings. In spite of that, I always do what I'm told no matter how badly it hurts. I talked to the others in our group and to our finance guy, Abacus. Although there were programs being used by other plants, the fact remained, we needed the data for government reports, and nothing had yet proved as comprehensive as our current program. The hatchet still hung over my job and over my head. This is truly a horrible weight to bear, and it chafed and cut into me every damn day.

Since it didn't look like I'd immediately lose my job, I turned back to trying to find a backup so I could take vacation. Les had made it clear that the engineers in my group had too much work to do to cover for me. Oddly, they didn't have too much work to cover for each other. My job was closely intertwined with the yields clerks and as I mentioned earlier, one of them, Lola, had actually done the yields part of my job when it was first installed. The light finally came on in my head. Since my boss wouldn't commit one of my coworkers to cover my job, I could train one of the clerks. Lola had already turned down the job, so I spoke to Lucy instead. She seemed interested and agreed to train/work the job if the company could reach an agreement with the clerical union. This was no easy feat. It was common practice in the refinery for union folks to temporarily cover salaried positions. The clerks had their own union (apart from the refinery group) so I had to negotiate with them on how to make this work. We did come to an agreement, but it was pretty devastating to me. Devastating, but better than nothing. In order to get a clerk to cover my job, I had to let all thirteen clerks pick their vacations first. I had significantly more seniority than most of the clerks but of course, none of that mattered in this situation. It was just one hell of a slap in the face that I had to let every clerk, all the way down to a clerk I had just hired, pick their vacation before I was allowed a selection. Of course that would mean I would rarely, if ever, be able to take off on a major holiday.

This became a common rant for me each time I met with Les. I had once truly respected this guy. Yet now, I couldn't understand why the rest of our group was allowed to cover for each other and yet my only option was taking the vacation days the clerks didn't want. I didn't understand why I had to be treated so exceedingly different from the rest of the group. Did not having an engineering degree earn me such disrespect? Was it because I was so much older than the young, up-and-coming engineers? Was it because I was fat and wore biker boots? Was I being discriminated against or was that just my perception?

Les eventually came up with the idea to have a contract engineer, Starling, cover my job. She happened to be a friend of his, went to the same church, and he thought she would be a good fit. He explained that if Starling wasn't on vacation, I could ask her to cover. I directly asked him to clarify his statement. Was he saying that even a contractor would get to pick their vacation before I did? Weren't contractors there to support the company? His response was, "You got a problem with that?"

Hell, yes, I've got a problem with that. I was a company employee with nearly forty years of service. How could this be fair? First, the clerks were given priority and now a contractor? Another straw was added to the weight I was now struggling every day to carry.

I wasn't ready to give up the fight just yet but looking back I realize a plan started to form in my mind. I still had my retirement goal and now I began to think about what I wanted to accomplish before that day came. I wasn't ready to retire, but my plan would take some time to implement.

In the meantime, I made a few attempts to bid on different jobs. I applied again to become an OLMC. After they selected someone else for the job, they explained to me I didn't get it because I had never been a production supt and everyone has to be a production supt before they get an area OLMC job. Sounds like a familiar argument, right? I was able to show them documentation where I had indeed worked as a production supt, but it was too late. They had already made their decision and notified the man that got the job. If they were going to lie to me at least they could come up with something more believable.

CHAPTER 28
(2011) THINGS THAT WILL FUCK YOU UP

Jumping tracks a bit but I need to wrap up my troubled relationship with my mother. I feel it's a part of my story I need to tell.

My mother, who was once so happy, energetic, and fun to be with, became an extremely negative person full of anger and hate. Since Mom didn't share her thoughts with me, I don't know what all it was that pushed her in that direction. I know the divorce was devastating financially and I know she loved my dad at one time. He was the one that asked for the divorce and boy did he bungle that, having brought home pictures of a woman in Thailand he was shacked up with. Mom also suffered through the loss of her mother and finding out things about her childhood that she never shared with any of us. When Grandma died, it set off another traumatic event that turned my mother against Steve and me. I had to convince Mom to go to the funeral. I bought the plane ticket to California for her, but Mom had the same social anxieties I suffered from and argued to stay home. During that argument, Mom was trying to think up any excuse not to go and said that she and Grandma had never really gotten along. I was shocked but for the most part, I thought it was all bullshit. I thought it was just another excuse to not face her fears. Steve on the other hand, was deeply, deeply hurt. He loved our grandmother, just as I did, but he didn't seem to have any compassion left for Mom. He essentially wrote her off that day, turning his back on her.

As Mom got older, she suffered from COPD and congestive heart failure. Out of five kids, Steve and I were the only ones still living nearby and could help her when she needed it. Steve would always help if I asked, but he'd gotten to the point where he wouldn't offer anything. I did what I could for her, what she would allow. The only time I lost patience was over computer stuff. I still think Mom did some of that crazy shit just to force me to come to the house so she would have someone to talk to. I wish she'd just invited me over for coffee and a chat instead of screwing up the computer all the time. I mean, seriously, how can you lose your entire email address book again, and again, and again? I'd try to spend time with her and visit but I really didn't care anything about the crap she watched on TV and that's all she seemed to want to discuss. I do understand more now and wish I'd been more patient. I wish I'd listened to anything Mom wanted to talk about while I was attempting to fix her damn computer. I know now because I sometimes wish my family would spend a little more time visiting with me.

Then one day, as fate (that bitch) would have it, Mom and I had a real discussion. I'd always tried to be respectful and nice to my parents or any elders. I never wanted to hurt anyone's feelings. Mom began asking questions that I couldn't answer honestly without hurting her. She was sad and lonely one second and then bitterly hateful towards everyone the next. I tried to encourage her to reconnect with her longtime friend, Carol, but she'd even grown to hate her. I think she was very jealous of Carol because all of us kids adored her. Carol was the most loving, happy person I've ever known. Mom raged on. Finally, as gently and compassionately as I could, I told Mom the truth. I told her that she didn't treat people well, that she was mean and negative about everything. I suggested that if she would just try to get along, it would all be so much better, with friends, with family. Maybe she would even be happier. Mom refused to look at me. She just said something like, "Well, there just isn't anything worth living for then, is there?"

Mom called me the next morning and said she was having trouble breathing. I jumped in the car and sped to her house. When I realized how bad she was, I called an ambulance, shocked that she had not made the call herself instead of calling me. She had terrible pain in her right shoulder (I know, it is backwards from anything I've ever heard). Her breathing terrified me. It was one of the most horrendous things I've ever witnessed, watching her gasping for breath, fear in her eyes as she tried in vain to suck in life saving oxygen, pain wracking her body. As the paramedics loaded her up, I started calling the family.

The local hospital confirmed it was a heart attack. They explained Mom had the "widow maker" and had given her an extremely large dose of the necessary medicine. Either the meds would help, or she would die. When Steve got to the hospital, I told him he had to go in to see her and to make sure and tell her that he loved her. Thankfully, he did. Mom was soon flown by helicopter to the heart hospital in Oklahoma City. It took us two hours to make the drive and by then Mom was sedated but she was still troubled. She said she was scared, so I told her to close her eyes, and I would tell her a story. Mom was a tomboy just like me and in her early years had loved riding and showing horses while living in California. I told her a story, taking her mind from the hospital room and putting her back on her favorite horse. I showed her how beautiful it was, unfolding the sights, sounds, and smells in detail. I talked low and soft, holding her hand. I did my best to help her feel the salty ocean breeze on her face, the warm sun on her skin. I reminded her of the gentle rocking motion of the horse as she rode along the beach, gulls cawing in the distance as the waves washed ashore. When I was done with the story, she was breathing easily. One of the nurses came in and said she'd never heard anything like that and hugged me.

Nurses allowed just a couple of us at a time to be with Mom. I left the room to let the other kids see her. When it was my turn again, she was in and out, but I told her I loved her. She smiled and said she was so surprised and so happy when Steve had come in and said that he loved her. She told me this several times, and

I was happy for her. One time she did respond with an, "I love you too," and I told myself to believe she knew she was saying it to me.

Doctors gave Mom more meds and an angiogram. They told us she was in the clear. I knew she wasn't. I stood there and watched her fading away. Literally. The color left her face, her body, and her hair. Another doctor came in and told us they had reviewed all the tests, and that Mom should be just fine. Steve, Diana, and I decided to go ahead and make the two-hour trip back home even though I knew we shouldn't, but I didn't say it out loud. Dotti, Charley, and Jake lived in OKC so we knew someone could be there if she needed anything. We were just coming into sight of the refinery when I got the call, the one I had been waiting for, the one I knew I would get. Mom was gone.

One of our cousins, Susan, came to town for the funeral and told us something about our mother that Mom had known for a long time. My mother was never sure who her biological father was, but we knew that. What we didn't know was that Mom's mother had been married to a German man who decided to use her as collateral in a poker game. He lost. Susan told us that Grandma was raped and got pregnant from that encounter. Grandma left town, went to California, and my mom was born. Mom didn't even know any of this until she went to her own mother's funeral and was told the story. My mother kept that secret for twenty-two years, never telling any of us, never sharing her grief, her anguish, her thoughts. Instead, my mother built a fantasy where she talked about her mother having had this wonderful affair with a Native American man, which I thought, explained Mom's beautiful long, dark hair and slightly olive complexion. She even used the name, Sioux, in her artwork in place of her real name, Sue. It was a fantasy that I fell for hook, line, and sinker. So much so that I legally changed my middle name from Sue to Sioux and eventually took a DNA test, then a second one. If there was any Native American blood, I didn't get a single drop of it, although I can say I do have a trace of African blood that nobody knew about.

As my mother learned the secret when her mother died, so I learned it when my mother died. I hated thinking about how this might have affected Mom all those years. I couldn't understand Mom not talking to her family. Was she ashamed? Was she sad? I'll never know. I struggled to handle the grief of her loss, the agony of her past.

We went to my mother's home to clear her belongings. Her landlord was wonderful to us, telling us to take whatever time we needed. We didn't take advantage of his generosity but instead wanted to wrap things up. I've seen families before that turn into monsters when a member dies, fighting over material things or money. Our family wasn't like that. We easily agreed what to do with everything and Diana did a great job in settling the finances.

There was just one snag. It was between me and my cousin Susan. As we packed up belongings, I decided I wanted to go into Mom's closet and go through her clothes. She was always so proud of her clothes. She didn't have much money so many of her clothes showed a lot of wear and careful mending. She also loved perfume. To go into her closet, surrounded by the familiar clothes and the subtle aroma, was like being hugged by Mom. I thought I might even save a blouse or two for myself for days when I needed to feel close to her. Susan, however, decided it wouldn't be good for me to put myself through that. I argued and argued, stopping just short of shouting and raising holy hell. My mind warred with wanting to tell her to get the fuck out of my mom's house and not wanting to make a scene. After all, she had come to help, all the way from California. I appreciated that, and I knew her intentions were good, but she wouldn't fucking listen to me. I couldn't make her understand how badly I needed that time alone in the closet, surrounded by my mother. She didn't relent, and I didn't want to make a scene, not on that day, not then. I have to admit, I hated her for that, and it took me a long time to let that go. At least, I'm trying to let it go.

Once again in my life, I didn't fight. I just walked away. I was angry, hurt, and totally lost. I ended up in Mom's spare bedroom and began cleaning out her desk. I took the time to look through everything to make sure there weren't any legal papers or mementoes I should keep. That's when I found two sheets of paper with Mom's handwriting. She had such beautiful handwriting. It was a list. Two full pages, front and back, of everything she hated about me. It was a list of every mean, hateful thing she had wanted to say to me but hadn't. I read every word. That evening, I tore the paper to shreds before burning it. I refused to keep it and punish myself with it. I did want to remember though. Remember not to kill myself with negativity, to not turn away from friends and family. I do have the tendency towards negativity, but it is so much easier to recognize and walk away from now. I simply tell myself I don't want to be like Mom.

I look back on my final day with my mother. I remember that last discussion. I clearly remember how softly she spoke the words saying it just wasn't worth living. You might think I'd even go so far as to blame myself for her death. But I don't. I was not responsible for my mother's thoughts and feelings. I had not treated my mother cruelly. Her happiness was not my responsibility, nor her hatred. My mother chose her thoughts, her feelings, her self-isolation, and loneliness. She chose her hatred. I do not take that burden, that responsibility onto my shoulders. I do wish I could have helped her more. Only she could choose to make her life worth living, or not. I hope someday we meet again, and her heart has healed.

CHAPTER 29
(2014/15) DOUBLE THE WORK, DOUBLE THE FUN

I had a tremendous challenge when we decided to upgrade our yields software. The software that Les continued to insist we didn't need—along with my job. I really enjoyed this type of work. It was extremely satisfying being in on the start/build of a new system. Although it was basically the same program, a refinery model, it had to be revised from the ground up to represent our refinery. We had a contractor that rebuilt most of the model, but then I had to clean it all up and make sure everything was functioning correctly. We were also able to get rid of any unnecessary data, streamlining the yields system. I had tremendous help from various sources to validate what data was accurate. I then happily deleted the unnecessary dead weight. We also had a team that worked on reporting and many other issues. Special thanks go to my "almost replacement" engineer, Kary, and our finance guy, Abacus. You guys rock! I'd also like to give extra thanks to Abacus. He was my information source. He remembered damn near everything and bailed me out many, many times. I also used that poor guy as a sounding board whenever I was stressed out about something. I wasted hours of his life bitching and moaning about everything. It wasn't a waste for me though. Abacus helped me see the big picture, helped me see things more clearly, and gave me balance. There were just so many times that I needed to vent, to release some tension or anxiety. He listened to it all. I really can't thank him enough. Keep this in mind if you have a bitch and whiner you work with. I understand this behavior gets old quickly. Take the opportunity to share your wisdom. Not all of us are born smart. If you recognize it as a need to vent, maybe you can have the patience to listen and allow them to get their panties out of a wad and relax. If they just won't stop bitching, ask them what it is they are trying to accomplish. You could even suggest they go away and think about it. Trust me, it works.

One thing the upgrade didn't do for us was provide a system to get data into the model. To do this, I built some new spreadsheets that were simplistic and easily updated. I even included instructions on one tab just to prove how much I wasn't going to be like Rudy. It was during all this work that I was finally able to replace the very last of the Rudyware spreadsheets.

We started testing the model software, and I did my absolute best to break it. I was good at that. Then I worked with the contractor to repair any issues. Once we had things working fairly well, I developed training slideshows on how to operate the new system. Although it was similar to the previous software, it took very different steps to get the same results, so it wasn't always intuitive. I started getting calls from IT and other yields analysts at our sister refineries asking for help. To keep me from spending too much time working on the issues, IT recorded one of my training sessions. I still got a kick out of training and helping other people.

We were still running the original program, but now I was running the new model simultaneously in order to build up the database. Our new reporting system wouldn't be able to access the old historical database. Since it was early in the year, I decided to build and run all the days from the first of January so that we would have a full year of data and year-end reporting would be easier.

Needless to say, my workload increased tremendously. In order to get all the work done, I bought more equipment and set up a dual screen office at home. I enjoyed the work, so it wasn't a big deal. Sure, it cut into my time playing World of Warcraft but running the model was almost as much fun as computer games.

It was a benefit to run both systems for as long as I did. Having the historical data already from the old system, I could run the new system and compare the two. It enabled me to root out any discrepancies and validated the accuracy of the new model. By the time our test run was to be complete I was feeling reasonably comfortable. We set a "Go Live" date.

As with many plans, things didn't work out quite as easily as they should. There were delays but no big issues, then more delays. All I had to do was keep working both programs. I ended up working seven days a week for a very, very long time. I worked like this for a year, actually. I was happy that I did all my overtime at home in my frumpy clothes and my dogs nearby. Nevertheless, it was a struggle.

I was surprised when even Les had to admit I had exceeded expectations. I received an above average rating that year. Not much above but the fact that they even moved a little was appreciated. Especially since all the overtime and work had been my idea. I wanted to make things as perfect as possible. I wanted the monthly and yearly reports to be easily accessible by the numerous people that used them. Nobody asked me to do this and thankfully, they didn't tell me I couldn't. Oh, and just in case you're not aware, salaried employees like I was don't get paid for overtime. We were supposed to be compensated with time off, but I normally didn't have anyone to cover for me so having more time off didn't really help me. After my efforts were recognized, I did feel my shoulders slump a little less, and I think I grew just a little taller.

I did still struggle with not feeling like a part of our team. It had been quite some time since I attended the two shift meetings with the rest of my work group. I was the only member of our team that wasn't allowed to attend. Instead, I listened to the meetings via conference call but wasn't permitted to ask questions. Occasionally, I would ask one of the folks in our group to ask a question for me since all of them attended the meetings. That was humiliating. I even explained to Les that I had the attention span of a two-year-old and could not stay focused on the conference call. I never knew if I was excluded because I asked too many questions, because I liked to joke around, or because "they" (?) just flat ass didn't want me there. I had a very legitimate work reason for being at the meetings. Hell, I used to help run those meetings back when I was a production supt. I never could get an answer as to why I was the only one in our group that was excluded. It resulted in me having to spend more time searching for info. Whatever the reason, real or imagined, this type of exclusion hurts.

Les tried to help by inviting me to their planning meetings in lieu of the shift meetings. My work, however, was entirely based on the past, not the future. It didn't help me to know what we planned to do, especially with how often plans change. Instead, I needed to know what had actually happened. I had too much work to do to sit in a meeting that would not be beneficial to me. Yet, I still was not allowed to attend the shift meetings in person. I swear to you guys, I did shower every day. I washed my hair and brushed my teeth. I quit smoking a long time ago, so it wasn't the lingering odor of stale cigarette smoke. I just didn't know what it was. Even if the meeting room was crowded, my job was such that they should have made room for me. Hell, I wouldn't mind sitting in a corner. I was used to that, and granted, I was comfortable there. But even that wasn't allowed.

I finally decided that it wasn't important for me to go to the meetings. I'd come to realize that I now knew the model software so well that I could tell what had actually happened in the refinery even if they didn't want to admit it. I felt like Neo in the Matrix. Someone would report that operators had lined up a product to go to a specific tank. I could see in the model that they had actually made a mistake and lined it up to another tank for so many barrels, caught the mistake, and then moved it to the correct tank. Thankfully, that was a very rare occurrence. Occasionally, they might report no change in a tank gauge, and I would tell them to check again. Who would have guessed that gauge was wrong? Me, I saw it in the model. It was awesome. Granted, they did regular audits on their tank gauges and rarely did anything slip by the area operators. That was another great thing about our operations, all the checks and balances we had to prevent or catch errors.

I would like to make a note here. I've mentioned our yields clerk, Lola. She wasn't just a thorn in my side. (OMG she was such a big, painful thorn in my side!) One piece of her job was to gather data and enter it into my software program. I bow down to her, as the Queen of the Matrix. Where my model gave me visual indications of all the connected flows, meters, tanks, etc., Lola worked only with columns of numbers. Her brain must have worked just like the visual display of the Matrix. She would see the numbers and immediately catch erroneous data. She single-handedly prevented numerous potential operating or environmental disasters by catching bad tank gauges that were near to overflowing or incorrect lineups. She was amazing. I have no idea how she did it but then, she was the nearly forty-year employee and had been doing this particular job for quite some time. If anything happened to get past the eagle eyes of Lola, I would then catch it with my model. Again, checks and balances.

It seems to me the challenging employees like Lola, or me for that matter, are often the most passionate. We just have to learn how better to harness that passion instead of ignoring it, or worse yet, trying to snuff it out.

CHAPTER 30
(2015) FIND THE PASSION, FIND THE SOLUTION

As much as I loved my job, I had been looking for other opportunities within the company. I applied for a few jobs but did not expect to get anything. Then, my dream job opened up. It was the same position that I had worked as my first salaried job. The position where I received such a high rating because of my phenomenal, positive, upbeat attitude. I would be the only applicant with experience in the job. I would have the advantage of being able to prove the high ratings I had received working the job. There was no way that anyone could legitimately rate higher for the position than me. Or so I believed.

I filled out my application and was one of several called for interviews. I was prepared. I was no longer the shy, intimidated female that couldn't speak up for herself. When they asked me how I would improve things or what ideas I had for change, I mapped it out for them with several well-thought-out plans. I even had color handouts for everyone. Several folks in that room knew I had excelled at this job before, and they were impressed with my improvement plans.

I waited anxiously for bidding to close and management to make a selection. After an unexpected delay, I checked with HR and was told the bidding had been reopened.

I am going to try to make a long story short here. I was told that after the job was posted and the deadline had passed to apply for the job, that a member of management had instructed HR to reopen the bid so that his candidate, the previously mentioned production supt, Erick, could apply. A candidate who did not know the job, who did not want the job, and who was not competent to work the job. A candidate who had a bad attendance record and presumably, more than one report of racist or sexual behavior against him. A candidate whom I personally had reported to HR for offensive racist behavior.

Yes, Erick got the job. Then he was instructed to implement some of the plans that I had laid out for them in my interview. He even came to me for help. He not only came to me for help but also had the audacity to ask me to do the work for him. Not gonna happen, dude.

Management lived with their mistake for quite some time. It was a known joke about how Erick wouldn't show up for work. On one hand, I did feel sorry for anyone who was forced into a job they didn't want. I just couldn't understand why management would make that choice when you had someone else pleading to be allowed to do the job. Eventually, I just couldn't stand how poorly the job was being performed, and I made multiple offers to management to help. I did not make my offer directly to Erick as I didn't want him taking credit for my work. It didn't matter anyway; they didn't want my help or at least they didn't take me up on my offer. Much later, Erick was moved to a different job.

Forcing alleged poor performers to another job might be a way for a supervisor to be free of a problem. It is not, however, a solution. There are all kinds of reasons people don't fit in a job; personality conflicts, disinterest, dissatisfaction, maybe their heart just lies elsewhere. Instead of sloughing off problems, management should seek out passions. Find the passion, find the solution.

CHAPTER 31
(2016) ADDING CUBES TO THE LEMONADE

When we reflect, we tend to see crossroads much more clearly. I saw this pothole in the road from the very first day. This quiet, unassuming, disastrous day was the day that Les told me the clerks and I would have to move our offices. This was the beginning of my irrevocable careening down a long dark road. I freaked at the idea I was going to lose seeing the little tree outside of my office window. Les explained that he and the rest of our team were moving to the third floor and wanted to know where I wanted to move. He said he thought it was important that whatever I picked, I should stay with the five clerks who worked directly with me. I was given three options: the third floor, a set of cubes intermingled with a contractor group (they had strict rules around any type of decorations that could be displayed in their area), or a solitary set of five cubes and a cubbyhole office up by the training group. I told him my first choice would be the third floor with the rest of our team; the second would be the solitary set of five cubes. He immediately said he didn't think there would be enough offices for us all on the third floor. I argued that there were several contractors on the third floor and surely, some shuffling could be done to keep us company folks together. After all, the main clerks were long-time company employees, ten to nearly forty years of service with extremely important jobs. I respected the contractors but believed that permanent company people should be given preference over contractors that come and go.

Again, I was told the third floor with the rest of the group wasn't an option. So why had Les even mentioned it in the first place? He said that if I chose the cubes that we would make some structural changes such as installing temporary walls. I finally gave in and chose the area with the five cubes. I turned in my proposed updates for the area along with a printed layout depicting the requested changes. Many of our offices have temporary walls so I didn't think I'd been misled, but sure enough, we never got the changes implemented.

The cubes were temporary glass panels that were about six feet high with openings in place of actual doors. We were right next to a training conference room so it would get very noisy on some days. When it got too loud, we would ask them to turn it down and/or keep their doors closed. They said it would get too hot/cold if they did and rarely did they adjust their volume. It was also a high traffic area, so people were constantly walking through the halls talking, their (communications) radios blaring. There was no way to block out the noise. On the quiet days, you could hear the toilets flushing in the next-door bathroom. These were the only offices I knew of that were right next to the bathrooms. I ordered some noise-canceling headsets for all the clerks. I also let them pick out some beaded curtains to hang over their open doorways to provide an illusion of privacy and paid for those out of my own pocket. It seemed like a good idea at the time but eventually got a bit obnoxious, so we tied them back out of the way.

Figure 62 *The cubes.*

My office was a dank, dismal little closet across the hall from the cubes. I still had a window, which was nice. It reminded me of a window in a jail where it is set too high to see out of. It did let the light in, so at least I could appreciate the sky.

We started getting ready for our move by first having everything in the cubes cleaned including the floors and walls. It was disgusting. Then, we got a big surprise. Les informed me that we were not allowed to take our own office furniture with us, which was the common practice. We would have to make do with the furniture in the cubes. I argued with Les that this was not common practice, that anyone who has ever moved was able to take their furniture with them. He adamantly refused. He wanted our current furniture left for whomever would be filling our old offices. This was a perceived slight. It was like a splinter in your sweater that rubs against your skin. Maybe it was more like the weight of straws piling up on your back. I did get one exception during the furniture debacle. I was allowed to take my sit/stand desk (ergonomic issues). Les wouldn't even allow me to take my locking cabinet for my confidential files. Fortunately, I found a small file cabinet and asked our facilities guy to move it to my office (without asking permission). I wouldn't have taken the risk of defying Les, but our clerk, Lola, also happened to be the union president (refinery union) and negotiations chairperson (clerks union) and she'd already been riding my ass about having confidential personnel documents open to the general public.

This is a good place to talk about the relationship between Lola and me. You ever have one of those people that just seeing them makes your anxiety ratchet up? Someone who challenges you, fights with you, and constantly argues that you are wrong? Someone who insists it is night when the sun is at high noon? Someone who tells you, "NO!" before you even ask the question?

That would be Lola and me. She was the biggest pain in the neck. She could possibly have single-handedly given me ulcers. And, without a doubt, she taught me more than any other person in the forty years I was there. If I needed advice, Lola was the one I asked. I might not like the answer, but I knew she would tell me the truth, no matter how badly I didn't want to hear it. She would tell me the truth even if it was something she did not want to admit. It took blood, sweat, and tears to reach some conclusions but I always knew I'd be smarter for having dueled with her.

We didn't always agree. Hell, most times we didn't agree. Fortunately, I was smart enough to know when to admit she was right, and I was wrong. I don't remember Lola ever admitting she was wrong. Once, or maybe twice, I think, she conceded an argument. I might have just dreamed that.

We had a short deadline to complete the move. We packed up our supplies and computers (at least we were allowed to take our computers) and headed to the land of the forgotten, the dreaded cubicles. We were shocked to find that we had little or no available electric or network. We got creative with extension cords and had them strung over the tops of the cubes and hanging from the ceiling. We had work to do, and we could not wait for electricians. This wasn't just some supportive, backlog type of work the clerks did. This was crucial payroll, shipping, and inventories work. How the hell did they expect us to work without having electrical power? I was to the point where I wanted to pull out my hair and gnash my teeth, but of course, that wouldn't help anyone.

The clerical jobs were such that we were required to retain reports for auditing or government purposes. We therefore moved our multitude of reports and file cabinets with us. The twist here was—our file cabinets got real offices (two connected offices) with doors that locked while the people got the cubes. This storage area became our new "Cave." I talked to our facilities guy, and he was more than happy to smuggle us a nice settee to place in the Cave so that the clerks could find some privacy if needed to make a personal call. The cubes afforded no privacy at all. One of our clerks did payroll, and she often had phone calls discussing sensitive personal information. As many times as I used this fact to plead for real offices, it was denied. It was suggested instead that the clerk just talk quietly.

I argued with Les continuously about the move to the cubes. His common response was that everyone was in cubes at the main offices at Houston. I would remind him each time that we were NOT located at Houston, Texas. We were located in Ponca City, Oklahoma, where people had offices. Offices with doors. I don't remember if he specifically mentioned the hated lemonade or if it was just implied. I had no idea how he could justify treating us so differently from all other company employees at our site, just because cubicles were standard practice at a separate company facility (non-refinery) in another state. If that is how he wanted to play, let's look at all the different standards. In our best practices benchmarking, we visited one site where the union president and the company plant manager shared the same office! No, I didn't think our company should implement that philosophy. Just like I didn't think everyone in Ponca should move to cubicles because that's what they do in Houston. For me, it always came back to why we were treated so differently? This exceeded the addition of a single straw on the old camel's back. It was more like the equivalent of an entire bale. My frustration, my sense of helplessness, my righteous indignation grew with each look at those sterile cubical walls.

I know that during this time I failed as a leader. I had learned long ago as an operator that the team takes on the attitude of the leader. I didn't always promote the positive attitude we needed to be happy in our given circumstances. I was struggling so much myself, but I should have been better for my direct reports. I still joked with them and did everything I could to make them laugh. I love to make people laugh. I brought homemade snacks and food, and we even had our own chili cook off one time. I bought them t-shirts for the occasion. I should have done more by having a better attitude. I just couldn't stifle my despair with how my people were being treated. Were they being punished just because of their relationship to me? Surely, it wasn't because they were "just" clerks. This group was so important to the refinery. As mentioned, they handled inventory data necessary for all our jobs, payroll, and shipping. You just can't get more important than that, and yet there they were, stuck in these awful cubes and I was powerless to help.

I did come up with an idea to keep the clerks' spirits up, work on teamwork, and make some stinkin' lemonade. The walls of the cubes were made of glass with a metal frame and solid backing. I found a colorful picture of a barn and the surrounding hillside that was like a coloring book picture. I made a graph and broke the picture down into the same number of pieces as we had glass frames. I bought erasable markers and numbered the cube frames; there were somewhere around fifty to sixty. I called the clerks in and gave them a scattered section of the picture so that they would be working in different areas and different heights—the cubes were four frames high and varying widths between the "door" openings. Once they had finished the first five pictures, I gave them five more. They had no idea what the finished picture would look like.

Figure 63 *First cube art started.*

As they started filling in the empty spots between finished frames, they realized they would have to make sure their picture matched up with lines from the nearby frames. Finally, they got to talking to each other. They shared markers. They swapped frames if they had one that was too low or too high for them to reach comfortably. They shared best practices, and it was something as simple as how to hold the markers to prevent fatigue. They also discussed safety by making sure everyone kept their markers off the floor so nobody would step on them, or step on the clerk if they happened to be sitting in front of the panels. They also figured out who was best at drawing the bold outlines and who didn't mind the mundane repetition of filling in the big areas. Once they had enough pieces filled in, they started recognizing the barn, the trees, and the hillsides. They got excited when they finally understood what they were working for, what

307

their final goal was. Even though their jobs were very different, it took all of them working together to create their final masterpiece and they had fun doing it. With the picture complete, the cubes took on a completely new feeling. Maybe it was the slightest twinkling of home. I know they took great pride and ownership in their work.

Once the drawing was complete, we had a meeting and discussed everything we had learned through our process. It took quite a while to finish the drawing. After all, they did have real jobs, and they always prioritized work before our team-building activity. I put together a PowerPoint slideshow outlining what we had learned as a team and as a leader, (how it helps to see the final picture or goal when starting a project). I tried to share our learnings with Les and other managers, but none of them was interested. They couldn't see how our drawing could have anything of import to share and was just a waste of time. I tried to explain to Les how we were finding ways to cope with being in the cubes and he didn't say we couldn't do it. I will point out that Les did try to support me in my out-of-the-box adventures and allowed me leeway in many things. However, I think he no longer appreciated my uniqueness or recognized what I could bring to the team. After all, it wasn't how he did things. But, that's just my perception.

Speaking of "out-of-the-box," we once had a town hall meeting with the company CEO, Greg Garland. Mr. Garland was a man who had come up through the ranks, quickly I might add. Of course, he didn't start as low as I was, but he did pay his dues. I had read some about his background and how he was ethical and did what he thought was right. What I liked even more, was how many times Mr. Garland made the reference of talking things over with his wife. Then he went on to discuss her thoughts and opinions. What this told me, is that he listened to his wife. I liked that.

During the meeting, Mr. Garland talked about his career and his "out-of-the-box" actions, etc. He mentioned having to fire some people who weren't handling things properly. Granted, the company did have a reputation for not firing salaried folks. They just moved them from one job of incompetence to another.

So, when it came time to ask questions, I took my turn and asked, "What is the most 'out-of-the-box' thing you've done?"

Mr. Garland did pause for a minute to think and then said it was when he fired the folks to get back on track. I was disappointed. I had expected so much more. I wanted more from this CEO, a man whom I had grown to respect. I believe what he did in firing those folks was guts, not out of the box. I wanted him to tell me he'd put a lowly operator on a high-level team to add diversity of thought to the group (kudos to Les). I wanted him to tell me that he'd initiated new people development training, a mentoring program that included even non-educated employees, was starting a company day care, or bring your dog to work day. I wanted him to tell me that passion was rewarded. I wanted something more. Still, I did not lose my respect for, nor my belief in Mr. Garland. He was young, maybe he'd do better next time.

We continued our team drawings on the cubes. We also had to start using permanent markers because people would run their fingers through the drawings, wiping off streaks of color. They often came by on night shift and really defaced the artwork. I have no idea why people would do this. As the clerks saw their work attacked, they were disheartened at times, but they would soon rally and fix the problem. There is something truly therapeutic in coloring. Let me reiterate—they did their jobs first. Most workers take an occasional break; hell, it is a requirement for the refinery hourly folks. The clerks did not have set break times. They did not go out to smoke. They did not sit in the lunchroom for breaks—or even lunch for that matter. They sat at their desks and worked. So, yes, I encouraged them to take a few minutes here and there to take a break and if they chose, to work on the cube walls.

Figure 64 These designs were based on the original artwork of Holly Kitaura. Please see her work at: https://www.hollyvision.biz

Figure 65 These designs were based on the original artwork of Holly Kitaura. Please see her work at: https://www.hollyvision.biz

Figure 66 *These designs were based on the original artwork of Holly Kitaura. Please see her work at: https://www.hollyvision.biz*

CHAPTER 32
(Post 2016) WHAT IS PERCEPTION AND WHAT IS REALITY

I continued to have my yearly reviews with Les, and of course, according to him, I couldn't hold a candle to the other members of my team. We discussed perceptions again, and Les reminded me it didn't matter what I did, it mattered how I was perceived. I did not get a response from Les however, when I asked him why it was only his perception that mattered and not mine. Each time we met, I continued to push for moving the clerks to real offices.

I should mention that by this time, I only had five clerks that reported directly to me, the five in the cubes. I still negotiated the contract for all thirteen clerks and worked union issues but the clerks in the refinery proper now reported directly to supervisors in their own areas.

I did what I could to make life in the cubes more tolerant. I bought each clerk an Iron Man mask so they could hide from onlookers in their open office if they chose. It was just a joke at the time but just recently, one of the clerks sent me a picture of two of them (jokingly) wearing their Iron Man masks. Cracked me up!

Figure 67 *Pepper & Lucy in their Iron Man masks.*

Each Christmas, the clerks would get presents from Santa Claus. Since they were union represented and I was salaried, I didn't want to do anything that might be misconstrued as favoritism or any other 'ism. So, I never bought them presents; Santa did. That's my story and I'm sticking to it.

The week of Christmas, presents would start appearing under their tiny Christmas tree. There would always be five presents. All five were the same item but a different design or color. It could be something small like Pez dispensers or some weird plastic bracelets that had flashing lights in them. Even the little items seemed appreciated. It was all for the fun.

During one meeting with all thirteen clerks, our group of five showed up with their flashing bracelets on. One of the area clerks asked what they were for and one of our clerks joked that they were GPS trackers so that I could monitor them. Our group got one hell of a laugh out of it, but I'm not sure whether the rest of the clerks realized we were just joking.

One year Santa brought stocking caps for our group. Not ordinary stocking caps, but ones that looked like different animals. I don't remember all the animals represented except for the unicorn. It had, of course, a single horn pointing up in the air from the wearer's forehead. The clerks donned their hats and walked up and down the hallways singing Christmas carols. As they walked into one engineer's office, he glanced up at the horn protruding from the clerk's hat and smiling, asked, "Are you happy to see me?" Ugh, men.

The clerks weren't above coming up with their own entertainment either. One clerk, Pepper, normally arrived hours before the others started showing up. She usually turned on the hallway lights, but, on this morning, she left all the lights off.

Do you remember I said the cubes were by the training center, and that it is a high traffic area? Well, the training center was just down from HR. Yes, this is leading somewhere.

Pepper hid in the dark cubes, knowing that Lucy would soon be arriving. One little "boo" from Pepper and Lucy ran screaming into the hallway. The hallway was empty except for the HR manager, a big dude named Russell, who screamed like a little girl and clapped a hand over his heart. Good thing he had a sense of humor. Yes, this was horseplay, and we could have gotten into a lot of trouble.

Oh, and we had snowball fights in the cubes. Santa brought some fake snowballs that really felt like soft packed snow. They even sounded like snow when you squished them. Fortunately, they didn't pack as hard as snow but were soft and fluffy but still weighty enough to give a good throw. Since the cube walls didn't go all the way to the ceiling, you could spot snowballs arcing up over the walls to splat on the clerk in the next cube. Snowballs

315

also shot out of the open doorways when innocent bystanders walked down the hallway.

Flashback: My brothers and I had many snowball fights over the years. Of course, Montana was the best. The worst snowball fight was in Oklahoma. I don't know if the last snowball to hit me was really hard packed ice, or if one of my booger-eating brothers had stuffed a rock into a snowball. The results were the same. The solid snowball struck me just above the forehead, about a half inch into the hairline. It split the skin open, and blood gushed out. Nothing seems to bleed quite as bad as a head wound. I still have the scar from that one too.

On the more serious days, the clerks and I took to drinking. They were just mocktails, but we had the appropriate glasses for our drinks—margaritas, mojitos, or beer. The beer mugs were double lined and had a golden liquid in between that was not only the color of beer but had a small head of foam on it too. They did keep your drinks cool, but since you taste with your eyes also, I never could drink from the damn things without my water or tea tasting like beer, and I don't like beer. The margaritas and mojitos though, they were good. We even caked the rims with sugar to make it look authentic.

One of the HR dudes, Owen, often interrupted our parties. We offered him a drink which he refused as he laughed, all the while looking over his shoulder. He finally couldn't stand it and asked if we surely, weren't drinking real alcohol because that just wasn't allowed. I insisted they were fake, but I also had the habit of always shaking my head the opposite of my verbal answer. If I said, "No," I would nod yes. If I said, "Yes," I would shake my head no. He skedaddled out of the cubes.

We really hated for anyone to be left out. We followed Owen back to his office, right next door to the HR manager. Then we loudly made a production of taking a drink in and setting it on Owen's desk. I have no idea if he had the guts to drink it or not.

So why make lemonade if you can have margaritas?

CHAPTER 33
(2016/17) SAY WHAT?

I continued to voice my angst with Les in our one-on-one sessions. I didn't hold back, even when it was directed at him personally. Les assured me that we had enough history and experience together that it would be a learning experience and that he appreciated the feedback. In fact, he always asked for feedback on his performance during those meetings. I eventually learned that he did not deal well with any negative feedback. I even pointed this out to him after explaining I would no longer offer feedback.

We had monthly staff meetings that the clerks and I attended along with the planning group and other engineers. Les normally ran those meetings and sometimes things went off the rails a bit. For instance, he once made an offhand comment about Asians taking touristy pictures and went so far as to mimic the actions. During the same meeting, he made negative references to a clerk working in one of the refinery unit areas. I was dumbfounded. Remember, this was the man who'd introduced me to leadership. He had included me in a team of people to learn the best practices of great leadership. I had once respected him and thought him to be a leader. I waited until after the meeting and went to his office to speak privately. I explained it was wrong to make racist remarks and that he should not air negative comments about another employee in front of a group. Again, he thanked me for my feedback.

I think it is safe to say my relationship with my formerly respected boss, Les, got a bit combative, verbally of course. I was still extremely frustrated that I could not get the clerks the respect they deserved. Then he said something that set me back. He asked if I was so angry with him that I wouldn't see any good he was trying to do. I believe one of my greatest emotional growths was being able to take information, put my personal feelings aside, and give all due consideration to the possibilities that I had missed something or maybe, I was just wrong. I thought about how angry I was, how angry I'd been for a long time, and realized it could be possible. I had such a bitter, gnawing ache in my stomach and heart that I could possibly just be angry, and my thoughts clouded. Was I giving him a fair chance? I really had respected him at one time. I realized that I had to let go of all my negative thoughts and feelings in order to view things fairly. I made a commitment to myself to be open-minded and give him a chance. I think I even wanted to be wrong about him, to respect him again.

I believe this way of thinking was one of my hidden super powers. I was good at asking myself, "What if..."

- What if I wasn't actively listening? Did I understand what was meant? Did I insert my own thoughts and feelings? Did I assume I knew what they meant?
- What if I missed something? Did I pay attention or was I thinking about what I wanted to say next? Did I need to ask more questions for better understanding?
- What if I am wrong? I have very strong opinions and feelings, but are they right? Am I giving the other person's view a fair and unbiased consideration?
- What if they are right?

I used the same type of strategy to prevent discrimination or favoritism type of thinking. First, let me say that I personally believe we are all prejudiced. Maybe our prejudice is prejudiced people. Maybe our prejudice is in favor of someone who has the same name as our beloved grandfather. Maybe our prejudice is against someone who favors the color blue, or looks like an ex, or likes cats instead of dogs. You get the picture. So how do we know that the decisions we make aren't based on our personal prejudices? It's easy. You just have to ask yourself. More importantly, you have to answer yourself…honestly.

- Would I make the same decision if the person had the same skin tone as me? Or a different skin tone?
- Would I make the same decision if this were a person I really liked instead of someone who is a bit more challenging?
- Would I make this decision for each person working for me?
- Would I make the same decision if I wasn't angry at this person even if I think my anger is justified?

Most of the time we supervisors make snap decisions based on years of experience. I believe we need to look at our decisions more closely and take the time to ask ourselves the prejudiced questions. Yes, it is okay to talk to yourself.

I want to go on a little more here about prejudice. I have a good idea how uneducated I have been, and am, about prejudice and racial tensions. I try to educate myself by researching and I can learn generalities, but I always keep in mind that every person is different and they perceive things differently. The first time I heard the term, "people of color," I was shocked. I had no idea that was an acceptable term. Being as old as I am, I remember different terms that were considered acceptable at the time but have since fallen out of favor. Now, I am educated enough that I wonder, whose favor? I want to be respectful, but I may inadvertently insult someone because I am unaware of what they personally consider respectful.

I want to do the right thing. I want to respect people. I do, however, have questions. The biggest question is why do we give so much power to specific words? Yes, I understand the hate behind some words. Only we can give them the power to hurt us though.

We can't stop people from saying hurtful, hateful words. So why don't we build our own personal power to protect ourselves from pain? Why don't we find more ways to teach our children to protect themselves from bullying and hate? My family raised me with the old, "sticks and stones" saying. It was a protective mantra that kids said to drown out things we didn't want to hear. It was supposed to teach us that words can't hurt us.

What if kids today used their strength of imagination to protect themselves? Technology and social media have opened the floodgates for unimaginable attacks. What if we use our imagination as armor? Armor that protects us from anxiety, fear, prejudice, or hate. I have. I am fixing to go way out in left field here, but bear with me. In my fictional novels, Grandmother, the gold dragon, has the ability to blow a calming dragon's breath that wraps you like a warm blanket, easing a troubled mind. In times of great stress or anxiety, I imagine a huge golden dragon with soft amber eyes. She blows out a gentle dragon's breath and I feel the warmth, the gentle weight. I feel my shoulders relax and my thoughts calm. I breathe in deeply, imagining the power of the gold dragon pulled into my lungs. Each exhale pumps the magic through my veins, lending me its strength. It is corny, I know that, but I always, always, feel somewhat better afterward. It is my form of meditation. Who says meditation has to be some formal guru, enlightenment kind of thing. Do what works for you. Use what you know; teach your kids to use what they know. Maybe they would don the imaginary, magical armor of T'Challa, the King of Wakonda. What if they could mentally call on the suit of Iron Man? Imagine yourself encapsulated in nuclear powered metal alloy with a cool British accented computer at your disposal. Never fear, we also have The Woman King, and if you remember, Pepper donned the Iron Man Rescue suit.

Now imagine that cruel, hateful words bounced off your imaginary armor and fall harmless and forgotten on the ground.

Wow, that would be cool. I know you guys are too grown up for this type of nonsense. I also think you probably imagined at least one of those scenarios. The cool thing is nobody has to know you do this. Do it for you, do it for your peace of mind, your protection, your—dare I say it—armor.

Even good words can go bad. I personally don't like the term, "Debbie Downer." It doesn't matter what word you use when you assign negative connotation with it. What happens if a popular influencer decides the word "bacon" means something hateful? Let's say "bacon" is the new "fat and ugly." Then, what happens when a server smiles and asks you, "Want some bacon with that big stack of pancakes?" Excuse me? You can wonder if she's calling you fat and ugly or you can say, heck yeah, bring on that bacon. I love me some bacon! Because bacon is just a word for a slice of delicious fried pork and doesn't have the power to harm you. Only you have the power to do that.

We can't stop people from using hurtful words. We can only change the effect it has on us. We have to stop giving words so much power to hurt us, to hurt our children.

With anything, there is the opposite side of the coin, the lack of words. As we know words may have the power to cause great pain, but words can also be used to heal. Combine kind words with an honest smile and you could change someone's life. How many stories have you read about a person who, at the last minute, does not commit suicide because of someone's kind words? One of the biggest things here is just taking the time to talk to people. Life today is so fast, so short. Take some time to share good words.

In learning to talk to others, especially people different from us, there are two phrases that I think carry a lot of power:

- "I don't know."—What if we admit to ourselves that we just don't know? Stop assuming we understand, that we know how people feel, what people want, or how people

323

need to be treated. What if we admit instead, that we don't know? It opens us up to the idea that we need to learn, to ask, to be open to others. What if we follow, "I don't know" with "Help me to understand."

- "What can I do to help?"—I can't count the number of times I just needed to feel like someone was on my side. I have been extremely independent and most often refused any offer of help. Nevertheless, it is an amazing reassurance to know that if you need it, someone has your back. I have always thought it takes a team to achieve the greatest results, but I've had to learn to let people help me. I feel it has made me more accessible. It has definitely made my life easier and better.

Too many times, I have stopped myself from speaking to people because I was afraid. What was I afraid of anyway? Hell, I don't know. Maybe I was afraid they would be irritated if I bothered them. Maybe they would laugh at me. Maybe I would embarrass myself by saying something stupid, which is undoubtedly something I will do again, and again, and again. But I don't stop trying. I've learned to start with a smile. I seriously have a resting bitch face. People are probably scared of my face. If they smile back, I say something small, something easy, like, "Good morning." I've noticed that many people will start chatting with me if I break the ice. Sure, I still accidentally say stupid stuff now and then because I haven't had a lot of practice with socializing. But I enjoy it. I've also noticed that folks start chatting with me more now that I look like someone's Granny. And don't get me started about the old men at the grocery store. But I still enjoy it.

Wow, I really took that train right off the rails. But some things I think are important to say.

CHAPTER 34
PERCEPTIONS, PERCEPTIONS AND PUTTING PAINT ON CANVAS

In spite of wanting things to be good between Les and me, it just didn't happen. I tried, I wanted it, but I felt that Les treated me as if I was so much less than the rest of the team. Remember, I not only went on what I saw, what was being done to my group, but Les himself was very forthright in his thoughts and opinions of me. During any discussion on wages, he reminded me that I would never be as important as the rest of the team. I argued but I don't think he understood my reference about "try to make dinner without salt." During performance reviews he told me what mattered more than what I did was the perception that he and others (a.k.a. senior management) had of me based on snapshots of my attitude. He told me that I was high maintenance because I took up too much of his time. He explained that these snapshots of me, these Polaroids, were used by others to gauge my value, my ratings. These people didn't know me. They didn't spend time with me. They were people I did not have a chance to influence. People who wanted a pretty picture instead of a documented history of good work. It was Les's job to represent me to "others" including senior management. After all, they only knew what they were told about me from these alleged snapshots they were shown. Since all this was so vague and I'd never seen any of these alleged Polaroids (yes, I know he didn't mean physical photos, that would just be weird), I asked a member of senior management for specific complaints against me and suggestions for remediation. I was told that my name had not even been mentioned during meetings with upper management. Humph, so where did the idea come from that I was in disfavor with upper management? I wonder.

Although Les complained that I was high maintenance, in reality, I was just begging for a crumb. All I wanted was a little honest acknowledgement or thanks for my work. That is why I endured so many things. I would get a small crumb here or there, even though I believed I deserved the whole cupcake. It was just enough to keep me pleading for more. (Very middle child syndrome of me. Oh, wait. I am a middle child.) That may be why I hadn't reported Les. I remembered and appreciated the few times he had actually seen me, had treated me with respect. Imagine how far I could have gone if given just a bit more of that respect.

In a later conversation, Les told me he'd heard a story from one of the upper-level managers. He was surprised to hear they had a pleasant experience and had enjoyed spending time with me. He refused to tell me who it was, and it didn't really matter to me. I was just curious if this person would have an influence on Les and make him cut me a little slack. As I reminisce, it could have been one of two people, and I'm hoping it was the former versus the latter.

The first occasion could have been when I went to a company approved concealed carry class. The training was promoted through the women's network, and I had a lot of fun. I was uncomfortable at first, going into the classroom not knowing who would be there. I did spot several people I knew and relaxed in spite of the fact I was carrying a 9mm pistol with me. I looked the crowd over and spotted one upper management person, Kara. I chose to be brave and sat down right next to her. We chatted and joked around during class and later, ended up side by side at the shooting range. I had the misfortune to be on Kara's right side. Every time she fired her pistol, the hot brass would be ejected out the right side and hit me in the chest. I was very thankful I was wearing a cotton shirt that didn't show any cleavage as the hot brass would have nestled right in there. As it was, the shells just bounced off my boobs. It did make it a little harder for me to aim, as I couldn't quit laughing.

I still maintain my concealed carry permit even though our governor has decided we don't need permits to carry concealed weapons. I disagree with this 100 percent. It's not the permit itself that makes the difference although the money you pay for it goes to great causes. It's the learning you get from the class. Everyone should be trained before being allowed to carry in my opinion. Did you know that it is not permissible to use a weapon to defend your property? It is permissible to defend your life or possibly the lives of others if you think you/they are in danger of losing their lives—but that's not a given. For example, if someone is stealing your car, don't shoot them. If someone is stealing your car and a family member is in the car AND their life has been threatened—you'll probably get away with shooting them if they are trying to run you over at the same time. But then why would you take the risk as your loved one is in the car? So many things to think about and no time to think. One thing I won't forget was when the instructor told us, "Never pull your weapon unless you fully intend to kill your aggressor." I wish everyone who owned a gun would attend one of these classes.

The second incident where a member of upper management might have enjoyed spending time with me could have been at one of my paint parties. I began hosting paint parties after my son, Jake, went to his first one. He said they had a lot of fun except there were some tight rules, such as, you only have so much paint and you have to paint the one picture the instructor picked out.

Figure 68 *John & Jake at a paint party.*

I began hosting parties where I supplied a ton of food and lots and lots of paint. I would also offer up five to eight different pictures for attendees to choose from and I would pre-sketch the design on the canvas for them if needed. I would also, however, be prepared to help anyone that wanted to paint their own design. I enticed everyone to attend the parties by telling them I would teach them the one big secret that would help them all become painters. People always waited so expectantly when we got started—they had to know the big secret. It's very simple, I told them. You have to put paint on the canvas.

That earned me many "duh" stares. But, over the next two to three hours I would show them how to use the paint, how to blend it, how to show their strokes, or how to hide them. You can't do this without using paint. You can't be shy about your paint—get it on the canvas. Most people act as if they are painting a house and trying to stretch the paint as far as they can—or they attended a class like the one Jake did where they could possibly run out of paint. I find the most interesting paintings are created when you aren't afraid to put paint on the canvas. It's not like I'm a great artist either. You don't need to be. Just relax and have fun. Painting is another very therapeutic hobby.

One party I did was for a family. The idea was that the family had to work together as the scene carried over from one panel to the next. It was a lot of fun to watch them work together.

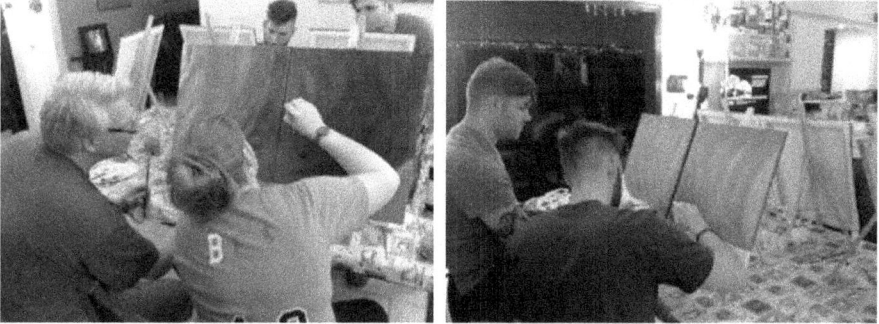

Figure 69 Family worked together to do a five-panel painting.

Another party was for a group of new hires and an upper-level manager, Pratt, was in attendance. It was the one and only time I instructed a party that I didn't host so I wasn't in complete control.

Several things went wrong that night. For the most part, it was fun even though we had to make do with the inadequate supplies we were given. I had fortunately brought some paint with me, or our large group would never have been able to finish.

For this group, I offered some sample pictures for them to try but I didn't pre-sketch the canvases. There were many impressive paintings that night. I wandered the crowd and offered suggestions as everyone painted…and snacked…and drank. There was one person, Kathy, in particular, who was having trouble with her painting because it was an original and didn't look like anyone else's. I kept encouraging her and told her I liked the colors she used and how she blended them together. The effect reminded me of something familiar, but I just couldn't put my finger on it. Finally, I got it; her painting looked like a tunnel through a copse of trees with all the shading and contrast. I loved it, but something was still missing. She continued painting, encouraged, but still seemed embarrassed by her freestyle work.

There was only one person that night that appeared to have imbibed a bit too much and that was our one manager, Pratt. That or he was just a total prick; maybe both. He finished his painting then took his wine glass and began stalking through the group, the group of younger engineers. Sure enough, he ended up gawking over Kathy's shoulder, as if she wasn't already self-conscious.

Kathy's painting was a bright upright oval of swirling greens and yellows surrounded by much darker, greenish, brownish streaks. Pratt stood over her shoulder and in the loud, obnoxious voice typical of someone who drinks too much, he proclaimed that he indeed, knew what it was a picture of and nudged Kathy's date, winking at him. They both stared at him, and he made more remarks that were suggestive.

Although I'd been across the room at the time, I saw that something bad was happening. I walked up during the last of the conversation and encouraged Pratt to move on. Kathy was really upset. She said that Pratt had insinuated that her painting was of a vagina. To make it worse, her date just laughed and agreed with Pratt.

As we wrapped up the paint party, I moved halfway up a staircase at the end of the room to take a picture of the large crowd. Everyone held their pictures up and that's when I realized what Kathy's freestyle picture reminded me of. It was so obvious from a distance. The only thing the picture needed was a shadowy form of an alien coming out of the bright oval. She was ecstatic when I told her, but we were out of time. She said she would finish it at home, but I don't know if she ever did. One thing I do know, she and her date went their separate ways soon after. Pratt, however, seemed to have really enjoyed himself that night but that was entirely due to the booze and his lack of manners, not to anything I had done. So, if this was the manager that associated me with a "good time," it was one of those situations where I was judged wrongly. If I had been in charge, I'd have taken the guy's keys, called an Uber, and kicked him out.

To be fair, Pratt did turn out a decent painting. That does prove what I believe, that you have to let go of your fears, your anxiety, your inhibitions, and let your creativity flow. That doesn't allow you to treat others disrespectfully, however. The same could be said for any work situation. Great instructors (Carlos), great training, should target reducing stress, not creating it. Hierarchical training groups don't always encourage free thought, free speech, or free actions. Sure, sometimes it is helpful, but it would be beneficial to gauge that before the training begins. If you don't, well then, it's on you when someone like me that can't keep their mouth shut…doesn't keep their mouth shut.

In spite of the fact that folks in upper management either didn't know I existed, or they actually enjoyed spending time with me, Les continued to insist that management held me in low esteem.

What is one of the worst things that can happen when you have a contentious relationship with your boss? In my opinion, it is when you have a personal health issue. Something that you need to share with your boss. Most health issues you can keep private or share with trained medical professionals. However, there are some things you may have to share, embarrassing as they are. I was sick and in such a way that I could still work but I could not come to work. Let me share a little back-story first.

My father moved back to New Mexico soon after receiving his cancer diagnosis. It was bad enough they told him there was nothing left to do but enjoy his final days. He did exactly that, and he documented it. He made several videos discussing his life, his work, and his experiences. We got DVDs full of pictures and videos. It was amazing. We also went to see him several times, and he didn't beat around the bush—he was dying and wanted to enjoy our time together.

My father was strong enough for both of us when I was with him. Alone, however, I struggled. I needed help. I found that help in the form of a fluffy, cuddly, Golden Retriever puppy I named Meesha. Her job in life was to help me through my heartache and she took to her job with gusto. The first day I brought her home I lay on the floor with her and couldn't quit sobbing as I thought about losing my father. She was there for me. Later, Meesha would come to my rescue when I overheated working in the yard. I staggered into the shower and turned the cold water on, slumping against the wall and sinking to the shower floor. Curt came in and wanted me to tell him what to do but my mind wasn't working. He kept trying to turn the water to warm, saying it was too much of a shock and I cried for him to leave it cold. He opened the window to let the AC cooled air out and then he left me sitting in the shower stall. Meesha wouldn't leave though. She pushed past Curt and came into the shower with me, sitting beside me. Every time I started to fall over, she would put her nose under my armpit or against my head and push me back upright. Water streamed from both of us as we sat there. I obviously survived, but I still struggle with the heat.

Meesha got old, as we all do. Her final day we lay on the floor together again and I sobbed at the thought of losing her. A week after Meesha died, I got shingles. The doc said that stress could bring it on. The blisters and swollen red rash ran from my spine, across my ribs, and just under my breast. The pain is unbelievable. It is not just a surface skin pain either. It is as if your insides are being torn apart. I wish I had never seen the *Alien* movies, but that is exactly what it felt like. Like a monster was deep inside of me, tearing its way out. I honestly thought all my internal organs were about to explode.

I didn't want to miss work because of shingles. I didn't have anyone to cover for me and working might take my mind off the pain. One big problem—I couldn't wear a bra. I don't know about you ladies, but I didn't like to be seen without a bra when I was young and skinny. I really didn't want to go to work unprotected now that I was old and fat.

My bosses had allowed me to work from home before—many times. Especially if I took a vacation day on Friday but still had to do my work. All I had to do was ask Les to let me work from home until the blisters and rash were under control.

I might have been embarrassed during that conversation with Les but instead, I got pissed. I tried to give as little health information as possible while requesting to work from home. Les pushed for more personal information. Fine, I thought, let's see who gets more embarrassed. I explained I could not wear my bra because of the rash and blisters across my back, ribs, and under my breasts. I also doubted that he nor anyone else would want to see me that way. Les explained he couldn't set up a new precedence of allowing me to work from home. I reminded him that working from home wasn't anything new. I did it all the time since I didn't have a backup. I also asked why he allowed one of his engineers to work from home when they were on long-term illness. He explained their illness was "..." (he did share the diagnosis) after all, and he stood by his decision. Les suggested that if I wanted to receive special treatment, I would have to get an order from medical.

I went to see our physician's assistant, PA, at medical and William was great. I'd always enjoyed working with him and he always did his best to help. I explained the situation, and he asked to see the blisters, which I showed him without any embarrassment. He felt bad for me but said, unfortunately, it wasn't his place to determine whether I could work from home or not. It had to be my boss's decision. I was a bit flummoxed. I asked William to document the fact that I had a condition that would temporarily keep me from coming to work. He was happy to do that.

I took the document back to Les and again asked for permission to work from home. I reminded him I was going home either way. I could keep my work caught up at home or he could find someone to do it while I was off sick. He finally agreed.

Health Insurance Portability & Accountability Act, HIPAA, is a federal law that protects sensitive health information.

As unwilling as I was to share my own health information with Les, I was even more protective of the clerks' information. The company and the US government have rules in place, such as HIPAA, to protect employee health information. Our little group had suffered several personal issues. I did my best to work with the clerks to handle each situation carefully and with respect to their privacy. A situation arose where one of our clerks went on extended sick leave. During one of my meetings with Les, he asked what was wrong with the clerk. I reminded him that HIPAA protected that information and that I could not give him details. The next time we met, Les said that he had checked and since he was my immediate supervisor, it was not a violation of HIPAA for me to divulge the clerk's personal information. I still refused. Since rules and regs can be confusing, I checked with our EAP (Employee Assistance Program) director. She adamantly upheld the HIPAA regs and told me not to share employee health data with anyone, not even my supervisor. Even the rest of the clerks were grumpy about not being able to wheedle health information from me about their coworkers. I am not sure where Les got his information or who had misled him, but I was going to follow the rules I knew to be accurate. This seemed to irritate Les quite a bit, but maybe that was just my perception.

Things came to a head for me not long after recovering from shingles. I felt like I couldn't take one more perceived injustice. I compiled a list of grievances and went to HR. I was prepared. I had notes. My major complaints were basically around being treated differently than my coworkers, the lack of vacation coverage, and the clerks being in cubes to name a few. I spent four hours with the HR manager, Russell, going over my complaints and specific incidents.

Eventually, HR notified me that the company would not do anything about my complaints. They had contacted Les about our discussion and Les informed them that vacation coverage for me wasn't an issue. We just had to come up with a plan (I don't know how many fucking plans he had already refused or ignored). HR also informed me that Les said that the clerks would not be moved from the cubes.

The next time I heard about my complaint to HR was during my next annual review. Les discussed how I had wasted four hours of Russell's time complaining. He asked why I had talked to Russell about not having vacation coverage. He asked if I thought Russell was going to cover my vacations. He then suggested maybe I should just take vacations around when work needed to be done. After all, if someone had to cover my work, then they would have too much work to do, and they needed to be free to do their important work.

I reminded him that I was a clerical supervisor and as such, could not contractually leave that part of the job uncovered. I ran inventory balances for every single day of the year. I also provided data for government reports twice a week, and the monthly inventory closing. Not to mention payroll closing for my direct reports. So, when exactly was I supposed to take off?

Les told me to come to him with solutions, not just problems. I point out that I always brought solutions but that he didn't find any of them adequate. I explained that my job would actually be easier if I got support in getting information from the multiple sources available. One report in particular, I could only complete after the production supts entered data into the spreadsheet. On one occasion, they fell way behind, and I was unable to run the reports until I had their data. He accused me of being unable to get along with the production supts. I was stunned and asked where he had heard that complaint. I asked if there had been complaints I could address and he said no, he hadn't heard anything negative about me from anyone. He said it was just his perception. He reminded me that I was being judged from these snapshots. I really didn't know how to improve my relations with someone else when it was only my boss who perceived the relationship as being poor.

I have pondered the whole perception thing. I can easily see how I gave out certain vibes. I really tried to respect and get along with everyone but not to the point of giving up my beliefs. If something was wrong, I sought to correct it.

So how do you change perceptions? I believe you have to find your voice. You have to get past being shy, being quiet and afraid. You have to be true to who you are and speak up for yourself. People will never get to know you if you hide from them. Most important—don't let people learn who you are from someone else's possibly biased opinions.

I often thought how easy personal interactions would be if I could hide behind a costume or mask. If I could pretend to be someone else. Then put my mask on and play the part. The more you practice speaking to people, the easier it gets. Yes, you'll probably embarrass yourself more than once. I have a big problem with saying the stupidest stuff and at the worst times. I don't mean to. I don't want to. But damn, it's crazy the shit that falls out of my mouth. It's as if my brain really doesn't have control over my mouth. But guess what? Time didn't stop. The world didn't end. I didn't get eaten by sharks. You won't either. Take several deep breaths, relax your shoulders, hold your head high, and try again. Most importantly, go easy on yourself. Learn to laugh at yourself. Be a duck. Let the unwanted stuff just run off your back. Eventually, people will get to know you. Maybe they'll think you're an oddball. Maybe they'll think you're an oddball with a great work ethic, an out-of-the-box imagination, an asset to the team. They don't have to like you. But let them know you. Let their perceptions of you be based on you and not some jibber jabber someone else spouts.

Les wrapped up the review by saying he would like to help me find a job at another refinery. I told him I didn't want to leave Oklahoma and go to another refinery. He said he thought it would be best. I could start over. I could almost feel those straws being laid on the pile. The weight was becoming unbearable.

My discussion with Les felt like company retaliation. I had to decide whether to take it beyond our local HR. Especially since the HR manager, Russell, had so obviously taken my complaint made in good faith, and allowed my boss to use it against me in determining my wages. I considered my options and once again, did not stand up for myself. I just did not want to be "that" woman.

Our HR manager, Russell, left the company not long after this. I wanted to be sure and tell him goodbye and congrats on his new job. I told him I was sorry I never got to work for him. Sure, he had betrayed me by telling my boss I had complained about him. I abhorred that about him. Nevertheless, he was extremely knowledgeable, and I went to him more than once for advice. He was usually able to get me to see the problem from a different angle, which helped me come up with a better solution. It didn't matter that I still felt the knife in my back each time I talked to him. I thought I could have learned more from him.

I know I was a challenge to management at times. Okay, more than one time, but I always fought for what I thought was right and that should count, right? I really didn't try to be a pain in the ass. Okay, well, there was this one time. I did mention that I will speak my mind and stand up for what I think is right when needed. I do try to be respectful. But, do you ever find yourself in a situation where what you're being asked is so damn stupid that you just can't keep the "you're shitting me" look off your face?

I was the administrator of an online operator log system. It had multiple capabilities and was a great tool. It was also temperamental. I had spent a lot of time learning the program, working with IT to repair glitches, and building new forms. The system security was designed to have one administrator who controlled and edited the program, especially since access to the system was audited every year.

One day, a production supt, Erick, came to me and said he wanted admin rights to the program. Instead of just saying no, I asked why he wanted admin rights. He was evasive. Eventually, Erick said he wanted to see what more could be done with the program. I told him he should instead concentrate on using all the tools that were currently available and suggested some areas where production supts hadn't been using the tool to its full capabilities. I also explained that there could be only one administrator.

Shortly after that meeting, I was called to the senior production supts office in the CCR to have a discussion with Erick and a very high-level manager, Jim. Jim led the conversation and said he'd like Erick to have administrator access. He went on to explain that Erick had the idea to actually get into the coding of the program to see if he could make it operate differently. I asked what was trying to be accomplished but Erick couldn't articulate what he wanted to do. Jim made one suggestion of an improvement, and I assured him the program already had that capability, but it just so happened that I hadn't been able to talk the production supts into using it. I took the time to explain why I thought accessing the coding was a bad idea and made suggestions on what they could do differently to increase the benefits of the program. Jim still wasn't impressed so I pulled out my hole card. I told them I'd be happy to call IT and have them give Erick administrator rights, but he would also have to take on all the work that went with it since "there can be only one." Erick would then be responsible for granting access to the program twenty-four/seven and conducting all the mandatory audits, just to name a few of the duties. Erick said he would not do those mundane, secretarial duties. I was allowed to leave the meeting, and Jim did not approach me about the subject again. However, as we all know, some folks just don't handle being told "no" very well.

So, yes, I did argue with one manager about spending money for women's restrooms and another manager I essentially told "no." I had probably pissed off some other managers and forgotten exactly how I accomplished that, but I do have a knack.

On the flip side, I also had managers that appreciated my experience, hard work, and diverse skills. One year, I was requested by my former senior production supt, Doug, to give a presentation on leadership to a group of managers in our Joint

Venture plant. Doug requested me due to my "diverse presentation skills." My boss, Les, whole-heartedly supported my participation. There really were reasons why I had respected him. (See, this is why I was also so confused. I had no idea where I stood with that guy.) The presentation went very well. I enjoyed the opportunity and received feedback that many of the managers went back to their home plants with a new perspective on leadership.

CHAPTER 35
(2017) NEW OFFICE, NEW OUTLOOK ON LIFE

Back at the cubes, I did what I could to keep up morale. We continued to update the artwork. People got to talking about it and made special trips to check it out. It increased the traffic and disruptions to the clerk's work, but it also increased morale.

Figure 70 These designs were based on the original artwork of Holly Kitaura. Please see her work at: https://www.hollyvision.biz

My office faced one end of the cubes. I always picked which art I wanted to stare at every day. I started out with the swimmers.

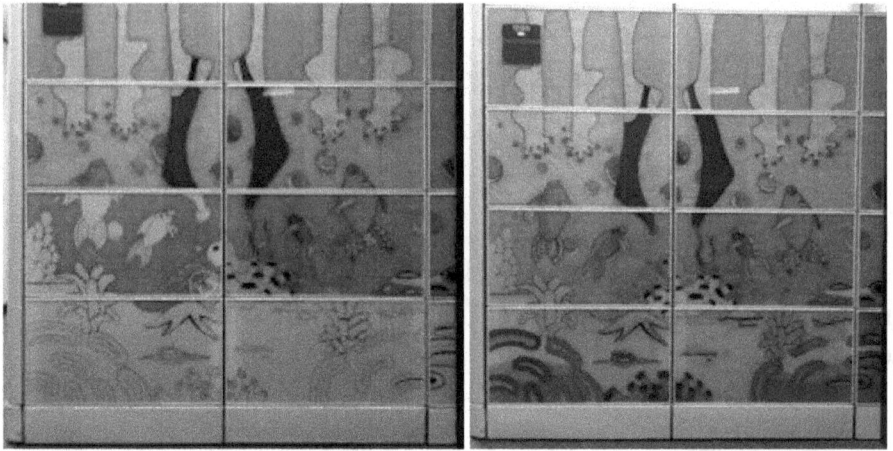

Figure 71 *Cube artwork (original by Holly Kitaura) across from my office door, in progress and then complete.*

My last pick was a nighttime scene. The clerks did an amazing job. I even bought some sparkly stars that we glued onto the artwork. Those sparkly little stars that faced my office and gave me peace also faced the busy, busy, high traffic hallway.

***Figure* 72** *Cube artwork facing my office door.*

I cannot confirm what happened next. What I do know is that:

- The refinery had a visit by a bunch of corporate big dogs.
- Our colorfully decorated cubes were located in a high traffic area for entering and leaving the building. Did the big dogs walk by our cubes? Don't know.
- Soon after, Les informed me that we would be moving out of the cubes and going to the third floor.

In exchange for moving to the third floor, Les told me I was expected to take on more work. Les also ordered the removal of every trace of artwork from the cubes before the move. I wonder if it was the sparkly stars that tipped the balance.

This move, like the previous one, came with conditions. This time, we were told that the only furniture we could use were the leftovers in empty offices on the third floor. We went through all the offices and realized that anything remaining had already been totally picked over when the offices were abandoned. Most of the furniture was damaged but we would make do with Elmer's Glue and duct tape if we had to. I picked the office I wanted and let the clerks pick their offices according to their seniority. We went through the furniture the same way, with some negotiations and trades going on.

I can't begin to explain how much this office meant to me. I don't know if it was the hard-won battle or the view from the windows. It faced to the east and each day I had the breathtaking view of the sun rising behind part of the refinery. I loved the cloudy, rainy days too. I faced my desk chair away from the window to prevent distractions but each time I walked into my office, I felt good. I felt at home.

Figure 73 *View from third-floor office.*

Figure 74 *View from third-floor office.*

Figure 75 *View from third-floor office.*

I decorated my office with brightly colored paintings. I also managed to scrounge a bookshelf where I put my diversity books and several of my Painted Pony statues. My office stood out like a sore thumb. I got numerous visitors that admired my paintings.

Figure 76 *Office bookcase with margarita glasses on top.*

As ecstatic as I was with our new digs, the lack of vacation coverage was always a sore spot with me. I did have Lucy and Starling if everything fell into place just right, but I couldn't count on their availability. I think I forgot to mention that part of our agreement was that if either Lucy or Starling's work group had an emergency or urgent work, they would be pulled off of covering my job and go back to their work groups. When I discussed this with Les, he told me I'd have to figure it out. In the meantime, he wanted me to take on more responsibilities from our group to make it easier for them to cover for each other when they went on vacation. I did as I was told and ended up permanently taking over some duties for shipping. I reviewed the sales of coke out of our refinery via truck and shipments via barges from the Port of Catoosa. (Coke is what's left after every ounce of quality product is boiled, pressed, and cracked out of the crude oil. Coke is a hard porous material that looks like coal or maybe lava rock.) I actually liked the work. It gave me an opportunity to work more closely with our shipping clerk. I took the spreadsheets and updated them, adding formulas to bring in current prices, fees, etc. Taking on this work was a small price to pay to get our offices on the third floor with the rest of the group.

Then one year, everything aligned. I don't know if it was Jupiter, Mars, or Aquarius. I checked the schedule repeatedly and found a three-week block that was open for both Lucy and Starling. I added my first ever three-week vacation to the schedule. I discussed this repeatedly with Les and wrote it on the calendar in his office, which was his preference. I added it to the electronic calendar in case any of the team used it, and, I included it on the clerks' schedule. Les and I discussed my upcoming vacation several times, and I reminded him that Lucy and/or Starling would just be covering one aspect of my job and that someone else would have to do other pieces. For instance, Starling was a contractor and could not act as a supervisor over company people, so if she worked the job someone would have to supervise the clerks. I also added data and ran reports on unit run rates and any deficiencies based on mechanical issues. We looked at all aspects of my job and had a plan to cover only what could not wait during my absence. I remember thinking it was almost a joke—how many engineers did it take to cover for one uneducated employee's job that, by the way, my boss wanted to get rid of? We had about six people lined up, but I don't remember if any of them actually were called on to complete any work.

The day finally came, and I loaded Curt and my two, tiny poodles, Maui and Maylay, in the RV and set off from Oklahoma on my way to visit the kids in Florida. The vacation was physically and mentally challenging for me. Curt had recently undergone eye surgery and had lost partial vision in one eye. Therefore, I drove the RV for the entire trip. We took three days to drive down and two very long days to drive back. Having Maui and Maylay with me added to the workload but reduced my stress in the big picture.

Figure *77 Maui & Maylay on the trip to Florida. Maui loved pillows!*

I have always loved driving across the country and the RV made it so much easier for someone like me with stomach problems. My dogs had their bed between the driver and passenger seat and although they were not exactly thrilled with traveling, they were happy to be with me. I had a serious discussion with Maylay about staying in her bed and not getting underfoot while I was driving. Like a little kid, she pushed it to see just how much she could get away with. She started by laying across the edge of the bed until her front paws touched the floor outside of her safe zone. Slowly, she inched forward until her entire front legs were laying outside of her bed. Next time I glanced down her butt was sitting on the edge of the bed, and the rest of her body was in the "no fly zone." Once I stopped laughing, I scooted her back into the safety of her bed.

Although I was driving, I did more sightseeing than may have been entirely safe. Normally, I drive as fast as I think I can get away with. On this trip, however, I slowed it down in the RV and relaxed instead of constantly pushing it. While Curt spent the entire trip staring at his phone, I saw the beautiful scenery. We passed through several states and by historical sites. The one thing that I think I liked most was driving past the Antioch Baptist Church, but then you would need to be a Charlie Daniels' fan to get that one. I really get a kick out of the little things.

Once we arrived, I was shocked when my granddaughters, Kinsley and Callie, just wanted to play with Curt. I had a serious heart-to-heart with myself over that. You see, Curt does not like people, especially kids, not even family. Okay, maybe he likes some of them, but he doesn't want anything to do with them. Unless, maybe, if it is for about five minutes and there is food involved. I willingly admit that his deep voice is mesmerizing and couldn't blame the girls for wanting to play with him. I also had to chuckle a bit when they got Curt to wear a tiara and wave a sparkly magic wand, something I had never imagined. All that said, the time spent with family was phenomenal for me. The girls put on a song-and-dance show for us, so I pulled my head out of my butt, quit my pouting, and enjoyed the time together.

My frame of mind began to change on that trip. I realized I was dedicating my life to the company and as hard as I tried, was getting very little appreciation for my efforts. Don't get me wrong, I was being paid well, really well, and I was beyond grateful for that. But, how many times can you talk to your boss about your job and hear him tell you if you keep complaining about not having vacation coverage maybe they'll just do away with your job so it wouldn't be a problem? How many times can you be told that the same rules don't apply to you, that you are uneducated, or that you just don't fit in? I decided that when I returned to work, I would continue to do my job to the best of my ability—eight hours a day, five days a week, period. I would stop checking email every five minutes from home just in case someone needed something—unless I received a phone call at home requesting a fix that couldn't wait until the next work day. I would still take vacation on Friday without coverage, but I wouldn't turn around and do the work from home just to stay caught up. I'd have to get my work done on company time. I understand that today they even have a term for this: "quiet quitting." I still followed my personal rule of always doing what I was told. I also helped anyone that asked, but they had to ask. At least this is what I told myself as I drove back from my vacation. It was on that long drive back home that I first started planning my retirement. For real this time.

A little more explanation of the extra work I did during my off hours. I mentioned I was the administrator of one program. This software was used by operators, engineers, supervisors, management, and mechanical folks. If there was a problem with the program and a user called the help desk, they were instructed to contact me instead. Even the help desk called me for help. We went to this program because it was supported by IT, but I guess they had a different definition. I actually enjoyed having that much control and not having to wait for someone else to do the work. However, when the program is used twenty-four/seven by essential workers, they need help when they need help, not when it's convenient. I was happy that this didn't happen a great deal of time during my off hours. Admittedly, I also felt good when I was able to help out.

Vacation over, I made it back to work with my new outlook on life. It didn't take me long to prioritize the work that needed to be caught up after having been gone for three weeks. Murphy's Law has slapped most of us on the wrist. I bet you have guessed by now that while I was enjoying a rare and much needed vacation, Mr. Murphy was back in my office lurking around and making everything that could go wrong, go wrong. Coverage on my job had been hit and miss with the misses being in the majority. I essentially had to go back and redo any work that had been done and then catch up on all the work that had been left untouched for various reasons.

I met with Les and updated him on my plan to get the work caught up. I also explained my new directive of working normal days/times. I also emphasized that I would do whatever I was told, and I would get my work done. I did question him on why Starling didn't do more of my work, asking why she wasn't dedicated to covering the job while I was gone. He reminded me that her work came first.

As time went on, I continued to attend different training classes in an effort to learn more, and possibly figure out why I was so often looked down on by management. I had given up ever being able to impress my boss, Les.

One training class was phenomenal and I could not quit talking about it. I discussed it at length with Les and loaned him my training material. He seemed impressed with the material, but I didn't see him put it into actual practice, at least not with me. Maybe he shared it with his engineers. There was just one thing that went whomperjawed during that class, and yet it turned into a teaching event.

Throughout the training, we were split up into small work groups. During one such session, an upper-level manager, Thad, who I'd personally considered a total jerk, was joking around and said something about knocking me upside the head. I didn't overreact; I just got really quiet. After some time spent thinking, I pulled Thad to the side and told him he should be careful about how he chose to joke around. I had, after all, been "knocked upside the head" by more than one man already. Young smart mouth that he was, I have to give him a lot of credit. Thad listened to what I said, and I think he was truly mortified by the incident. He was apologetic, and I believed he actually meant it. I accepted his apology and had more respect for the guy after that.

On a separate occasion, I went to a training class that was entirely on how to fit in, how to influence others, and most importantly, how to get along with your superiors. A college professor had developed the training and after it was seen by a member of management, it was thought that frontline supervisors could really benefit from it. I couldn't help but think this training was designed with me in mind. I think I was the first one to sign up. I was excited. There was no way I wouldn't benefit from this training. There was no way I wouldn't learn something that would benefit my career. There was no way I could have been so wrong.

During the training, we were instructed that in order to get your boss's favor, you have to dress like them. We received instruction on what color socks to wear with which shoes. Almost all of what he had to say was directed at the young, male engineers. I looked behind me at the bevy of female engineers, many of which had that familiar "you're shitting me" look on their faces. One woman in particular had on bright orange sneakers and she made some comment about this sure wasn't going to work for her. I did finally raise my hand and ask the professor how women in a refinery setting were supposed to dress. He was somewhat at a loss but then suggested we mimic females in upper-level corporate jobs—long skirts or pantsuits. Again, I looked at the group of female engineers sitting in the class all wearing their mandatory fire-retardant coveralls and leather work boots, hard hats tucked under their chairs. These women worked in a REFINERY. I seriously wanted to ask the professor if he realized how flammable some clothing or even hairspray was; or how any type of nylon, or for shit's sake spandex, would melt if too close to a heat source.

The professor went on to explain that "facts don't matter," "job interviews are a scam," and "it's all about how much they like you." (Also known as, "the company is going to do what the company wants to do.") I couldn't believe that a company-paid instructor actually said this out loud. It is one thing for me to be a paranoid female that assumed these conspiracies were true. But to have a hand selected college professor, hired by the company, tell us these things were true was horrendous.

I remember one male supervisor, Jarod, that questioned whether the professor was serious about this. I didn't disrupt the training any further, especially since I had literally gotten so mad that I developed a migraine. It wasn't until after the training that I took some time to talk more with the professor. I found out it was my boss, Les, that had requested this training material. The professor also told me that it was designed more for the engineers who would be promoted up the corporate ladder, not for people like me. I asked him if the hiring techniques that he suggested would actually be against the law. You know, since it promoted discriminating against anyone that didn't look/act just like the boss. He stuttered to a stop. I was glad I managed to make it all the way home before I puked.

In spite of my boss, Les, thinking so little of me, I did receive special thanks from other managers for all the work I did to help their area personnel. Les was surprised to hear I had been given a special thanks and asked what it was for. He liked to share these types of accomplishments at our staff meetings along with service anniversaries. I showed him the thank you cards I had received and explained how I had earned them. I sat up a little straighter at the end of our next staff meeting as Les went through and thanked different individuals for their contributions. I waited, but my thanks never came. I don't know how much it would have meant coming from Les anyway, but it would have meant a great deal to be recognized in front of my peers. The same thing happened again after a long, especially difficult turnaround. Every single person in our group, including the clerks who report to me, were personally mentioned by name and thanked by Les. Everyone but me. The slight was a little thing really, in the big picture. A little thing no bigger than a straw.

CHAPTER 36
(2017/18) THE TIME IS RIGHT

Still in my old job, I continued to train our clerk, Lucy, on all aspects of my job. It didn't matter that she might not be covering for me for vacation. I always operated on the big bus theory. If a big bus runs me over, how would essential work be completed? I don't think the company ever realized how much I was a company person. Yes, yes, I bitched, complained, and raised hell about a lot of things I thought were wrong. But, remember my goals. I really wanted the company to be the best that it could be. I didn't want to leave unexpectedly and the company to have difficulties running government reports. I didn't want my replacement to have no idea how to do any piece of my job. I developed even more training materials and stored them in a common access location where any approved company person could access it.

I began coaching Lucy on how to handle union/company issues. We discussed hypothetical personnel issues. Lucy was one of those people who got along with everyone, who everyone liked. Yep, she was pretty much the total opposite of me. Lucy was accepted. Lucy also deserved every damn bit of it. She was single-handedly the hardest working person I had seen since moving into a salaried job. We had faced extreme personnel shortages over the years, and I had seen Lucy cover multiple jobs across the refinery. One time it was so dire we got her a laptop so she could be in one area working the job while training a new clerk and simultaneously log into another area to handle issues that popped up. You might say she was the best Whack-a-Mole player ever. Whatever popped up, wherever it was, Lucy was all over it. There was also a lot of stress during these times. She handled it probably better than I did although once or twice, I thought I was going to have to cut her off the excess coffee.

Several times during this period, I had to re-justify my job. Les continued to tell me that other plants were using different methods to do the same work and that we should do away with my job. Each time this happened, I would go back to finance and IT and outline what it would take to do away with my job. I would then have to reassure my union-represented clerks that if they did away with my job, their jobs may change but they would still have a job. I came from the refinery, and I had been on strike. I had always been under a looming threat of job loss. This was different. I was made to feel as if this was a personal punishment. I had gotten the clerks to the third floor, but I was going to constantly pay for it.

One of our clerks, Pepper, had a service anniversary come around. The company had a great program where employees got to pick out gifts based on years of service. We also got to have a party, the size and content also being service based. As her supervisor, I informed Pepper of the amount she would be able to spend for her party and worked with her on when/where/what she wanted. I ordered the cake and made reservations at a local restaurant. We had a great time. I gave a short speech and thanked her for her outstanding service. I think everyone realized my thanks were genuine and from the heart. This was how it was supposed to work.

The day drew near for my forty-year service anniversary. After just having Pepper's celebration, I knew how early the supervisor was notified of the upcoming event. I waited…and waited… to hear something, anything, from my supervisor. Eventually, I reminded Les of my upcoming anniversary.

Things didn't go as well as I'd hoped. Since Les had often complained that I was high maintenance, I did as much of the work as possible for my own celebration. Kind of like buying and wrapping your own Christmas presents. Les did tell me to let him know whatever I wanted him to do, and he would do it. I honestly believed it would be held against me if I did ask for help. It wouldn't be the first time Les had done that to me. In spite of the fact that forty years should have garnered a large celebration, even according to company rules, I downplayed everything. The company allowed an on-site cake and cookie type gathering and an off-site dinner. I scheduled it all. I even ordered cupcakes instead of cake because normally, your boss helps to serve the cake, after they give a congratulatory speech.

Normally, a celebration of so many years of service would be held in the cafeteria with the whole refinery invited. I chose not to do this. I couldn't see forcing Les to participate in a big celebration. I had checked with Les on the availability of our shared conference room (he said he didn't need it) but decided not to book it on the off chance something would come up and he would need the room. I didn't want to inconvenience him. Instead, I scheduled my forty-year celebration to take place in the hallway across from the restrooms. It wasn't so bad, the coffee pot and sink were right there too so hey, coffee and cupcakes! Woo hoo! The clerks had printed up a banner for me and we hung it over a couple of tables sitting just across from the men's restroom and set out the cupcakes. Just before the scheduled start time, Les came to my office and said he needed the tables to set up food for his group (he had ended up using the nearby conference room after all—you know conference rooms, lots of chairs, lots of tables). Les said I needed to remove my forty-year anniversary cupcakes and punch. We had a large table in one of the clerk's offices that we used just for such purposes and I suggested he place his food there since it was right across the hallway from the conference room doors making their trips back and forth easier. The clerk wouldn't be in the office anyway since she was helping with my anniversary celebration. I explained that I thought this was more logical since I'd already sent out a refinery-wide email telling everyone the celebration was taking place in the hallway.

Les insisted it would work better for him to have the tables, and I could move to the clerk's office. He also instructed me to coordinate his food delivery and setup once I had removed my forty-year anniversary celebration items.

I did as I was told. I did it as I choked back tears. I did it with every breath catching in my throat. I did it trying not to let anyone see the absolute, final defeat, the last damn straw that broke the camel's back.

I personally removed all traces of my forty-year service anniversary just minutes before my scheduled celebration. I handled the setup of Les's lunch. Most of the folks that showed up in the hallway for the celebration eventually wandered into my office and asked what had happened. I directed them to the office next door for cupcakes. Others just left confused, not knowing what happened. I did my best not to show my total humiliation, my defeat. I'd made a decision. I couldn't take anymore. My career was ending over a few fucking cupcakes.

It is amazing how the little things build up. It's often not one big thing that breaks you. It is the constant drip, drip, drip that wears a hole in your well-being. The proverbial straws that get piled higher and higher on the camel until the weight of the accumulation breaks the camel's back. We had been trained on this at work, what we called your emotional bank account. You add value to the account by treating people well. Withdrawals are made from this account when you break trust, show disrespect, treat people poorly. Or, we can go by the old saying, "One aw shit wipes out a thousand atta boys."

I took stock of my situation. I had won the battle and got the clerks into real offices, just like their counterparts. They were now being treated as part of the planning group. They interacted with the engineers and seemed to fit in well. I had our hardest working clerk, Lucy, fully trained on my job and although I had no idea what the company would do, she was positioned to be the first clerk ever to move into a salaried position like mine. At least, this was the plan I had been working toward for so long. There was no longer a reason for me to stay and be so totally and utterly disrespected. I'd never thought of myself as a quitter, but the only other option was to file an ethics complaint. Over cupcakes? Seriously? I just didn't want to be that woman. Although I know the company would take an ethics complaint seriously, any violation would be based on the predefined list of offenses. If my complaint didn't fit a known category, it would not be considered an actual violation. There was no way I could prove age, education, or religious discrimination. They didn't have a "square peg" protection against discrimination. I could see where the things that had happened were a personal insult but realized it would not constitute a company-recognized ethics violation. It was just an asshole being an asshole. My son, Jake, works for HR in another company and confirmed all this.

Reflection has made me think I should have taken this further. The way I was treated was wrong. I was doing the best thing for me at the time, but I failed to protect the women who would follow me. Even though my treatment didn't fall into a predefined violation, my supervisor's actions should have been brought to light. Everyone has a boss. Was this the type of behavior Phillips 66 wanted to allow? I think not. I still believe in our company. Sure, they could have done some things better, but then that goes for each and every one of us. I should have done better. I should have laid my problems at their feet before I left and let them handle the situation.

Many people have mused over when the "right" time was to retire. I had talked about retirement my entire career as a "someday" kind of thing. Once I actually looked at my circumstances, my finances, my goals, my dreams, my wants, and desires, I laughed to realize this was the perfect time. Sure, I was upset over how things had gone, but I'd been upset before. I considered where I thought the company and my job would be going. I considered where Lucy's job and career would be going. I was so happy to have made it forty years and accomplished all I had. Now the timing was right to do one more thing that was extremely important to me. The time was right to attempt to get Lucy into a job she deserved. My decision to retire was mine and mine alone. Once the decision was made, I was happy with it. I didn't have regrets.

I told Les I was retiring. I explained that Lucy was fully trained and would be the perfect replacement for me, listing all of her qualifications. I added that if Lucy were awarded the job, I would do everything in my power to help her even after I left. I would answer every phone call, every email, or come in and sit right beside her if needed. I swore to do this for Lucy, and only for Lucy.

I went to HR and told them the same.

I scheduled my retirement dinner at my favorite local Mexican food restaurant, Enrique's. I picked there because I could invite everyone in our work groups without exceeding costs. I also picked it because there was no privacy and the traditional farewell speech by my, soon to be former boss, Les, could be omitted without it looking like an insult. We had a great time.

Okay, maybe I do have one regret about retiring. Whoever you are, if anyone has read this far, I'm sorry if I never got to work with you. I know I wasn't everyone's cup of tea. There were others though, that really saw me. I'm funny. I'm passionate. I'm driven. I'm loyal. I'm honest. I may be a little slow intellectually but there are rare moments of brilliance. I give credit where credit is due. I love animals and more importantly, they love me. Well, that may not be important in the work setting...or is it?

2018 Retired—I am very lucky in so many ways. I do not dwell on what I walked away from, on what I lost. It took me about sixty seconds to drop all the stress from my old job and to realize the joy of absolute freedom. I don't remember ever being in the position to literally be able to do what I want when I want. This is crazy! This is amazing

As it turned out, Lucy was promoted into my old job. She rarely needed help and only in the very beginning. I answered every call, every question. Eventually, a problem did arise. She didn't have a trained backup so she could take vacation. Sound familiar?

I was contacted with an offer to come back as a contractor to provide vacation coverage for Lucy. After I agreed, I learned that most of my former coworkers had sworn I would never come back, even though I had explicitly informed Les and HR that I was willing to do just that. They must still have those damn Polaroid snapshots in their desks or hanging on their dart boards. I just don't know. What I do know, is that they didn't know me at all.

I got set up as a contractor and worked my old job a few times to allow my new boss, Lucy, who was my former employee, to go on vacation. I did my best to always respect her position and authority. I never forgot I was a contractor, and that I was there to support her. I was no longer a supervisor or a company employee. It did get difficult a couple of times when people came to me with a problem. Old habits I suppose. I directed them to the appropriate company employee and only did the specific work assigned to me. Not that I didn't offer opinions on occasion. I mean, after all, I really do have trouble not saying what I think. I really enjoyed being back. At the end of the day, I couldn't wait to get back home. Lucy was also lucky in that soon after she got my old job, Les was transferred to another site. She ended up with a great boss that treated her well and respected her. Awesome. So happy for her.

Although I retired early, my career with the company had provided me with a comfortable retirement. Top that off with a brilliant financial man, thank you, Richard, and I could possibly live my normal life for many years to come. I will always appreciate the company for what they have given me over the years. It wasn't a perfect career, but tell me where you can go and find that. I'd bet there aren't any openings if such a place exists.

I did a lot of financial planning around my retirement. I paid off the house because I couldn't handle the thought of the economy tanking and losing my home. Our vehicles and tractor were paid off so the only thing we still paid on was the RV.

The RV situation was a real heartbreaker for me. We could afford the payments, but I had to admit that it was a lot of money. We had to take the RV out of town to get the Mercedes chassis serviced and the last maintenance check we had on it cost nearly $500. The RV had been my idea. It allowed me to travel even if my stomach was acting up. It also allowed me to take my beloved dogs with me. I like long road trips. Curt, however, does not. I made a major mistake by breaking him in by taking him on that long, long trip to Florida. Curt now has no desire to travel.

My original thought was to get a dog to travel with me once I retired, in lieu of my husband. I'm going to refrain from making a joke there. My retirement gift to myself was a goldendoodle puppy, half golden retriever, half poodle that we named Mavis. She would be big enough to possibly act as a guard dog and provide some protection when I traveled solo.

I've had a lot of dogs in my life and raised many from puppies. Mavis tested every amount of patience I possessed. My intent was to train her thoroughly in order to make traveling easier. I read several books on new, updated training methods. My understanding was I could reward good behavior, and everything would be just fine. The problem was I never got any good behavior from Mavis to reward. She stretched my last nerve to the breaking point. At one time, I even contemplated taking her back to the breeder.

Fortunately, I discussed this with our veterinarian. She gently explained to me (she tried not to look at me as if I was an idiot) that dogs are like kids and need accountability for their actions. I went home and immediately went to work on explaining to Mavis what "no" meant and the consequences for violations of rules and regs. Mavis is still full of piss and vinegar, but she also turned out to be the absolute smartest, most dedicated dog I've ever owned. That is saying a lot after my beloved Meesha. Obviously, she was smarter than I was for quite some time until I finally got a handle on her. She has been with me nearly every single day since I brought her home. She worships and adores me. As much as she exhausts me, she makes me laugh until I almost pee my pants. She doesn't allow me to be sad, to feel sorry for myself. We just don't have time and energy for that. The only problem still remaining: she hates to ride in a car or RV.

Figure 78 Mavis saying hello to Jake.

I finally made the decision to get rid of the RV. I really didn't want to travel by myself or with a dog who was going to cry and whine the whole time. I also didn't want to have to dope the poor dog for anxiety. If I had known that COVID would turn into the pandemic it was, maybe I would have reconsidered. But, it's too late now. I try not to grieve over the life I thought I would have. I thought Curt and I would take the dogs and enjoy taking trips and getting away. But the time comes when you have to realize what is fantasy and what is reality. Curt doesn't like traveling. Mavis doesn't like traveling. RVs are expensive. I comfort myself with the idea I can buy a little pull-behind camper if I need to. Or better yet, find a dog friendly hotel.

CHAPTER 37
(2020) FINDING A NEW PASSION, A NEW SOLUTION

COVID-19 lockdown and fear of exposure became extremely stressful. Curt and I are both considered high risk. He is content to stay at home all day every day, but the confinement began to tell on me. Something like this also makes you consider your own mortality. I contemplated my life and my death. I realized how unhappy I was at home. I couldn't take the loneliness any longer. I thought about my kids and what I would leave behind for them. In my mind, there was only one way out.

I put my affairs in order. I checked and rechecked my finances and my beneficiaries. I tried to keep Curt out of the loop as I searched for a way out. I needed someone to help me, but it couldn't be anyone local. I searched online to find exactly what I needed, something that would end my suffering. You can find just about anything online nowadays.

I found exactly what I needed. Something to free me from the mental and physical confinement of life during lockdown.

I bought a Jeep Wrangler. In times like these, you need to turn to what makes you happy. Sure, I had to burn a little of the kid's inheritance, but I think one of them would take the Jeep if I was run over by a bus. I have always loved the outdoors and driving. There's just something about a Jeep Wrangler. I've owned many over the years and ended up trading them for something more practical. The time had finally come in my life where I was able to throw practicality out the window. After years of owning plain white, black, or gray vehicles to not attract unwanted attention (after the red truck fiasco), I ordered a Jeep that is a "bikini-pearl" color. It is a greenish-blue Caribbean Ocean kind of color in my opinion. I ordered the Rubicon Recon edition, so it has bright red seat belts.

Please understand that I in no way mean to downplay the horrors of the COVID pandemic. I lost friends and loved ones to the horrible virus. Many of my family caught COVID and were lucky enough that they didn't need hospitalization. As many of you know, the mental toll was extremely difficult for so many, many people. People separated from loved ones, unable to attend school or social functions. I hope we never see something like that again, but I try not to think about what horrors will be released as the ice melts.

Mavis still doesn't like riding in a vehicle. Maylay on the other hand, loved to ride in the Jeep. She has a little box that I strapped to the seat to raise her up enough to see out the window. Maylay loved it when I took the top off the Jeep, and we drove out around the lake. She also loved it when we drove around town, and she smelled all the smells. I started taking pictures of our little trips, always shooting out Maylay's window so I'd catch her looking at different sights. I found the freedom I needed with that little Jeep. I seriously couldn't drive it without smiling, especially when Maylay was with me. Maui, Maylay's sister, has been gone for about a year now. I wanted to make sure that Maylay and I enjoyed as much of our remaining time together as possible.

Figure 79 *Maylay (going blind) and Grogu getting ready for a Jeep ride. Yep, both have on their seatbelts.*

Figure 80 *Maylay checking out the entrance to the Drummond Ranch. This is where the Food Network star, Ree Drummond, and her family live.*

Figure 81 *Maylay and her teddy out for a Jeep tour: City Hall, Osage Nation Heritage Trail, Poncan Theatre and the old RR Depot.*

June 2022—Maylay

A tiny angel arrived in Heaven today. The sweetest little girl, a tiny five pounds, six ounces, with the softest apricot and white curls. I have long believed that her fur had a hypnotic quality that would calm your mind and lull you to sleep just by cuddling her closely. I imagine her wings will be made of the same magic fluff.

More than sixteen years she has stayed by my side. Even when her sister, Maui, earned her own wings and left us, Maylay stayed with me. I think she's always known how much I needed her. She would demand to be held so that I would take a moment and breathe. She demanded treats for no good reason at all other than to get me out of my comfortable chair where I was content to

369

waste the day away. She demanded her own pillows in my bed so that any time I reached out she would always be right there, right where I could always find her, touch that magical fur, and drift back to sleep.

Now her time has come to take her place in Heaven, and it is time for me to let her go. She leaves knowing she takes a piece of my heart with her. She leaves knowing we will be apart only for a while.

Today I will celebrate her regained youth, her now healthy body, and those huge brown eyes once again clear and bright. I smile to think of her ears perked up and listening. Was she really hard of hearing these past few years or had she just chosen to ignore my commands?

I ask this one last thing of her, that she waits with Maui and Meesha and all the others that came before, until the day I will be with them again.

Goodbye my heart, my love, my friend. Until I'm with you again.

This is the end of my tale. The moral to this story? I have learned that I am not a camel. The straws I felt accumulating for so many years were of my own making. I chose to see them as a burden, not an opportunity. Damn, I hated hearing that back then. "It's not a problem, it's an opportunity." Nevertheless, it is true. Sure, some of those opportunities suck dog biscuits, but everything tastes better with a little Head Country BBQ sauce on it. It just takes a bit of fortitude, a bit of gratitude, and a whole lot of attitude. The attitude you choose is entirely up to you. Nobody can force it on you. Choose wisely, grasshopper.

I hope that you can find your own Mavis, your own Maylay and Maui. A dog, a cat, a person who loves you unconditionally, who makes you laugh. Take the time to breathe the fresh air, to soak in the sun. Allow the wind to dry your tears. Find your peace. Don't smile for the dumbass bastards. Smile for yourself. Smile for your happiness. Smile for your well-being. Find your own reasons to smile.

As for me, what if nobody ever reads this? That's okay. I grew a little just writing it. I cried a little. I faced a few demons. I healed a little. I challenge you to do the same.

Addendum:

One of the great folks that reviewed this material asked me to not just tell a story but to teach what I've learned. Looking back at my notes I decided to list the key items again without any of the backstory. Just a quick refresher of the wisdom I was trying to impart in this book.

On being different, don't be different just to be different. Be different because that is who you are, how you were born. Be different because that is the skin you're comfortable in. If you are just being different to shock someone or get attention you're doing it for the wrong reason. Just be YOU. There will always be a price to pay for being different. Being true to yourself is the only thing that makes it worth the cost.

Don't be your own worst enemy. Plenty of people will be in line for that job. Don't beat yourself up. Don't make yourself sick with stress and worry about things you can't control. We choose how we react. Choose to be happy, choose to have fun, choose to rise above. You'll have a hell of a lot more fun having fun. Don't waste your time on being angry. Oh, go ahead and be angry. Righteous anger is empowering. Then LET IT GO and figure out how to make a change. Seriously, flip the switch, lose the negativity.

Don't be afraid of people that challenge you personally or professionally, they will help you grow. Don't make it personal even if they do.

There isn't always a big win. Celebrate all the little victories. It may be nothing more than making a coworker laugh. Remember you touch people's lives every day in ways you don't even realize. Make it a good memory.

I've never not been introverted. But now I always ask myself, who do you want to be? Do you want to be better than your weakness? Challenge yourself.

I hate to ask for help, but you have to know when you need it, and you must be willing to accept it.

Don't forget that you don't know what you don't know. It's easy to take a few facts, judge a book by its cover, and jump to conclusions. But before you do, realize that you don't know all the facts, all the issues, all the background of what seems to be right in front of your face. As Mama Odie said, "You got to dig a little deeper."

I loved my job. Too bad that wasn't always appreciated. Leaders need to learn to recognize passion in all its weird, difficult, chaotic wrappings and harness that incredible power.

ABOUT THE AUTHOR

Figure 82 Left to right, Me, Diana, Dotti and Steve. Family game night. Mom loved playing cards with us, and we wanted to include her one last time. Oh, that's Mom in the cardboard box.

I grew up a rough and tumble tomboy with two older brothers and eventually two younger sisters. I rode horses and Harleys. I learned how to shoot, and qualified expert marksman in the US Army Reserve. When it came to getting a job, I hated to consider anything that would box me into an office. Instead, at 19 years old, I went to work at an oil refinery. From day one, everyone told me I did not fit in. Five years in, they said a woman would never last in this type of work. Ten years in, and I was battle worn with the scars to prove it. Twenty years in, my boss said, I was a

"Square peg that didn't fit into the company's round holes." Thirty years in, another boss said if I wanted to take vacation, I needed to figure out a way to do away with my job. Forty years in, I had climbed the ladder as far as an "uneducated" woman could go (or so they said). I had watched all these naysayers come and go. There were times I believed the stories that I did not belong, that I did not fit in. Nevertheless, I always stayed true to myself, and I did my best to help others along the way. I retired after 40 years of service at just 59 years old. I was wealthier and so much wiser. What was the main thing I learned along the way? Do not be your own worst enemy. Do not pile the weight of proverbial straws onto the camel's back. I learned how to free myself.

My retired life is so much calmer, easier, less stressful, boring, less fulfilling, and could be depressing if I let it. Instead, I choose happiness. I choose to leave the negativity behind. I choose to enjoy every little thing that I can. I love my family, even the pain in the ass ones (you know who I'm talking about). I love clouds, sunrises and sunsets, the smell of rain, most of nature actually, except the dang tornadoes. I read, write, paint, ride around in my gnarly little jeep, spend time with my dogs, host sewing groups and paint parties, and truly enjoying having lunch with good friends.

PS—I don't care what Steve tells everyone. He is older than me.

www.ingramcontent.com/pod-product-compliance
Lightning Source LLC
Chambersburg PA
CBHW072133090426
42739CB00013B/3177